Channel Islands

Edited and Produced by Brian Bell
Photography by Alain Le Garsmeur

APA PUBLICATIONS

THE INSIGHT GUIDES SERIES RECEIVED SPECIAL AWARDS FOR EXCELLENCE FROM THE PACIFIC AREA TRAVEL ASSOCIATION.

CHANNEL ISLANDS

First Edition

© 1989 APA PUBLICATIONS (HK) LTD
Printed in Singapore by APA Press Pte Ltd
Colour Separation in Singapore by Colourscan Pte Ltd

APA PUBLICATIONS

Publisher: Hans Johannes Hoefer
Managing Director: Julian Sale
General Manager: Henry Lee
Marketing Director: Aileen Lau
Editorial Director: Geoffrey Eu
Editorial Manager: Vivien Kim
Editorial Consultants: Brian Bell (Europe)
          Heinz Vestner (German Editions)
Updating Coordinator: Hilary Cunningham (N. America)

Project Editors

Helen Abbott, Diana Ackland, Mohamed Amin, Ravindralal Anthonis, Roy Bailet, Louisa Cambell, Jon Carroll, Hilary Cunningham, John Eames, Janie Freeburg, Bikram Grewal, Virginia Hopkins, Samuel Israel, Jay Itzkowitz, Phil Jaratt, Tracy Johnson, Ben Kalb, Wilhelm Klein, Saul Lockhart, Sylvia Mayuga, Gordon McLauchlan, Kal Müller, Eric Oey, Daniel P. Reid, Kim Robinson, Ronn Ronck, Robert Seidenberg, Rolf Steinberg, Sriyani Tidball, Lisa Van Gruisen, Merin Wexler.

Contributing Writers

A.D. Aird, Ruth Armstrong, T. Terence Barrow, F. Lisa Beebe, Bruce Berger, Dor Bahadur Bista, Clinton V. Black, Star Black, Frena Bloomfield, John Borthwick, Roger Boschman, Tom Brosnahan, Jerry Carroll, Tom Chaffin, Nedra Chung, Tom Cole, Orman Day, Kunda Dixit, Richard Erdoes, Guillermo Gar-Oropeza, Ted Giannoulas, Barbara Gloudon, Harka Gurung, Sharifah Hamzah, Willard A. Hanna, Elizabeth Hawley, Sir Edmund Hillary, Tony Hillerman, Jerry Hopkins, Peter Hutton, Neil Jameson, Michael King, Michelle Kort, Thomas Lucey, Leonard Lueras, Michael E. Macmillan, Derek Maitland, Buddy Mays, Craig McGregor, Reinhold Messner, Julie Michaels, M.R. Priya Rangsit, Al Read, Elizabeth V. Reyes, Victor Stafford Reid, Harry Rolnick, E.R. Sarachandra, Uli Schmetzer, Ilsa Sharp, Norman Sibley, Peter Spiro, Harold Stephens, Keith Stevens, Michael Stone, Desmond Tate, Colin Taylor, Deanna L. Thompson, Randy Udall, James Wade, Mallika Wanigasundara, William Warren, Cynthia Wee, Tony Wheeler, Linda White, H. Taft Wireback, Alfred A. Yuson, Paul Zach.

Contributing Photographers

Carole Allen, Ping Amranand, Tony Arruza, Marcello Bertinetti, Alberto Cassio, Pat Canova, Alain Compost, Ray Cranbourne, Alain Evrard, Ricardo Ferro, Lee Foster, Manfred Gottschalk, Werner Hahn, Dallas and John Heaton, Brent Hesselyn, Hans Hoefer, Luca Invernizzi, Ingo Jezierski, Wilhelm Klein, Dennis Lane, Max Lawrence, Lyle Lawson, Philip Little, Guy Marche, Antonio Martinelli, David Messent, Ben Nakayama, Vautier de Nanxe, Kal Müller, Günter Pfannmüller, Van Philips, Ronni Pinsler, Fitz Prenzel, G.P. Reichelt, Dan Rocovits, David Ryan, Frank Salmoiraghi, Thomas Schollhammer, Blair Seitz, David Stahl, Bill Wassman, Rendo Yap, Hisham Youssef.

Distributors

Australia and New Zealand: Prentice Hall of Australia, 7 Grosvenor Place, Brookvale, NSW 2100, Australia. **Benelux:** Utigeverij Cambium, Naarderstraat 11, 1251 AW Laren, The Netherlands. **Brazil and Portugal:** Cedibra Editora Brasileira Ltda, Rua Leonidia, 2-Rio de Janeiro, Brazil. **Denmark:** Copenhagen Book Centre Aps, Roskildeveji 338, DK-2630 Tastrup, Denmark. **Germany:** RV Reise-und Verkehrsuerlag Gmbh, Neumarkter Strasse 18, 8000 Munchen 80, West Germany. **Hawaii:** Pacific Trade Group Inc., P.O. Box 1227, Kailua, Oahu, Hawaii 96734, U.S.A. **Hong Kong:** Far East Media Ltd., Vita Tower, 7th Floor, Block B, 29 Wong Chuk Hang Road, Hong Kong. **India and Nepal:** India Book Distributors, 107/108 Arcadia Building, 195 Narima Point, Bombay-400-021, India. **Indonesia:** Java Books, Box 55 J.K.C.P., Jakarta, Indonesia. **Israel:** Steimatzky Ltd., P.O. Box 628, Tel Aviv 61006, Israel (Israel title only). **Italy:** Zanfi Editori SRL. Via Ganaceto 121, 41100 Modena, Italy. **Jamaica:** Novelty Trading Co., P.O. Box 80, 53 Hanover Street, Kingston, Jamaica. **Japan:** Charles E. Tuttle Co. Inc., 2-6 Suido 1-Chome, Bunkyo-ku, Tokyo 112, Japan. **Kenya:** Camerapix Publishers International Ltd., P.O. Box 45048, Nairobi, Kenya. **Korea:** Kyobo Book Centre Co., Ltd., P.O. Box Kwang Hwa Moon 1 658, Seoul, Korea. **Philippines:** National Book Store, 701 Rizal Avenue, Manila, Philippines. **Singapore:** MPH Distributors (S) Pte. Ltd., 601 Sims Drive #03-21 Pan-I Warehouse and Office Complex, S'pore 1438, Singapore. **Switzerland:** M.P.A. Agencies-Import SA, CH. du Croset 9, CH-1024, Ecublens, Switzerland. **Taiwan:** Caves Books Ltd., 103 Chungshan N. Road, Sec. 2, Taipei, Taiwan, Republic of China. **Thailand:** Far East Publications Ltd., 117/3 Soi Samahan, Sukhumvit 4 (South Nana), Bangkok, Thailand. **United Kingdom, Ireland and Europe (others):** Harrap Ltd., 19-23 Ludgate Hill, London EC4M 7PD, England, United Kingdom. **Mainland United States and Canada:** Graphic Arts Center Publishing, 3019 N.W. Yeon, P.O. Box 10306, Portland OR 97210, U.S.A. (The Pacific Northwest title only); Prentice Hall Press, Gulf & Western Building, One Gulf & Western Plaza, New York, NY 10023, U.S.A. (all other titles).

Chinese editions: Formosan Magazine Press Ltd., 6 Fl. No. 189, Yen Pin S. Road, Taipei, Taiwan, R.O.C. **French editions:** Editions Gallimard, 5 rue Sébastien-Bottin, F-75007 Paris, France. **German editions:** Nelles Verlag GmbH, Schleissheirner Str. 371b, 8000 Munich 45, West Germany **Italian editions:** Zanfi Editori SLR. Via Ganaceto 121 41100 Modena, Italy. **Portuguese editions:** Cedibra Editora Brasileira Ltda, Rua Leonidia, 2-Rio de Janeiro, Brazil.

Islands do not need to be as inaccessible as the cartoonists' proverbial desert island to hold an enduring fascination for many people. The Channel Islands could scarcely be more accessible, lying just off the coast of France and served by a wide range of ships, hydrofoils and aircraft from France, Britain and much further afield; yet the larger islands attract a surprising number of satisfied customers

Hoefer

Bell

Garsmeur

again and again, and the smaller ones occasionally come on the market, allowing dreamers to imagine that they too might one day own their very own island

Like so many other holiday destinations, however, the Channel Islands have been striving to rid themselves of an outdated bucket-and-spade image and attract a more sophisticated class of visitor. But how? Should they try to cater more comprehensively to the tastes of continental Europeans and visitors from even further afield? Would that mean lessening their appeal to their traditional English customers? Can they please both? What impact will the Channel Tunnel between England and France have on them? As the islands' tourism officials pondered the problems of success, *Insight Guide: Channel Islands* turned its attention to the bailiwicks' culture and attractions

The award-winning *Insight Guides* series began in 1970 with a colourful book on Bali, put together by **Hans Hoefer**, a West German photographer and disciple of the Bauhaus tradition. The success of his novel design, combining top-quality photography with "insightful" text, soon blossomed into the Singapore-based Apa Publications, whose guides now cover countries and cities on every continent.

Brian Bell, the project editor for *Insight Guide: Channel Islands*, first became involved with Apa through writing a chapter of *Insight Guide: Great Britain* and went on

to edit Insight Guides to Ireland and Scotland. As a journalist with wide experience in newspapers and magazines, he was impressed by Apa's approach to travel guides because it combined detailed reporting about what makes a country tick with a bold photojournalistic approach to illustration. In a crowded publishing market, Bell believes, too many guidebooks content themselves with anodyne prose and picture-postcard photography. Yet a country's warts, he argues, shouldn't be omitted; they can be as interesting as its beauty spots and usually make it more enticing to the adventurous traveller. When the Channel Islands project was first broached, however, Bell, displaying his Northern Irish scepticism, wondered whether the islands were large enough to justify a whole book. Were they sufficiently varied in character? Would there be too few visual contrasts?

Bell, then deputy editor of the colour magazine published with *The Observer*, Britain's oldest Sunday newspaper, turned for advice to two of his colleagues. **Alain Le Garsmeur**, one of Britain's most respected photojournalists and a regular contributor to the magazine, happened to be a Jerseyman and had no doubts that visually the islands had a lot to offer. And **Colin Smith**, *The Observer*'s chief roving reporter and husband of a Guernsey "donkey" (as the islanders used to be disrespectfully called), sketched out the islands' dramatic history and drew attention to their current controversial role as tax havens. Bell needed no further convincing. *Insight Guide: Channel Islands* was already taking shape in his mind.

Le Garsmeur, whose portfolio included several magazine assignments featuring the islands, left Jersey at 18 to attend a school of photography in Britain. Like many young people, he found permanent island life claustrophobic, but retained an affinity for islands in general; one of his most memorable assignments was photographing lemurs on Madagascar for the World Wildlife Fund. Today, based in London, he thinks of himself more as a European than a Jerseyman, but still cares enough about Jersey to worry whether it is developing too fast. These days he finds the gentler pace of life on Guernsey more akin to the Jersey he used to know. All the same, he can never quite escape from Jersey: once, when photographing at 8,000 feet (2,500 metres) in Bhutan, he stumbled across a herd of Jersey cows

To ensure that the book's text would combine authority with objectivity, Bell assembled a writing team of both insiders and outsiders. For several of the chapters, particularly those detailing the unique way in which the islands run their affairs, he turned to two very experienced freelance journalists, **Edward Owen** and his wife **Willa Murray**. Since they settled in Guernsey in 1965, they have written about virtually every aspect of Channel Islands life for U.K. national newspapers and magazines as well as for North American and European publications. Murray was the last national journalist to interview the legendary Dame of Sark, Sibyl Hathaway, before her death, covering her 90th birthday for *The Times*, *Daily Telegraph*, *Sunday Times* and *The Scotsman*.

When Owen and Murray arrived in Guernsey, most of their neighbours at Pleinmont, in the south-west corner of the island, still used the Guernsey-French patois as their daily language. Since then, they have seen the comparatively simple communities they first knew grow into prosperous and sophisticated offshore finance centres—a development Owen has reported from the outset as local correspondent for the London *Financial Times*.

But has it all been a change for the better? Owen and Murray admire the way the Channel Islands have diversified their economies and the job opportunities this has brought for islanders, especially young people, but they believe the point has been reached where local politicians must give much greater priority to conservation and restraint on growth if the islands' character is not to be sacrificed.

The same thought is voiced by Colin Smith, who chose to write about the tiny feudally-run island of Sark, where cars are still banned. He notes with regret the increasing number of "essential tractors" and the almost Disneyland feel created by the influx of tourists during the season. Nevertheless, Sark remains one of his favourite places. Smith, brought up in England's West Midlands, began his journalistic career as harbour correspondent of the *Guernsey*

Ridsdale   *Owen*   *Murray*

Evening Press and soon afterwards met the Guern who was to become his wife. Most summers, he spends at least a month on the islands, which are "as

Earl   *Shipley*

foreign as I want to be on holiday" and certainly more peaceful than many of the places he works in as *The Observer*'s trouble-shooting foreign reporter.

Over the years, he says, he has found that most Guerns seem to be a bit in awe of Sarkees, perhaps because, lacking an airport and often isolated by winter gales, they have retained a more separate identity than most Channel Islanders. Guernseymen, he thinks, find the inhabitants of Britain's last feudal fief somewhat exotic. "Listen to those Sarkees speak!" they'll exclaim when they hear the rolling Rs—although, to the average visitor, the two accents are indistinguishable. Even more mysteriously, he has heard Guerns confiding that Sark butter is better than theirs—despite the fact that it comes from identical golden Guernsey herds.

Rivalry between the two main islands, Jersey and Guernsey, has become no less fierce with the passing years. Both are competing for tourists and for offshore investment and, because their inhabitants, when they leave on business or on holiday, are more likely to be heading for England or France than for the other island, there is a great deal of ignorance on each island about what the other one is really like. It was a situation that reminded Brian Bell of his native Ireland and convinced him that a good recipe for civil war would be to let a Jersey or Guernsey writer loose on the rival island.

Lake   *Smith*   *Fisher*

Instead, he asked a complete outsider, **Stuart Ridsdale**, to report on both islands. Ridsdale, a writer with a leading London public relations company, is no stranger to Apa's approach to complex societies: he spent two years as as editor at Apa's Singapore headquarters. Later, in 1986, he became one of the first travellers to cross out of China along the Karakoram Highway to north Pakistan.

Abraham

Even that journey, however, seemed mundane when compared with his flight between Jersey and Guernsey in one of Aurigny Air Services' 18-seater Trislanders. Low cloud and heavy rain combined to turn what should have been a pleasant dash across a few miles of sea into a fist-clenching excursion he wouldn't forget. But he had nothing but praise for the pilot who, navigating through a cocoon of cloud the whole way, behaved with the precision of a professional.

For a portrait of Alderney and a candid view of conservation and wildlife on the islands, Bell turned to Guernsey journalist **Tim Earl** who travels the world leading birdwatching trips and lists Alderney high among ornithological wonders. The island's other attractions include a relaxed way of life lost from his Guernsey birthplace. Earl has been a research biologist, banker and special interest tour operator but now, as a writer, enjoys poverty and inner peace. A senior reporter with the *Guernsey Evening Press*, he finds that journalism relieves some of his frustrations by giving him a licence to investigate some of the less welcome changes taking place in the islands.

The chapter on Herm and three other contributions came from **Chris Lake**, a feature writer with the *Jersey Evening Post* and author of several books, including *These Haunted Islands, The First 50 Years —A History of Jersey Airport* and *The Battle of Flowers Story*. An English teacher before he turned to journalism, he finds island children pleasingly tame compared with their counterparts on the U.K. mainland. "How can you have Hell's Angels," he says, "when the maximum speed limit is 40 miles an hour?" As Jersey relies increasingly for its revenue on its offshore finance industry, Lake sees the balance of power moving perceptibly away from the politicians and towards the lawyers and bankers.

Like Lake, **Rob Shipley**, author of the chapters on Fishing and Sailing, turned from teaching to the *Jersey Evening Post*, with a stint as a professional fisherman in between, skippering a crabbing vessel. He is still much involved with the sea, enthusiastic about scuba diving, underwater photography and anything to do with boats. He has written extensively on the local fishing industry and on maritime subjects ranging from windsurfing to the America's Cup yacht race. In 1987 he set sail across the stormy seas of journalism as editor of a new magazine, *Jersey Now*.

The ability of Apa Insight guides to focus on unique aspects of their locations suggested a chapter on the remarkable Jersey Wildlife Preservation Trust set up by the world-famous naturalist Gerald Durrell. For this, Bell had to look no further than his wife, Connecticut-born freelance journalist **Diane Fisher**. An admirer of Durrell's work, she points to his Jersey zoo when she hears people condemn all zoos as prisons for animals, reminding them of its widely recognised work in saving species from extinction and returning them to the wild.

For more information about the Channel Islands' world-famous cattle and for the detailed information needed to compile "Travel Tips", Bell signed up **Stuart Abra-**

Continued on page 305

TABLE OF CONTENTS

pretty little paradise, run with military precision by the Major

Part Three

Part Four

Maps

OTHER INSIGHT GUIDES TITLES

THE MELTING POT

The Channel Islands are not really in the English Channel at all, but lie scattered along the Gulf of St. Malo, their closest point to France being just eight miles (13 km) from the Cherbourg peninsula. They are not sovereign states, nor are they colonies. They are British, but do not belong to the United Kingdom. They are partly in the European Economic Community, partly outside it. They do not bow the knee to the government of Great Britain, but loyally (if anachronistically) toast the Queen of England as "Our Duke of Normandy".

Such contradictions multiply to give Jersey, Guernsey, Alderney, Sark, Herm and their smaller brethren a distinctive appeal. They have their own language, but everyone speaks English. They have their own banknotes, but deal in familiar pounds and pence sterling. They hold elections, but there are no party politics. They flourish in a democratic age while preserving the western world's last bastion of feudalism. They form the setting for *Bergerac*, a popular British television detective series, yet they have one of the lowest crime rates in Europe. They attract international financiers and rich tax exiles who drive Porsches and Jaguars, yet nowhere does the speed limit exceed 40 miles an hour (64 kmph).

French influence: It's the Gallic flavour that is most attractive to the taste of English visitors, who still dominate the tourism statistics. Street names like Colomberie (Dovecot) and Rouge Bouillon (Red Spring) give them the feel of an English-speaking province of France. So do the croissants and long French loaves in the bakeries.

The Channel Islands have a combined population of just 134,000, yet rivalries—as ferocious as the tides that pound their shores—exist between them. When natives of the two largest islands, Jersey and Guernsey, refer to each other as *ânes* (donkeys) and *crapauds* (toads), the humour in their remarks is laced with a touch of contempt. To an outsider, these attitudes can be baffling. After all, the two islands have more similarities than differences—so why does each behave as though the other does not exist? History is partly to blame, but today's insecurities can probably be traced to the realisa-

tion that good times can always turn bad, that there may not always be enough tourists to go round, that offshore financiers may find a more appealing home for their money.

Victor Hugo, who wrote *Les Misérables* during his 16-year exile in Guernsey, called the Channel Islands "pieces of France which fell into the sea and were gathered up by England". Geographically, he was right: the islands belong naturally to France rather than to England. Yet they were ruled by France for only 200 out of the 900 years during which they were at the centre of a tug-of-war between the two countries. No matter; they have absorbed a distinct Gallic fla-

Preceding pages: Renoir's "Enfants au Bord de la Mer"; transatlantic influence in a Battle of Flowers parade; a ferry leaves for England; Mont Orgueil Castle, Gorey; horse-drawn carriage in Sark; dressing-up for the parade. Left, the French factor. Right, Jersey's Battle of Flowers queen.

vour from their immediate neighbour.

Renoir, for example, who appraised Guernsey's light with a painter's eye, also noticed how "the Anglo-Saxon miss sheds her prudery when she arrives in Guernsey". Hugo, for his part, was prepared to broaden her mind still further: ignoring Anglo-Saxon decencies altogether, he lived on the island with both wife and mistress, introducing them respectively as "*Madame, la mère de mes enfants*" and "*Madame, mon amie*".

Feudal chic: The past has a strong appeal for many tourists and in no other part of Britain is the tradition of preserving tradition so stoutly established. The telephone directories of the islands are littered with names

dominant, French is the official language in the island and has equal status with English in Guernsey. Much of the law-making is an Anglo-French affair.

The result is that they are "tight little islands"—unsurprisingly insular in outlook, more than a little complacent, sometimes a bit illiberal. When "Swinging London" was at its height in 1969, Jersey made the headlines by expelling a 21-year-old Portuguese girl who had come to work, quite legally, in a knitwear factory. The reason for her unacceptability: she was about to become an unmarried mother.

Sark lagged even further behind the times. Only in 1974 were married women given the

like de Carteret and de Veulle, descendants of the Norman knights rewarded with land by William the Conqueror 10 centuries ago. Michael Beaumont, the Seigneur who rules Sark today, is successor to the feudal lords of the manor who held sway in Norman times—though, before succeeding his formidable aunt, Sibyl Hathaway, who was Dame of Sark from 1927 until her death in 1974, he had led a thoroughly 20th-century existence as a guided weapons engineer with the British Aircraft Corporation.

A Norman-French patois is still spoken occasionally by about 15 percent of Jersey's population. But, although English is now

right to have their own bank accounts and to own property.

To many visitors such differences stir feelings of nostalgia. In the dusty lanes of Sark, where cars are banned, it is refreshing to encounter horse dung rather than petrol fumes. In the age of the jumbo jet, you fly to Alderney in a tiny 18-seater Trislander of Aurigny Air Services, whose in-flight magazine includes a diagram of the cockpit layout—on the assumption, perhaps, that you might wish to reach forward and take over the controls.

As a holiday destination, the islands can exploit two valuable resources: sea and sunshine. There are unspoiled bays and coves, with shellfish in rock pools. Hugo mused poetically about the "Aegean of the Channel" and Queen Victoria, visiting Jersey in 1846, found that St. Aubin's Bay reminded her of Naples.

Then there is the contrast between the superb shoreline and the lush rural interior. The farmland has been subdivided between heirs for so many generations that there is a patchwork profusion of small fields and scattered dwellings. Pretty cottages have a bygone charm and the towns are undisfigured by skyscrapers. The restaurants offer delicious lobsters and fresh vegetables.

Money talks: But the islands aren't just

playgrounds. Traditionally they have been a market garden, providing England with early fruit, new potatoes and fresh cream. They are a breeding ground for Jersey and Guernsey cows, among the world's leading milkers. And, in the past quarter-of-a-century, they have become tax havens; not that any resident would dream of describing them as such—the preferred euphemism would be "offshore finance centres" or "special tax regimes". The result, though, is

Left, away from the seaside, farming dominates. Above, a voluntary station-mistress at Alderney's small railway.

predictable: a recent hunt through Jersey's telephone directory revealed nine butchers, seven bakers and 69 accountancy firms.

In the narrow lanes of St. Helier and St. Peter Port, brass plaques list the international bankers, insurance agents, trust administrators and multicurrency fiduciary deposit managers who thrive in the bracing financial atmosphere of these offshore city states. The Chase Manhattan is there; so is the Bank of India, the Banque Nationale de Paris and about 50 others. St. Helier, someone said, has become like a scaled-down financial centre—little Zurich.

Nor have the smaller islands failed to benefit from the financial boom. The well-dressed passengers you see on a horse-drawn carriage on Sark may well be the directors of a company set up on the island for tax purposes; they will have popped over from London for the day to attend a statutory board meeting in somebody's house.

But the easy-going image of a tax haven could not be more misleading. The islands are crawling with customs and immigration officials, determined to deny smugglers and illegal immigrants a back door into Britain and the European Economic Community. Foreigners entering the Channel Islands are entering Britain, and their image of tax haven life is quickly shattered.

Seeing stars: There is a glamorous side to being special tax regimes. Tour guides in Jersey and Guernsey, like their counterparts in Hollywood who identify film stars' mansions, will point out the homes of TV personality Alan Whicker, thriller writer Jack Higgins and pop singer Gilbert O'Sullivan. Guernsey can even lay claim to a fully-fledged film star, Oliver Reed, a recognised connoisseur of the island's pubs.

Whatever the virtues of tradition, the Channel Islanders are ever adapting to change. Having been farmers, fishermen and innkeepers, they became expert in the 1960s and 1970s in fitting brass nameplates to bankers' doors.

Now they have passed through those doors to become accountants, advocates and computer programmers. They have also ensured that their islands continue to be anomalies and, as the continent to which they cling becomes increasingly standardised, that stubborn individualism remains their greatest asset.

Puis affiegerent ozlean
Les contes de fallebzy fuff
Talbot et aultres leurs ge
Qui y traueillerent moult
Et la firent de grans ba
Du coste de beausse et foul

CATALOGUE OF CONQUESTS

The Channel Islands today are regarded as romantic places, ideal destinations for holidaymakers looking for relaxation. The image isn't always accurate, but it is at least an improvement on their traditional role. The islands, throughout history, have served as stepping stones for plundering armies on their way to new conquests. Like many similar places around the world, the Channel Islands were, for centuries, prey to scourges of nature, easy pickings for passing pirates, and reluctant pawns passed between warring rulers. If today's inhabitants seem to overemphasise their proud independence, it is because they remember their turbulent past.

As elsewhere, earliest recorded history celebrates the survival of the fittest. More than 100,000 years ago, Stone Age men in Jersey banded together to hunt for game. Their prey included the elephant and the woolly rhinoceros. Excavations at La Cotte de St. Brelade, a cave on Jersey's southwest coast, provide tantalising traces of palaeolithic activity on the island, then still connected to the French mainland.

It wasn't until around 6,500 B.C., when the great Ice Cap melted, that the Channel Islands were separated from the rest of Europe. Today, at very low tide, evidence can be seen in Jersey's St. Ouen's Bay of a "submerged forest" that dates back to early neolithic times.

Detective work: Farmers supplanted hunters in about 5,000 B.C. Villages began to take shape. The remains of pottery and flint tools resemble those found in northern France. Burial mounds, containing passage graves, survive. One Jersey burial mound, at La Hougue Bie, is an impressive 177 feet (54 metres) in diameter. Excavations at the Les Fouaillages mound on Guernsey have unearthed the work of builders spread over 1,500 years. Fragments of tools and weapons and a large gold neck-ring (on display in the Jersey Museum) provide clues to the

Preceding pages: Gallic influence at work in St. Peter Port; valuable *vraic* (seaweed) at L'Etacq in Jersey. Left, the Normans go into battle.

trading links and relative prosperity of the Bronze Age, which came shortly before 2,000 B.C.

As with much of Western Europe, the Channel Islands' early history is a catalogue of invasions. Defensive earthworks on the coasts of Jersey and Guernsey date back more than 5,000 years and were augmented in the Iron Age by the Celts, who arrived in 800 B.C. from France and Germany.

Developing iron weapons turned the Celts into fearsome opponents, and subjugating the horse had made them mobile. Hoards of buried valuables, including more than 15,000 coins, suggest that the Celts felt threatened. Certainly, they were no match

mains of a Gallo-Roman settlement in Alderney show that they visited the islands at all. Occasionally Roman coins are still found, usually dating from the third century and identifiable as originating in Alexandrian mints.

God squad: The early Christian era was a period of comparative peace. Parishes grew up around stone churches and missionaries gave their names to areas such as St. Sampson in Guernsey and St. Brelade in Jersey. St. Helier founded a hermitage on a rock near the present town. St. Magloire established a monastery on Sark, which had been inhabited from early times.

The peace was shattered in the ninth cen-

for the Romans.

When Rome's conquering legions marched across Europe in 56 B.C., they swept the islands, along with what is now France, into their province of Gaul. Jersey, it is thought, became "Caesarea", Guernsey "Sarnia" and Alderney "Riduna". They were ruled from what is now Lyons, but the evidence is that rulers such as Mark Antony and Justinian left "the islands in the sea between Gaul and Britain" largely to their own devices, much as the British parliament does today. The Romans left surprisingly few traces; only coins and trinkets, unearthed centuries later, and the excavated re-

tury as the Vikings arrived in their Scandinavian long ships in search of booty. Again and again, houses were burnt, people murdered, crops and cattle carried off and prehistoric tombs rifled. Norse words began to enter the language, not least the word *ey*, meaning "island", which provided the last syllable for Jersey, Guernsey and Alderney. The Norsemen were also expert sailors and farmers— skills which they left the islanders as a permanent legacy.

In 911 A.D., Charles the Simple of France, tiring of the endless devastation, tried to buy off Rollo, chief of the most feared band of raiders, by giving him land that was later to become the Duchy of Normandy. It was not enough: in 933 A.D. Rollo's son, William Longsword, wrested more territory from the Breton lords, probably including the Channel Islands. The end result was that the feudal system was firmly in place.

Rollo lives on today in the curious *Clameur de Haro*. An islander who feels that someone is damaging his property can summon two witnesses, kneel before the offender and call out: "*Haro, Haro, à l'aide mon Prince, on me fait tort*" (Rollo, Rollo, my Prince, come to my aid, I am being wronged), followed by the Lord's Prayer, also in French. The offender must then stop whatever he is doing until the case is heard in

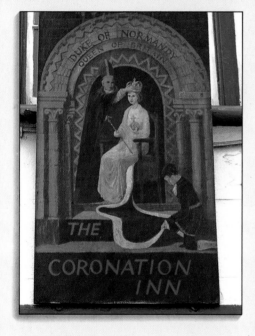

a court of law.

The medieval cry, originally used to prevent murder or robbery, is far from defunct and can still be effective. It has been uttered in recent times to stop people felling trees and, in a more contemporary context, to force a building contractor to remove a crane that was violating the air space of a newsagent's shop in St. Peter Port.

William Longsword's successor, William the Conqueror, captured the English crown

Left, cavalry charge by the Normans. Above, the Anglo-Norman connection celebrated on a pub sign.

in 1066 when he won the Battle of Hastings, thus bringing England within the same jurisdiction as the Channel Islands. The sequence of events has not been forgotten: because England was added relatively late to the Duke of Normandy's offshore properties, islanders today jokingly refer to their dominant neighbour as "a possession" of Les Isles Anglo-Normandes—a reverse of what most people would think.

After 1066, the centre of power shifted to London. But the islanders went on paying their taxes to Rouen, William's Normandy capital, and the islands changed hands frequently within the families of the dukes of Normandy. Sark, for example, was handed over to the monks of St. Michel.

Stark choice: The enlarged kingdom, however, lacked stability. When Richard the Lionheart died in 1199, his brother, John, succeeded him; but Brittany preferred the claim of his cousin, Arthur. Fighting broke out and Arthur disappeared, presumed murdered on the orders of John.

In 1204, Normandy broke away to become part of the kingdom of France and John fled to England. The islanders were torn: should they swear allegiance to England or to France? It was a particularly difficult decision for families with possessions in both countries.

The better offer came from King John, who promised the islanders "the continuance of their ancient laws and privileges", thus laying the foundation for the self-government they still enjoy. There were other considerations, too. First, the islanders had to consider that England, with its superior naval power, might defend them more effectively against raiders; and second, that the King of England, being farther away than the King of France, might interfere less in the islands' affairs.

The theory was sound. But in fact the tug-of-war between England and France was just beginning and Mont Orgueil Castle, built early in the 13th century on a Jersey promontory overlooking the French coast, became a lasting symbol of the islands' beleaguered state. Geography, too, dictated their plight: they were strategically placed to shelter the opposing fleets from each other and from the elements. They were, therefore, fated to remain at the centre of a struggle that would continue for centuries.

Like the Third Reich's invaders in 1940, England's 13th-century rulers found that the islanders had infuriatingly independent minds. They insisted, for instance, on being governed according to their ancient customs; but English administrators, who were by now used to laws being formally codified, could never quite be certain what those customs meant in practice.

What became known as the Hundred Years' War between Britain and France subjected the islands to frequent hit-and-run raids between 1337 and 1453. At the outset, the French dangled a tempting carrot in front of the islanders: join France in return for a firm confirmation of self-government. England's Edward III was forced to match the offer. In a charter which was profoundly to affect the islanders' future, he allowed them to "hold and retain all privileges, liberties, immunities and customs granted by our forbears or of other legal competency, and that they enjoy them freely without molestation by ourselves, our heirs or officers".

Even so, the raids continued. France invaded twice in 1338, capturing Guernsey, Alderney and Sark. In 1373 the Constable of France, Bertrand du Gueslin, overran all of Jersey except for Gorey Castle, which withstood a siege from July until September, when it was relieved by the English fleet. In 1380 the French captured Jersey again and held it for two years.

Within four years of Henry V's triumph over the French at Agincourt in 1415, virtually all of Normandy except for Mont-St.-Michel was an English province. His dream was to unite the two kingdoms, which would have oriented the Channel Islands permanently towards the closer of the two cultures, the French. But after Henry's death the tide was turned by a 17-year-old peasant, Joan of Arc, who inspired the French forces to rout the English. By the end of the Hundred

Preceding pages, John Copley's "Death of Major Peirson", portraying the Battle of Jersey. Left, Du Guesclin attacks Mont Orgueil Castle. Right, Jersey's Grosnez Castle.

Years' War in 1453, the tables of history had been turned again and Calais was the only part of France held by England.

Family feuds: Peace was short-lived. In 1455 the islands were caught up in an internecine English feud, the Wars of the Roses, which dragged on for 31 years. Families were split between loyalty to the House of York and support for the House of Lancaster. The French, taking advantage of the diversion, mounted a successful attack on

Mont Orgueil (Mount Pride) in 1461 and held the islands as part of Normandy for the next seven years.

In 1483 Edward IV of England and Louis XI of France agreed that the Channel Islands should be neutral territory in any ensuing conflict between their countries. Pope Sixtus IV reinforced the treaty by issuing a Papal Bull pronouncing "sentence of anathema and eternal damnation with confiscation of goods" on anyone who infringed this neutrality. Soon afterwards, the islands were divided for administrative purposes into two bailiwicks: today's Jersey and Guernsey.

The Papal Bull of Neutrality didn't rule

out preemptive strikes. Even Sark couldn't escape the feuding and in 1549 was seized by the French. The island, which had prospered in the 13th century, had been abandoned by the monks in 1412 when they could no longer withstand the countless pirate raids, and belonged more to birds than to either Britain or France. For the next nine years the French proceeded to fortify it. Their presence there was a thorn in the side for the larger islands. Finally Sark was liberated by Flemish adventurers who returned it to the English crown. Elizabeth I later granted it to Helier de Carteret, a member of one of Jersey's leading families, under a typical condition of feudal tenure: that he kept at

stronghold throughout the Middle Ages. The buccaneers were finally driven out during Elizabeth I's reign, a period of consolidation for the islands. As trade flourished, Sir Walter Raleigh, while governor of Jersey for a brief period, oversaw the building of another addition to the island's skyline: Elizabeth Castle in St. Aubin's Bay. Every monarch added to the fortifications. In Henry VIII's time a stolid fortress, Les Murs de Haut, came to dominate the approaches to Alderney's Longey harbour; rebuilt, it was to become Fort Essex in the 19th century.

God's law: By now the islands had evolved legislative assemblies, known as the States, which helped stabilise internal affairs when

least 40 loyal subjects there. He found willing colonists and provided them with housing, the titles to which still give the owners the right to a seat in the island's parliament, the Chief Pleas.

De Carteret found Sark "so full of rabbit-holes and heather, briars, brambles, bracken and undergrowth that it looked impossible to cultivate. There were no tracks down which a cart could safely pass, nor harbour where a boat could unload safely." Nevertheless, farming was developed and a safe harbour (the tiny Creux Harbour) was cut from the rocks to provide safe anchorages.

Alderney, meanwhile, had been a pirate

anarchy reigned in neighbouring nations and were to be the foundation of eventual self-government. Their religious orientation had changed, too. During the Reformation from 1547 until 1558 "the venom of Martin Luther's heresy", as the Roman Catholic church called it, swept through Normandy and across to the Channel Islands. Roadside crosses were smashed and Latin services swept away. Few of the islanders spoke English and the new English prayerbook had to be translated into French for Edward VI's subjects in the Channel Islands and Calais.

Influenced by the Huguenots, the islanders adopted the Calvinist model of the new

Protestant faith. Dancing or gossiping on Sundays, which were reserved for church-going, meant a jail sentence. Absentees from the quarterly communion were thrown in the stocks. If anyone at a party sang lascivious songs or told licentious stories, everyone present was fined. The unrepentant were excommunicated, "cut off as septic limbs from the body of Christ, as Adam was expelled from Paradise by a flaming sword".

The Presbyterian ethic didn't drive out the ancient belief in witchcraft, which lingered through the 17th century and into the 18th. At best, someone might whisper of a neighbour: "She has the hidden knowledge." At worst, someone might be subjected to a ing a pair of white, weatherproof stockings knitted in Jersey. Strict quality control was enforced, with inspectors being appointed to ensure that three ply rather than two ply wool was used.

Stocking up: Knitting was so profitable a business that it employed both men and women. Jean Poingdestre, a lieutenant bailiff of Jersey, wrote: "The greatest part of the inhabitants are knitters. There be many houses where man, wife and children, beginning at the age of five or six, have no other employment, and may be said to make everyone a pair of stockings every week; which must, according to my account, come to more than 10,000 pairs weekly."

flogging or be executed.

On the economic front, though, things were improving. The islands' fishing fleets had discovered the rich waters off Newfoundland and at home the knitting of stockings and fishermen's sweaters — still known as "jerseys" and "guernseys" — became the most important industry. The Tudors had set the fashion with their liking for knitted stockings, and it is recorded that Mary Queen of Scots went to her execution wear-

Left, Henry VIII's ships of war, and Queen of Elizabeth I. Above, Essex Castle on Alderney, begun in 1546 by Henry VIII.

Rectors forbade knitting in churches because the noise of the needles drowned out the sermon. And the authorities began to get worried: so irresistible were the profits that men were beginning to neglect the harvesting crops and collecting seaweed (*vraic*) used for cooking and heating. In 1608 a new law was framed: "During harvest and *vraicing* seasons all persons shall stop making stockings and work on the land on pain of imprisonment on bread and water and the confiscation of their work."

There was comparative peace until England was torn apart by its Civil Wars, the bitter conflict between Parliament and Charles I over freedom in politics and religion. Jersey's sympathies were with the King; Guernsey's with Parliament. On two occasions Jersey's Elizabeth Castle gave sanctuary to the King's children, Charles, Prince of Wales, and James, Duke of York. When the King was beheaded in 1649, Jersey proclaimed the Prince Charles II and he spent much of his time on the island with a generously large group of courtiers, including a jester. As a reward to their supporters, Charles and James granted them land on the eastern seaboard of America; it was to become known as New Jersey.

Jersey's loyalty to the monarchy incurred the wrath of Parliament. In 1651, after the

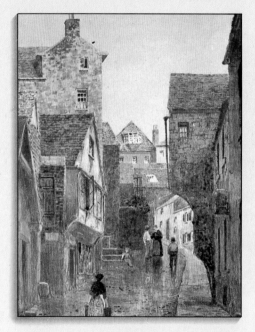

Royalists were defeated by Cromwell's Roundheads, Charles became a true vagabond prince. A fleet of 80 vessels under Admiral Blake was despatched to crush the Royalist resistance. The Roundhead troops landed at St. Ouen's Bay and quickly took St. Aubin's Fort and Gorey Castle. Elizabeth Castle capitulated after a 50-day siege, but Castle Cornet held out for nearly nine years. It was not an easy occupation: the troops billeted themselves in churches and ignored ancient charters by press-ganging able-bodied men into the forces. Jersey remained under Parliament's rule until the monarchy was restored in 1660.

On the prowl: Towards the end of the 17th century, the islands steadily grew more prosperous and, in an uncanny echo of today's concerns, the States complained that too many houses were being built. With the French fleet less of a threat, fishing business with Newfoundland flourished.

In Jersey, new ploughing methods improved the yield of parsnips. St. Peter Port, now a free port, profited by acting as middleman to smugglers, who were tolerantly regarded by most islanders. Tobacco was a favourite commodity, shipped secretly by night to the Devon coast; customs men realised what was going on when they noticed that the islands were importing far more tobacco than their inhabitants could possibly hope to smoke on their own.

Sark's fortunes began to fluctuate. The de Carteret family remained rulers until 1720, strengthening their holding by giving support to Charles II. But the sixth Seigneur, Sir Charles de Carteret, got into debt and, with Queen Anne's permission, sold the island. It then changed hands regularly.

Methodism reached the islands in the 1770s and the church's founder, John Wesley, visited Guernsey where the religion had taken hold. But a more telling indicator of the times were the dozens of round towers (later called Martello towers) springing up around the coasts.

As various wars erupted between England, France and Spain, enterprising sea captains grew rich as armed privateers, licensed to plunder merchant vessels of the current enemy. Scores of brigantines and cutters prowled the seas around the islands, most often preying on French traders. Jersey's fine martello towers were built as beach defences in anticipation of more trouble from France.

It was a wise precaution: in 1781, Jersey was invaded by French troops led by a soldier of fortune, Le Chevalier de Luxembourg, who had vowed to drive out the privateers. But he lost a hard-fought contest that came to be called the Battle of Jersey. As a protection against further attacks, Fort Regent was built on a granite hill overlooking St. Helier, but proved to be redundant: the French never invaded again.

Right, the traditional Jersey bonnet. Left, Guernsey's capital, St. Peter Port.

When the French returned in 1789, they came as refugees, fleeing from the French Revolution. Thousands of aristocrats sought refuge from the guillotine and were joined by an estimated 3,000 priests who refused to swear loyalty to France's new constitution. It was a lucrative time for the islands' boatmen who ferried them across. Builders benefitted, too, as the aristocrats invested whatever wealth they had salvaged in erecting manor houses.

When France declared war on England in 1793, Jersey became a counter-espionage centre and an operation based at Mont Orgueil was set up to smuggle fake banknotes into France to undermine confidence in the Republic's currency.

The brigands were having a heyday. By now piracy was promising such guaranteed profits that old ladies were known to invest their savings by buying shares in the privateers. As a business, it required little capital since some of the ships themselves were vessels taken in combat: the *Union*, for instance, had started life as the *Los Dos Amigos*. So much French brandy was plundered that Guernsey was dubbed the bonded warehouse of British merchants.

Eventually, Napoleon Bonaparte's patience ran out. "France can tolerate no longer this nest of brigands and assassins," he fumed. "Europe must be purged of this vermin. Jersey is England's shame." Taking him at his word, the English built Fort Regent as a defence. But the threat never materialised and the privateers survived, finding new opportunities during Britain's war with the United States in 1812.

Peace breaks out: The French threat finally ended with the English victories at Trafalgar in 1805 and at Waterloo in 1815, and a period of prosperity began. Retired army and navy officers began to settle on the islands, attracted by the low cost of living, and a few French arrived to open hotels.

One helpful consequence of the islands' strategic importance was that the roads had

Left, traditional Guernsey flower seller. Right, old Jersey water trough.

to be improved to allow soldiers to be moved more easily from place to place. Usually it was far faster for Jerseymen to get from St. Helier to St. Aubin by boat round the coast than to travel through the narrow, meandering country lanes. "Two carts meeting each other could not pass; one or the other must back until it reached the nearest field or gateway or some other recess to which it might retreat during the passage of the other," said a report to Britain's Board of

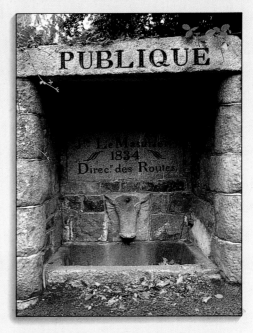

Agriculture. "To this little circumstance in their internal economy, and the disputes which it engenders, may perhaps in part be attributed to the remarkable proficiency of the Jersey populace in swearing." Such a situation would not be unfamiliar to drivers in today's car-clogged lanes.

The military's attempts to upgrade the roads were not appreciated by the farmers. One resisted with a gun, and another raised the ancient *Clameur de Haro*, forcing the issue to be taken to court. (He lost.)

Another cause for frequent dispute in Jersey was the bitter rivalry between the politically radical party, whose symbol was a rose, and the conservatives, who wore a laurel leaf. A guidebook of the time reported that Laurel and Rose supporters hated each other "more bitterly than do rival actors or singers. They seldom intermarry, seldom salute each other in the public ways; and they, for the most part, carry their mutual animosities into every transaction of their lives, legislative, judicial, municipal and private." Yesterday's bitter rivalries could not be further removed from today's scene, when politicians are elected as individuals and parties do not exist.

Economically, great changes were taking place. Stocking-making didn't survive Britain's Industrial Revolution and was

Conqueror to the Augustinian Order of Cherbourg, who farmed it; but the religious community had all but died out by the 16th century and Guernsey's gentry began using Herm as a game preserve. But in 1815, granite quarrying became big business, bringing in its wake shops, a school, a hotel and a lilliputian beehive-shaped jail. Thereafter, Herm passed through the hands of wealthy men who liked the idea of owning an island. One famous tenant in the 1920s was the novelist Sir Compton Mackenzie; another tenant raised wallabies there. Finally, in 1946, the island was bought by the States of Guernsey for use as a resort.

The smuggling business, known colloqui-

largely replaced by a large entrepot trade which exploited the islands' ability to sail under the U.K.'s tariff barriers. Thus, leather might be imported tax-free from France and exported as shoes to England.

Guernsey's first glasshouses, built in 1792, were used for growing dessert grapes but became a source of unimagined wealth as tomatoes, introduced in 1865, took over. Within 90 years, tomatoes accounted for 75 percent of Guernsey's income and employment of the local people.

Shooting parties: The 19th century brought important changes to Herm. The tiny island had been given by William the

ally as *La Fraude*, was changing too in the 19th century as customs men tightened their grip. As in Devon and Cornwall, violence often erupted on moonless nights as the authorities pounced on contraband cargoes of spirits and tobacco. An advertisement placed by the British customs in a Jersey newspaper in 1823 gives a graphic account of one such encounter; it offered a £50 reward for information about an incident in which "Humphrey Oxenham, being out on duty about one o'clock of the morning of Thursday, June 19, saw a smuggling vessel in the offing and some carts on the beach, which were accompanied by upwards of 40 smugglers, armed with bludgeons, who surrounded him, struck him a violent blow above his eyes, which knocked him down, and, whilst on the ground, beat him severely, until James Hudie, an extra boatman, came to the assistance of Humphrey Oxenham, on which the smugglers dispersed."

Nor were the smaller islands exempt from the pressures of the age. Sark's idyll was disrupted when traces of silver and copper were discovered and the Sark's Hope Mining Company began trading in 1834. But early dreams turned to tragedy when a cutter carrying the first silver to England diverted to Guernsey when the captain returned to visit his sick wife. The vessel ran on to the

land "England's shield". The English began building an ambitious 3,300-foot (1,000 metre) breakwater in 1847 to counter a French naval build-up at Cherbourg. Alderney, they said, would become the Gibraltar of the Channel. It was a project so worthy of the mighty British Empire that Queen Victoria herself paid two visits to see its construction. But the architects hadn't bargained for the pounding of the seas and the ferocity of the westerly gales. By 1864, it was abandoned as hopelessly expensive and England agreed "temporarily" to bear the cost of maintaining the incomplete breakwater. The arrangement was more than temporary: by the 1980s, maintaining the Victo-

rocks, sinking with the loss of both crew and cargo. On the same day, seawater flooded the mine's profitable lower galleries, putting an end to the venture. The 16th seigneur, the company's principal shareholder, was forced to mortgage the island to pay off his mounting debts.

The tourists of the time, denied the inducement of a silvermine, looked to Alderney where they marvelled at the massive fortifications. Napoleon Bonaparte called the is-

Left, smugglers at a deserted spot in Jersey. Above, encountering history in a Guernsey gallery.

rian white elephant cost Britain more than £500,000 a year.

Waiting for war: Fort building was, all in all, a safer business to be in. Military architects specified the finest quality of stone, selected shades of granite to set off their design and, to keep that traditional touch, included arrow slits and moats that had very little to do with 19th-century warfare. In Alderney an impressive half-circle of coastal forts was created, from Fort Clonque to Essex Castle.

The islands' reputation as a place of refuge brought in exiles from many countries— Poles, Hungarians, Italians, French—during

1848, when revolutions erupted all over Europe. The most celebrated refugee, Victor Hugo, a politician as well as a novelist, poet and playwright, arrived with a price on his head in 1852 from Paris, where he had violently opposed the rule of Louis Napoleon.

Typifying the traditional rivalry between Jersey and Guernsey, both claim to have pioneered Britain's distinctive posting box. Jersey says its octagonal model was adopted by the novelist, Anthony Trollope, at the time a Post Office surveyor; Guernsey claims its first-pillar box appeared in St. Peter Port in 1853.

New, fast steamships were making the islands more accessible to both tourists and

planes kept watch for U-boats. The war passed the islands by and they were even considered safe enough to house German prisoners-of-war. Only sugar and petrol were rationed.

In the 1920s, buses put the railways out of business and many retired English people, attracted by the genial climate, easygoing lifestyle and low taxes bought comfortable houses with spacious grounds and ran smart cars about the islands.

Modern life was kept at a distance. Electricity didn't come to Alderney, for example, until the 1930s and, apart from the telegraph service, instant communication with the outside world depended on one radio-tele-

wealthy new residents. The first railway lines were built in the 1870s. Telegraphic communication with England followed. Hotels sprang up, schools and libraries were opened, and cattle farming flourished. However, industries such as knitting, oyster fishing and cider-making were dying out.

Peace reigns: The 20th century was ushered in on an exuberant note. A Battle of Flowers, held to commemorate Edward VII's coronation in 1902, became a regular festival symbolising the islands' fecundity. Even World War I failed to spoil the tranquillity: although many natives joined the forces and Guernsey-based French sea-

phone. Sark's Court of Chief Pleas outlawed cars and motorcycles, on the grounds that they would ruin the island's charm. When one persistent doctor shipped in a car, he was forbidden to use it unless it was pulled by a horse.

The Channel Islands might not have been Britain's South Sea Islands, as one guidebook claimed, but they were a delightful and hospitable little world. By 1939 Guernsey's modern and efficient tomato industry was producing 35,000 tons a year and Jersey's potato yield was 10,000 tons. Both islands did well from cattle exports. As Europe talked of war, the Channel Islands regarded themselves as the safest place on earth.

Don't call us: When war was declared the States of Jersey and Guernsey pledged to King George VI the services of "Your Majesty's Norman subjects" and many islanders, although exempt from U.K. military service, joined the British armed forces. His Majesty's government, however, had given so little thought to the position of the Channel Islands that it was unsure whether to communicate through the lieutenant-governors of the bailiwicks, both militarymen, through the War Office or the Home Office.

When, in September 1939, Jersey asked London for anti-aircraft and coastal defence guns, the War Office, unable to supply even island in newspapers as "the ideal resort for wartime holidays this summer".

By the middle of 1940, things looked less rosy. All British troops had been driven out of France. The Channel Islanders, realising that German forces were now just eight miles to the east of Alderney, felt utterly vulnerable. What support could Britain offer given their defeats? Perhaps total evacuation ought to be considered?

Since the 1920s, Army chiefs had argued that the islands had no strategic value for Britain—and, anyway, they would be impossibly expensive to defend. On June 19, 1940, the long-awaited decision was taken: they would be demilitarized. All army per-

a Bren gun for at least a year, said it thought the chances of an attack on Jersey were "somewhat remote". Certainly, the conflict seemed far away as 1939 gave way to 1940. Ration books were prepared, and a few elderly gentlemen with ancient firearms stood guard over power stations and reservoirs.

However, life went on as usual; cargo boats still called, the mail still arrived. And Jersey felt so unaffected that it advertised the

Left, French workers provided the islands with much needed immigrant labour. Above, making lobster pots in Jersey in the 1930s.

sonnel were evacuated. So were the lieutenant-governors. Civilians were ordered to hand in all weapons to their local parish constable. But in London the military experts were reassuring: "There need be no fear of the Germans taking any advantage from the British decision to demilitarize the islands."

There was a great deal of dithering about whether to evacuate the islanders to the U.K. Finally voluntary evacuation was offered, but without any guidance as to the wisdom of accepting it. Initially shipping offices were besieged and there was a run on the banks. Defiant posters appeared: "Why run away?"

In the end, 90,000 people chose to leave the islands and 80,000 stayed. Many found themselves packed like cattle on boats normally used to haul coal or potatoes.

Sabotage strategy: On Jersey valuables were buried; savings withdrawn from banks; houses, farms and cars abandoned; several thousand pets destroyed. In Guernsey a publican abandoned his bar, inviting his neighbours to help themselves to the liquor.

In Alderney, communications were particularly bad: the telegraph cable to England was out of order and radio silence was obligatory. A meeting of the States was convened and the town crier invited the island's 1,400 people to assemble. A notice

from the island's *de facto* leader, the autocratic Judge F.G. French, set out the stark options: "I have appealed to Admiralty for a ship to evacuate us. If the ship does not come, it means we are considered safe. If the ship comes, time will be limited. You are advised to pack one suitcase for each person, so as to be ready. If you have invalids in your house, make arrangements in consultation with your doctor. All possible notice will be given."

Enough fishing boats arrived at Alderney on June 23 to take off the entire population; so people, expecting the worst, took to the boats. During the voyage to England, three

children were born on one ship. Only 19 islanders stayed behind—and 12 of those were soon persuaded to flee to Guernsey. On Sark, reassured by the example set by the Dame, Mrs. Sibyl Hathaway, a forceful lady who had ruled over the feudal island since 1926, hardly anyone left.

In London, the authorities were divided on one question: should the Germans be told the islands were undefended? If they knew, they might invade. If they didn't know, they might attack. Either way, the islands were sitting ducks. On June 28, a gloriously warm summer day, the *Luftwaffe* put an end to the dithering: it first bombed and machine-gunned Guernsey, then Jersey, killing 33 people. The government asked the U.S. ambassador in London, Joseph P. Kennedy, to inform Germany through the American Embassy in Berlin that the Channel Islands had been demilitarized and were no longer a legitimate target for bombardment.

Phoney war: The invasion seemed to the islanders a long time in coming. Everyday German planes flew overhead on reconnaisance missions, but none landed. The Germans expected to find the islands defended because aerial photographs revealed columns of lorries, assumed to be troop carriers, approaching the harbours of both main islands. The lorries were, in fact, transporting Jersey potatoes and Guernsey tomatoes not British troops.

Then, on June 30, a lone *Luftwaffe* pilot upstaged the cautious German naval command by touching down on Guernsey. There was no resistance. Satisfied that the island really was defenceless, the Germans flew in a platoon of soldiers. The next day a detachment of naval assault troops and a company of Infantry Regiment 396 flew into Jersey. Troops on motorbikes and officers in cars drove into St. Helier and St. Peter Port. Alderney was occupied on July 2 and Sark on July 4.

For the first time, a part of the British empire—one just 90 miles from the English coast and the monarchy's oldest possession—had been abandoned to an enemy, without a shot having been fired.

Left, a German gunner gets the islands in his sights. Right, Nazi soldier meets British bobby.

Life under the *Wehrmacht*, Germany's armed forces, began in a cordial enough way. True, a curfew was imposed, the sale of spirits was banned, listening to any radio station not German-controlled was forbidden, carrier pigeons were outlawed, and clocks were put forward one hour to conform to Central European time. But church services were allowed, prayers for the Royal Family and the British Empire could be said, and civilians could travel between Jersey and Guernsey.

Such "correct" behaviour, it was reasoned, would counter propaganda about German barbarity and reassure the English that they had little to fear when England fell, as it inevitably would, under Hitler's rule. Anticipating that day on celluloid, the Germans filmed their army invading the virtually deserted island of Herm and claimed, for propaganda purposes, that it was the Isle of Wight.

Soon there were more Germans per square mile on the islands than in Germany, and there was no question about their purpose. Major-General Count Rudolph von Schmettow, Commander of the Channel Islands, a Silesian nobleman, was generally regarded as being courteous and civilised—but he was under direct orders from the Führer to turn the islands into "strong naval fortresses as quickly as possible, employing all forces and means available". After the war, Hitler had decided, Alderney would become part of France, while Jersey and Guernsey would remain German outposts.

Chalk and cheese: The Germans began to administer the islands as part of France, believing the islanders would be glad to be liberated from the British colonial yoke. They found it hard to understand the people's loyalty to Britain, and soon found much to disapprove of in their easy-going ways: the high illegitimate birth rate, the heavy consumption of alcohol, the presence

of retired plutocrats who devoted their time to golf and bridge. The Germans deplored the wide gap between rich and poor and regarded social provisions as being much behind the times. Reform, they vowed, must be a priority, and by 1943 they were able to report: "The face of the islands has been changed completely; it has become more serious and more European."

But they found it almost impossible to come to grips with the islands' feudal system

of government. What sense did it make to judge a 20th-century traffic offence by reference to 11th-century practices? Reluctantly, they decided to leave untouched this "constitutional nature reserve". For one thing, they were too thin on the ground to change everything overnight; for another, it soon became clear that it was in their interests to let the locals go on running their everyday affairs while the troops concentrated on making the islands impregnable.

Even so, the inexperienced German chiefs issued many unworkable orders. All photographic apparatus had to be handed in, they decreed; they were deluged not only with

Preceding pages, the Germans march in. Left, the Dame of Sark confronts German officers. Right, German observation tower at Noirmont Point, Jersey.

cameras but also with lenses, tripods and developing tanks. All weapons must be surrendered, they ordered; a strange selection of hunting weapons such as spears, tomahawks and blunderbusses descended on them—the legacy of the colonial careers of former administrators who had retired to the islands.

Many such people, who had devoted their life to the British Empire, now felt abandoned by Britain. Why, they asked bitterly, were the Channel Islands mentioned so seldom in BBC broadcasts? Had they been totally forgotten? In fact, the Home Office had advised the B.B.C. not to make direct broadcasts to the islands for fear of reprisals

shops—clothes, jewellery, clocks, gas fires—to send to their families in Germany. Since they paid in *Reichskredit* currency, issued only in occupied territory, this was in effect a form of respectable looting. Cars were requisitioned in return for eventual and inadequate compensation in *Reichsmarks*.

Prices soar: As the shops emptied, some were converted to other uses, such as soldiers' canteens. Others began selling secondhand goods, such as old kettles and worn clothes, at fancy prices. Soon flour, sugar and butter had to be imported from France. So did two-thirds of the meat ration.

The Germans took a particular interest in food production, bombarding experienced

by the Germans, who might, it was argued, confiscate all radio sets and so leave the islanders in complete ignorance of what was happening in the outside world. The argument was probably correct: when the war started going badly for the Germans, they did confiscate all radios. At first there was more than enough food on the islands for those remaining; too much, London thought, since the surplus would help sustain the invaders. Financially, things looked less rosy: many taxpayers had left, taking their bank accounts with them.

When the troops first arrived, they rapidly bought up everything they could find in

farmers with unwanted advice and demanding regular supplies of statistics. Glasshouses in Guernsey had to start producing green vegetables instead of flowers and tomatoes. Wheat, oats and barley largely replaced potatoes in Jersey's fields. "Agricultural commandos" were appointed to ensure that farmers were not supplying a black market.

Fishermen were closely supervised. Permits were issued only to those "who for family reasons are unlikely to flee" and, unless escorted, they had to stay close to shore. As a result, catches were inadequate. The regulations governing fishing boats became so restrictive that, even when the seas were teeming with mackerel and mullet, the fishmongers had little to sell. In June 1942 fish was rationed.

Tea ran out within a year of Occupation. By 1943 black market supplies were costing £25 a lb (less than a half kg). Soap ran out early in 1941 and soon sugar was short. With each deprivation, the islanders became more inventive, concocting such delicacies as carrot jam.

Smokers turned to substitutes such as water-cress leaves and dried rose petals. They also tried cultivating tobacco plants and found, to their joy, that they flourished in the Channel Islands' soil. The States tried

Collisions involving German troops were frequent enough for driving on the left was abandoned in favour of the continental system of driving on the right. Gradually road-signs were translated into German, turning Castle Cornet into *Hafenschloss* and Petit Bot Bay into *Grüne Bucht*.

Close screening: Schools had to add German lessons to their curriculum, but not enough teachers could be spared from Germany to ensure it was effectively taught. When the few English language films trapped on the islands—such as *The Barretts of Wimpole Street*—at last lost their appeal through repetition, German films were imported. A galvanised pipe ran down the

unsuccessfully to license the growers, some of whom were raising thousands of plants, and then turned their attention to how best to tax the tobacco grown. As a result the black market price of tobacco soared to 10 times its controlled price.

As petrol supplies diminished, vehicles were restricted to transporting troops or to essential services such as distributing milk. Bicycles were requisitioned, and soon rusty old crocks that might once have fetched a few shillings were changing hands for £10.

Left, Jersey displays a defiant victory sign. Above, a German band concert.

centre of cinemas; Germans sat to the right of it, locals to the left. Cinema-goers were instructed that it was in order to applaud comedians and heroes. Many locals turned, instead, to amateur theatricals, although the choice of plays had to be approved.

For lovers of military bands, there was no shortage of entertainment. For frustrated lovers among the military, official brothels were opened in St. Helier and St. Peter Port; the girls, imported from France, were permitted the more generous rations usually reserved for heavy workers.

Respecting the Hague Convention, the Germans did not insist that Channel Island-

ers undertake any war-related jobs which might indirectly harm their fellow countrymen. But they did tempt some workers, particularly from the local Irish community, with high wages and better food rations. In reality, of course, anyone who grew potatoes or produced milk on the island was indirectly working for the enemy.

The grip of rationing tightened. An adult was allowed half a pint of milk a day and seven lbs (three kg) of potatoes. Gradually the amounts decreased: by the end of the war the bread allowance had fallen from four lbs (two kg) a week to one lb (half kg); the meat allowance from 12 ozs (330 gm) a head to one oz (28 gm) a week, and a one lb (half kg) packet of tea cost up to £30 on the black market. Thievery became commonplace. Crops were stolen and some took advantage of the curfew to sneak into farms and milk the cows. Ingenuity (and necessity) produced parsnip coffee, blackberry leaf tea, carrot pudding and seaweed jelly. Curtains were made into clothes. Shoes were soled with wood.

The black market in food smuggled in from France began flourishing early in the Occupation. "It was interesting," remembered one doctor, "to watch people who lost weight at the early part of the Occupation gradually put it on again as they overcame their scruples."

Friend or foe?: The moral question faced by everyone was: to what extent should they cooperate with the enemy? Clearly the islands were too small for an effective resistance movement to develop, as it did in France. But at what point did passive cooperation shade into cordial collaboration? It was a delicate balancing act.

One resident remembered many years later: "There was no organised resistance as there was in France, because in a small country like this there would have been nowhere for them to hide. In France you could blow up a train and be hundreds of miles away by nightfall. There was not much sabotage, but plenty of passive resistance. Our motto was: if you couldn't hinder you didn't help. There was a great deal of hiding of food, of falsifying returns of potato crops, that sort of thing."

Left, before the food shortages, life of a kind goes on.

As so often in such situations, however, some girls cooperated closely enough to become pregnant. They were derided as "Jerry bags". Some personal grudges were settled as people informed on neighbours who had kept a radio set hidden or hoarded too much food.

There were small acts of defiance, too. When supplies of Jersey's postage stamps ran out, the artist, Edmund Blampied, designed a new set with King George VI's cipher "GR" hidden in the scrollwork.

Soon the islanders became pawns in the battle of wills between Winston Churchill and Adolf Hitler. When Britain detained German citizens working in Iran, Hitler threatened to deport all British-born inhabitants of the Channel Islands. Unknown to the islanders, lists were drawn up.

Hitler's madness: The *Wehrmacht* were unenthusiastic about the idea: they had more than enough women and children on their hands in refugee camps and, with 36,000 much needed troops pinned down in the Channel, were already referring to Hitler's "island madness". But the Führer's personal orders could not be ignored for ever and in September 1942 the threat was finally carried out. More shiploads followed; eventually 2,000 British-born islanders were interned in Germany.

Even more ruthless retaliation was feared. The Germans reserved the right "to nominate certain members of any parish who will be liable to the death penalty in the event of any attacks against communications, as for instance harbours, cranes, bridges, cables and wires, if these are made with the assistance or the knowledge of the inhabitants of the parish concerned". The threat was not taken lightly. As Charles Cruickshank points out in his official history, *The German Occupation of the Channel Islands*, it was realised that "every man, woman and child could have been gassed and incinerated in a single day in one of the larger and more efficient German concentration camps". Such a grim prospect did not stop Churchill from planning nuisance raids on the islands. Bad weather put an end to most of these operations before they even began, but one Royal Navy action ended in disaster when E-boats sank the H.M.S. Charybdis in October 1943 with the loss of 462 lives. At the burial of the 21 bodies washed up on Guernsey, the entire population of around 5,000 turned out to mourn, surprising the Germans with such an uncompromising loyalty to Britain.

Gradually the face of the islands changed as up to 15,000 imported slave workers, including Russians, Poles, Spanish Republicans and European Jews, poured in 17.5 million cubic feet (half a million cubic metres) of reinforced concrete. Anti-tank walls six feet (two metres) thick appeared on beaches. Gun emplacements ringed the coast: Jersey had 16 coastal artillery batteries, Guernsey 15, Alderney five and Sark one. Old granite towers and mills were turned into observation posts. Concrete strongpoints were surrounded by fixed

work." A Russian recalled that the German guards "tried to get out of us every ounce of labour and energy they could on as little food as possible. Our term of usefulness was generally accepted by the Germans to be six months. After that we were expended." Soon Jakob, Gustav and Adolf—as Jersey, Guernsey and Alderney were coded in the construction plan—were far better fortified than the coast of France. At one point there were 42,800 enemy personnel on the islands—two to every three remaining native islanders. Yet the islands, which were eating up one-twelfth of the *Wehrmacht's* resources, had little military significance, even as a jumping-off point for Operation Sealion, the

flame-throwers and barbed-wire entanglements. Narrow-gauge railways were built to transport the concrete. More than 150,000 mines were laid.

Hard labour: The human cost was appalling. On Alderney, where an S.S. concentration camp (Sylt) was set up, as well as three labour camps (Norderney, Borkum and Helgoland), there were no civilians to witness the ruthless regime. It was "work, hard physical work for 12 to 14 hours a day, building the fortifications," one French survivor said later. "Every day there were beatings and people's bones were broken, their arms or their legs. People died from over-

invasion of England. The Occupation was about prestige. Commonsense was a low priority.

As supplies of soap ran out and medicines became scarce, it wasn't just the morale of the islanders which deteriorated. The Germans, at first delighted by their posting to such a pleasant location, soon became bored. Apart from occasionally turning the anti-aircraft guns on overflying RAF planes, there wasn't much to do. Also, as postal deliveries became less frequent towards the end of the war, the German troops, hearing of British bombing raids on Germany, worried increasingly about the fate of their families.

By the beginning of 1944, the tide of war had turned decisively against Hitler. But, worried that the Channel Islands might still be used as stepping-stones for an Allied assault on Europe, he repeated the order: the islands must be held to the last man and the last bullet.

Uncertainty grows: The action on D-Day, June 6, was concentrated elsewhere: on the beaches of Normandy. With rations down to three months' supply, the islanders were left to wait out the rest of the war and found themselves in a frustrating situation: besieged by the British navy. Because fuel was scarce for the supply vessels that hadn't

troops, and Alderney had 3,500 Germans plus the slave workers. The poor diet encouraged ill health: tuberculosis, arthritis, jaundice and diptheria became common. Some troops were on the verge of revolt. Islanders listening into BBC broadcasts on illegal home-made crystal sets heard of food being sent by the Allies to Russia, Greece and Italy. What about the Channel Islands, they wondered. Had they really been abandoned?

As autumn turned to winter in 1944, there was no coal and no gas and not enough wood for fuel. Electricity was due to cease at the end of the year. Communal kitchens were set up. The bailiff of Jersey summarised the stark facts to the German commander:

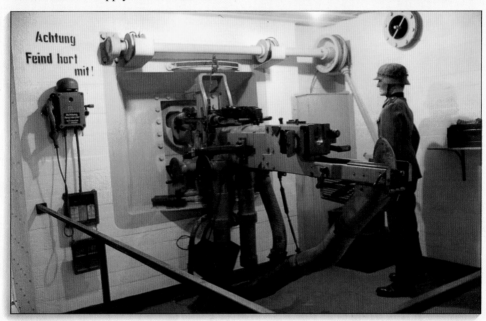

already been destroyed, the Germans began using Rhine barges to supply their "beleaguered Atlantic fortresses". These boats were low enough to creep under British radar screens but they couldn't be used in rough seas, so supplies became more uncertain than ever.

In the autumn of 1944 there were more than 90,000 mouths to feed. Jersey contained 39,000 civilians and 12,000 troops, Guernsey 23,000 civilians and 13,000

Left, German command bunker at Noirmont Point, Jersey. Above, relics in Guernsey's German Occupation Museum.

Butter: 2 oz. weekly ration. Sufficient to last until December 31.

Sugar: 3 oz. weekly ration. Sufficient to last until November 18.

Salt: for bakers only. Sufficient to last until November 30.

Macaroni: Sufficient to last until November 15.

Dried beans: three rations of 7 oz. remaining.

Cheese: 4 oz. ration. Sufficient to last until October 15.

Tinned vegetables: one ration remaining in stock.

Tinned fish: one ration remaining in

stock.

Tinned milk: one ration remaining in stock.

Matches: one ration of four boxes per household remaining in stock.

Dripping: not enough for one ration.

Oil (cooking): enough for one ration of under half-pint remaining.

Saccharine: enough for two rations of 100 tabloids remaining.

Soap: None.

Soon, one milkless day a week was announced, extended in January 1945 to three days.

Hitler had a dilemma. He couldn't let civilians starve and hadn't the resources to

However, the same dilemma had to be faced: the Germans might take more than their share and again the Occupation would be prolonged.

But the risk had to be run, and food parcels were duly delivered at the end of 1944 by the International Red Cross. The German response was to hand over the parcels but seize locally grown potatoes and cereals. They also told the islanders that, if they were accepting free gifts of food, they could not justify hoarding secret stocks of tinned soup or fruit or bottles of wine and that all such stocks must be handed over. Houses were raided to ensure that this order was obeyed.

Power cut: In January, telephones were

move them to Europe, so it would be best to hand them over to Britain. On the other hand, three-quarters of the people were working for the troops, directly or indirectly, growing food and running utilities such as electricity and water; so how could they be spared?

In the end, Hitler asked Britain to evacuate all islanders except those fit to bear arms. This created a dilemma for Churchill. Naturally, he wanted to liberate as many Channel Islanders as possible; on the other hand, leaving the Germans with most of the food would prolong the Occupation longer than necessary. An alternative was to send food parcels and medical supplies to the islands.

finally cut off. Electricity supplies, which had been limited to one kilowatt per house per week, ended completely. It was forbidden to cut wood for fuel. Down to their last few matches, people tried to keep alight a paraffin-soaked piece of string. To conserve food, no household was permitted to keep more than one dog; all others were killed.

There seemed to be fewer pets, anyway, and people began to notice the increasing number of advertisements for missing animals in the "lost and found" columns of local newspapers. The horrifying answer to the mystery soon emerged: hungry troops were catching and cooking cats and dogs.

Ironically, if the Germans had shipped in fertiliser as well as cement and grown more of their own food to start with, the islands might have become self-supporting. One plan, early in the Occupation, had been to turn Herm over to cattle fattening, but the idea came to nothing. As the end of the war neared, they turned desperately to planting potatoes and fishing. But it was too late.

When Hitler's death was announced on May 1, 1945, a German Army newspaper printed in Guernsey ran the headline: "Führer dies a hero's death". The islanders reached for their Union Jacks, but they weren't able to wave them in public for another week, until surrender documents

beaten up. But, mostly, ecstasy was in the air as British soldiers handed out lemonade, chocolate, cakes and soap. A child given an orange started bouncing it: never having seen one before, she thought it was a ball.

On Sark, British soldiers could not be spared to guard the German prisoners and the task was left to the redoubtable Dame of Sark. From May 10 until May 17, she took charge of 275 Germans, ordering them to return confiscated radio sets and to remove mines from the harbour. The British Home Secretary, Herbert Morrison, praised Mrs. Hathaway for having been "almost wholly mistress of the situation" throughout the Occupation.

were signed. Churchill had ruled that Operation Nestegg, the liberation of the Channel Islands, should not involve an assault that might cost civilian lives.

Free at last: There were scenes of jubilation but also of violence as H.M.S. Beagle and H.M.S. Bulldog liberated the islands after four years, 10 months and seven days of Occupation. In Jersey, some girls who had consorted with the Germans were rough-handled and a few black marketeers were

Left, a gun emplacement camouflaged as a house. Above, Red Cross supplies keep starvation at bay.

Alderney, the ultimate fortress which, according to one estimate, would have cost a quarter of a million lives to capture by force, was liberated peacefully on May 16. Four days later, 2,332 Germans were taken as prisoners-of-war to Britain, leaving 500 behind to begin the massive clean-up.

A *Guernsey Evening Press* editorial summed up the mixture of jubilation and apprehension: "As the gates of Liberation and Freedom swing upon their hinges, the durance of captivity passes like a dreadful dream, and there opens before us a prospect impossible, as yet, either to realise or to visualise."

Hitler's plan, had he won the war, was to turn Jersey into one giant holiday centre as part of the Third Reich's "Strength through Joy" programme. What happened, some would say, was not all that different.

The economic need to win back holiday-makers was evident from the first day of peace—even though the islands were in no state to receive them. The economies of Jersey and Guernsey had to be rebuilt and Alderney needed a complete overhaul. Many houses were damaged, some beyond repair. House rents, living costs and taxation had all gone up and domestic servants, the more affluent discovered, were practically unobtainable. Some shrewd U.K. business-men, seeking to escape from the grim eco-nomic prospects on the mainland, snapped up houses at inflated prices, leaving return-ing ex-servicemen and the poorer evacuees unable to find affordable accommodation.

One major problem was what to do with the fortifications, air raid shelters, munitions dumps, gun emplacements and subterranean hangers. Were they an eyesore, a unique tourist attraction or both? One islander in exile in the U.K. had written with prescience in 1944: "What is a disfigurement of the landscape today will be a historic monument tomorrow." In many cases the problem was theoretical anyhow, since the concrete was solid enough to defeat the demolition teams. In glasshouse-covered Guernsey, the dy-namiters didn't dare try.

Normality returned slowly. Gradually those evacuated in 1940 began to come back. German time was changed back to British time and *Reichsmarks* were exchanged for sterling at 9.36 to the pound.

Warm welcome: Alderney, evacuated in 1940, had suffered most. So great was the devastation that some observers thought her best left abandoned. But soon the islanders started drifting back. The first contingent arrived on a stormy December day to be greeted with "Welcome Home" placards made by German prisoners of war on the orders of the British army. Surprisingly, relations were tolerably good between the remaining Germans and the returning is-landers, and the Germans, before they were finally shipped out in June 1946, gave a farewell concert in the Lyceum Cinema.

Prompted by the UK, Guernsey assumed financial and administrative responsibility for Alderney. For the individual, though, picking up the pieces after more than five years was a heartbreaking business. It cer-tainly wasn't made any easier by the curious decision of Judge French to allocate the islanders' scattered furniture and belong-ings by means of a free-for-all; the people lined up and, when a whistle was blown, ran forward to grab whatever goods they could. It was a sure way to create ill-feeling, and it did.

Nor could the past be easily forgotten. There were demands that known collabora-tors—mistresses of Germans, profiteers and informers—should be punished. But from whom should the pound of flesh be extracted? At what point did disgraceful behaviour become treachery? It was easy enough to claw back profits made from the Occupation: a 60 percent levy on such prof-its was imposed in Jersey; in Guernsey, 80 percent of the first £10,000 of profits were seized, then 100 percent. But, in identifying traitors, the British authorities found it diffi-cult to separate hearsay from hard evidence, and there were no criminal prosecutions.

Calls for reform: In facing the challenges of peacetime, many of the islanders who had spent the war in the U.K. were determined not to return to the prewar rule of a paternal establishment; they had experienced a more robust political climate in the U.K. and demanded reforms in the States. More democratic election procedures were intro-duced. These brought experienced business-men into government, laying the foundation for the prosperity to come. Due concession was made to tradition, however: it was de-cided to keep French as the language for formal and ceremonial occasions, so that,

Preceding pages:joy as the islands are liber-ated; in the shadow of yesterday's grave-yard, today's Jersey beach. Left, tourism became a major post-war priority.

even today, the islands' parliaments vote *pour* or *contre*.

As older people tried to forget the Occupation, a younger generation began to discover it. Two Guernsey schoolboys began collecting some of the relics still to be found in bunkers, tunnels and slit trenches: gas masks, satchels, helmets with the original owner's name inside. As their collection outgrew their attics, their activities formalised themselves into "The Society for the Preservation of German Occupation Relics". Eventually this became the Channel Islands Occupation Society, which today runs filmshows and talks about wartime life and publishes an 80-page annual magazine.

lies, the Independent Broadcasting Authority Act became the only Westminster legislation applying to the Channel Islands. It decreed that Channel Television must produce at least three-and-a-half hours a week of local programming, buying the rest from the Independent Television network. Making a virtue of its size, the station avoided trade union opposition to new technology and became the first ITV station to take advantage of the compactness and flexibility of electronic newsgathering equipment.

Midas touch: In the early 1960s, as more and more of the British Empire's colonies were granted independence, many expatriates in those countries, fearing for the future,

One last territorial squabble between Britain and France was played out in 1953. It centred on ownership of the offshore reefs, the Minquiers and Ecréhous, and was fought out in the International Court at the Hague. England won.

In a postwar world chasing economic prosperity, it became a matter of policy that islanders should have first call on the limited land and housing. Television, too, had to tailor itself to island life. The commercial station, Channel Television, became Britain's nearest equivalent to community TV, closely reflecting the needs of the people. Adding to the constitutional anoma-

looked around to find a safer haven for their capital. With the abolition of a 200-year-old law limiting interest rates to a maximum five percent, Jersey made its bid to become a tax haven—or, as it prefers to call itself, an international finance centre.

Gradually the face of tourism changed. In the old days, the Channel Islands had catered for honeymooners and the conventional family holiday: two weeks living in a guesthouse, with most days spent on the beach. It was "going abroad" made easy. Jersey was seen as a comfortable, cosy destination and, keen to retain its quiet image, refused to let one of its most celebrated tax exiles, Sir Billy

Butlin, build one of his holiday camps on the island. In the 1960s, as cheap package tours lured many British families to the Mediterranean, the Channel Islands found themselves with more middle-aged couples, who demanded a better class of hotel and restaurant and who were looking for alternatives to sunbathing. About half the holidaymakers were return customers—an enviable endorsement of the islands' popularity, but a worry to the tourism authorities because that meant the average visitor was getting older; even today, more than 60 percent of tourists are over 45. Would the next generation of tourists forsake the Channel Islands?

Jersey began wooing the more sophisti-

trade and soon busloads of nurses, teachers, salesmen and Rotarians were being discharged into hotel lobbies.

Guernsey's tourism chief echoed the words of countless other populations throughout the world: "The islanders hate tourism, but they like visitors." But not too many, of course. A ceiling was placed on the number of beds licensed to visitors: 25,000 in Jersey, 15,000 in Guernsey.

Almost European: When Britain joined its old foe, France, in the European Economic Community in 1974, the Channel Islands were uncertain which way to jump. Accepting the EEC's rules could undermine their agricultural and financial services indus-

cated visitor. Capitalising on its abundant supplies of seafood and fresh vegetables, it started a gastronomic festival in 1965. Activity holidays—walking, windsurfing, horse riding—were designed to appeal to the health-conscious younger set. To give tourists something to visit, museums were spruced up and cottage industry attractions, such as glass-blowing, were created. Both States discovered that there was money to be made in the low season from the conference

Left, Jersey cow joins the export drive in 1956. Above, celebrating Jersey's Black Butter night.

tries. In the end, a compromise was hammered out: the islands became subject to the EEC's external tariff on industrial goods and to certain parts of its Byzantine Common Agricultural Policy; but they did not have to harmonise their taxes or conform to the rules governing the free movement of workers and capital, and cattle were excepted so that the purity of the Channel Islands strain could be preserved. The States, having gained the best of both worlds, congratulated themselves on their triumph over the anomaly-hating bureaucrats of Brussels.

Also, aware that 80 percent of Jersey's visitors and 90 percent of Guernsey's came from Britain, the tourist chiefs saw an opportunity to spread their net wider. The average French visitor, for instance, was younger and spent more.

When the French and other Europeans began expressing interest in the islands' history, the States, which had never been particularly conscious of their heritage, opened a maritime and wrecks museum in an old Guernsey fort and revived the noonday gun-firing ceremony at the 13th-century Castle Cornet.

In the 1970s, the oil crisis gave a new significance to the islands' sunshine statistics as solar panels began appearing on rooftops. The high oil prices also hit air fares, and British Airways stopped flying to Guernsey, to local dismay. But, as inflation ravaged Britain, Jersey's prices still looked cheap to Continentals. The French in particular began flocking over to buy English woollens and pop records and to eat gourmet food at affordable prices.

Crisis point: But population pressures were stretching the islands to breaking point. The water supply was inadequate. So were rubbish disposal facilities. Roads weren't good enough. The well-heeled immigrants were demanding efficient services, but Guernsey had more cars than workers. Jersey erected that familiar totem to modern living, a multi-storey carpark. Hospital, police, fire and ambulance services all required expansion. The tourism industry had to import seasonal staff, such as waiters and chambermaids, first from Portugal, then from Scotland.

Even Sark's tranquillity as an offshore Ruritania began to be eroded by day-trippers. Did such visitors, the locals asked, benefit anyone except the wagonette owners? Many brought packed lunches and were rushed around so fast by their tour guides that they didn't have time to stop and buy a postcard.

Other aspects of the modern world began to impinge. In 1979, an automatic telephone exchange was installed on Sark because spare parts could no longer be found for the old manual exchange. But the efficient new technology was not welcomed. Islanders liked the old days when there weren't any telephone numbers; when you simply told the lady operator who you wished to speak to and she would connect you, even if the

person was in the grocery shop or visiting neighbours.

Also, you could have too much of a good thing, even millionaires. Tax exiles such as golfer Tony Jacklin and boxer Billy Walker had brought the islands useful publicity, but too many rich people, the States felt, would unbalance their economies. Restrictions were imposed. Suddenly it seemed easier for a rich man to get into the kingdom of Heaven than to settle in the Channel Islands.

Immigrants to Jersey were expected to buy an expensive house and had to be able to contribute £10,000 a year in taxes to the island's coffers. Even then, the number was limited to 15 a year and all applicants had to

be interviewed. Guernsey adopted a two-tier approach to housing: there was to be a fixed stock of 1,200 houses on an open market, available to newcomers; the rest, in a closed market, could be bought only by natives. What's more, the newcomer could expect to pay between three and five times as much for a house on the open market than the native would pay for a comparable house on the closed register.

The rules defining residents became so complicated that native-born students who had left for long study courses (such as medicine) found it difficult to get permission to return home to practise their profession.

One couple who had continued to own a house on Guernsey while they worked abroad for 20 years were refused residents' licences when, at retirement age, they tried to return to the house.

Alderney prided itself on being less restrictive, but it too had its fair share of problems. An influx of middle-aged wealthy settlers unbalanced the population; there were too few children on the island. Also, some natives felt that the rash of new house-building was making the island look suburban, detracting from its rural appeal.

The big boom: The 1980s have seen a financial bonanza. Margaret Thatcher's new Conservative government in London saw

Europe, the Channel Islands were enjoying virtually full employment, no public debt and healthy budget surpluses.

Although the States owe allegiance to the Queen rather than to the U.K. government, they realised that they could be badly hurt by the actions of the politicians at Westminster.

The fears aren't purely imaginary. One Labour spokesman accused the islanders of living off the proceeds of tax avoidance and encouraging "fraudsters, shysters and tricksters". It was intolerable, the party stated, that British territory should be "a bolthole for money that shuns the light". Nonsense, declared the States, most investment money now comes from non-U.K. sources and,

the decade off to a good start by relaxing exchange controls. This meant that British residents no longer needed Bank of England permission to move money to the Channel Islands and enabled them to use the Channel Islands as a base from which to trade on world money markets. Non-resident company registrations rocketed. The banking and fund management industries became a magnet for billions of pounds. As unemployment soared to new heights in most of

Left, the lure of tax-free goods on Guernsey. Above, hydrofoils boosted inter-island travel.

what's more, makes the U.K.'s balance of trade look a lot healthier by adding to its invisible earnings. Prudently, though, they drew up plans to break the monetary union with the U.K. if necessary.

They also resolved to keep their image clean, expertly juggling the two sometimes contradictory qualities demanded of a tax haven, confidentiality and respectability. An investigation was quickly mounted in 1985 when the U.S. alleged that millions of dollars of Mafia drug money, chased out of the Caribbean, was being laundered through the Channel Islands. No evidence of organised crime transactions was found.

Embarrassments occur regularly, however. Eleven bars of gold bullion from Britain's biggest robbery, a £26 million raid on a Brink's-Mat warehouse in 1983, turned up in Jersey. And, in 1987, it was discovered that Channel Island companies had handled part of the wealth of Ferdinand Marcos, the deposed president of the Philippines. One top banker neatly summed up the situation when he said: "You will notice the corollary between crime and secrecy, and therein lies our dilemma."

The head hunters: There are other dilemmas. The banks alone employ 3,000 people in Jersey and 1,500 in Guernsey and face acute staff shortages. As often happens on

wares in display advertisements: "Looking for a new offshore base? There are no house purchase restrictions, and the lack of red tape makes it ideal for the smaller business."

As finance and tourism brought in more riches, agriculture began to wilt. Guernsey's tomato growers couldn't match the low fuel costs of their Dutch competitors or compete with the cheap exports of Spain and Portugal as they joined the EEC. The heyday of the "Guernsey Tom" was over.

Short of space, both principal towns have been clawing land back from the sea. St. Helier, already using 14 acres (nearly six hectares) of reclaimed land east of the harbour, is now creating a whole new area of

small islands, many of the brighter young people leave to build careers on the mainland, and immigration restrictions mean that the banks can import only specialists. As a result, local school-leavers are often offered jobs in finance before they have even taken their examinations. Poaching staff from rivals is the other common solution.

Financial institutions wishing to set up shop on the larger islands today are confronted with a "No Vacancies" sign. At best, they must wait patiently, as they might after applying to join a select gentleman's club in London. Hoping to take advantage of this situation, Alderney began trumpeting its

town by infilling 35 acres (14 hectares) west of the harbour. St. Peter Port has reclaimed 30 acres (12 hectares) for a marina, car park and container marshalling yard.

Now, as ever, there is a new wave of French invaders. But, as befits the islands' affluence, the newcomers are hoteliers and chefs, seeking to replace tomato soup and cod steaks with *escargots a la Bourguignonne* and *truite Grenobloise*. It's the latest of many revolutions, but at least it is being realised with the kitchen knife rather than the sword.

Above, the long arm of the law in Jersey.

POLICEMEN IN PULLOVERS

For the first half of this century (and for many centuries before) 11 of Jersey's 12 parishes policed themselves without paid assistance from men in blue uniforms. The philosophy was that each parish was an extended family and looked after its own. This meant that, if someone committed a crime, the head of the parish (the Constable, or *Connétable*) and his honorary, part-time policemen—including the *Centenier* (his right-hand man), Constable's officers and *vingteniers* (the on-the-beat kind of PCs)— would be called out. But the paid police of St. Helier would not be alerted—unless the crime was too large for the parish to handle.

In simpler terms, the Constable was the father; his men, elected within the parish, were big brother; the rest of the parish were family; and, as in all families, if a younger son got out of hand the older, wiser lads would quickly bring him to heel.

Red tape: The system dominated crime prevention and fighting. In 1950 there were 233 honorary police in Jersey and only 50 full-time, professional men who wore uniforms and were controlled by the Constable of St. Helier. If a crime took place outside the town or if a criminal fled and hid in a house in another parish, the uniformed branch could not enter that house or arrest that man without the permission of the other parish's Constable or Centenier. It was an odd state of affairs, satisfactory in the Jersey of 500 years ago—but in a Jersey which was growing and developing as a tourist resort.

As far back as 1919, Guernsey had done away which such a system. After all, for every budding Sherlock Holmes that emerges from a completely volunteer, unpaid police force whose members could range from farmhands to quarrymen, how many ponderous Dr. Watsons might there be? The States, reaslising this problem, allowed a "real" police force to be established in the 1950s. By the 1960s, it was dealing effectively with most of the major crime committed on Jersey.

"Most", however, didn't accommodate the sex crimes committed by the notorious "Beast of Jersey". Between 1960 and 1971, "the Beast" (Edward Paisnel) terrorised the island and, in so doing, highlighted one of the main flaws in Jersey's police system: the lack of cohesion between the honoraries and the paid. During any investigation after a crime, the honorary policeman had to be in attendance because only he had the power to enter a home without a warrant—a privilege denied the paid officials. Only an honorary policeman (usually the Centenier) could formally charge a man and so, for a decade, the paid and unpaid police got in each other's way in trying to unmask the Beast.

Even when Edward Paisnel was caught, it was more through luck than judgement. His excuse that he was "on his way to a fancy dress party" when he was arrested (initially for a traffic offence) seemed rather tame when a mask, wig, gloves and large blue coat with inch-long nails protruding from the shoulders were found in the back of his car.

As the "Beast of Jersey" affair unfolded in court, the States were encouraged to rethink their policing policy. Honorary police might be fine for settling domestic disputes, such as when a paternal visit from an honorary would be more welcome than a knock on the door from a man in blue; but they weren't so good when a villain confused the police with some premeditated, subtly thought-out crime.

In the 1970s the paid police force were given more power. Nowadays they operate from the main police station on Rouge Bouillon (there is a smaller, sub-police station at St. Aubin) and nearly all serious charges are made here. Only an honorary policeman (often the Centenier) can formally charge a suspect. This means, for example, that if a St. Clement man is arrested, the Centenier of St. Clement will be invited to St. Helier police headquarters to charge the man. The next morning the Centenier will present the case at St. Helier's magistrate's court. If the crime is a serious one, it will be referred to the Royal Court; if not, it will be dealt with by the presiding magistrate.

The main arbiter of justice in Jersey, the Bailiff, presides over Royal Court, aided by his deputy and a panel of Jurats. A similar panel operates in Guernsey, although Guernsey courts also have the power to pass judgement on criminals arrested in Sark (which has no professional policeman), Alderney (which has two) and Herm.

Jersey's honorary police have a wide range of powers which would be the envy of many UK officers, who operate within tightly defined rules and regulations. They can order petty criminals to attend a parish inquiry at the local parish hall where, depending on the severity of the crime, the offender will be warned, fined, or referred to the magistrate's court for a sterner sentence. They can also set up road blocks and can flag down a car if they think the driver is breaking the law.

Looks deceive: While Jersey's paid police have now established themselves as the real threat to big-time crime in the island, visitors should never underestimate the powers of the honorary police. If you find yourself involved with the law, don't ignore the little man with the roll-neck sweater, pipe and carpet slippers who shuffles his way alongside the burly, blue-uniformed police sergeant and into your cell. He's the man who's going to charge you.

GOVERNMENT BY "AMATEURS"

The Channel Islands' system of government provokes very varied reactions from outside observers. Visiting international bankers praise it for its virtually unshakeable political stability. Christopher Murphy, a former British Conservative member of parliament who has a holiday home on Sark, has spoken admiringly of the islands' non-party "consensus" style of politics. On the other hand, left-wing critics at Westminster, such as Labour spokesman George Foulkes, tend to see the system as an unholy alliance of surviving feudalism and freebooting capitalism, lacking many of the elements of 20th-century democracy.

Local politicians feel that some of their detractors, ignorantly or wilfully, ignore the islands' constitutional history, treating them as a corner of the United Kingdom that has obtained home rule, whereas they have never been part of mainland Britain. Channel Islanders, it is pointed out, have been running their own affairs for centuries—ever since, in fact, they chose to be linked to the English Crown rather than to France.

That choice was a lucky historical chance (or perhaps shrewd 13th-century thinking) because if the islands had remained part of Normandy, as they were at the time of the Norman Conquest of England, they would undoubtedly have long since been absorbed into metropolitan France. As it was, in return for staying loyal to the English Crown when King John lost his French possessions, they were granted, in 1215, rights and privileges that amounted to self-government, subject only to Royal assent through the Privy Council.

Softly, softly: The islands' parliaments evolved gradually from the Royal Courts established by the constitutions of King John. The bailiff, who presided over a court of 12 *jurats*, began to consult other leading members of the community—Les Etats, or the States, as they came to be called—about

Preceding pages, Rozel Harbour in Jersey. Left, Jersey's coat of arms. Right, official ceremonial takes to the streets in Guernsey in full force.

the running of the island. It was not until the mid-18th century that the separate functions of the Royal Court and the legislative body, the States, were clearly defined, and not until the 19th century that elected representatives began to sit in the States.

Under a postwar reform that followed the German Occupation in World War II, the number of elected deputies was increased, and the *jurats* and rectors who had previously sat by right in the States were dropped.

The parishes continued to be represented, and the *jurats* were replaced by 12 senior statesmen, known as senators in Jersey and *conseillers* in Guernsey, whose purpose was to bring political maturity and continuity to the more democratic island parliaments.

Jersey's States Assembly now consists of the bailiff or deputy bailiff, 12 senators, 12 parish constables, 28 deputies, the dean of Jersey, attorney-general and solicitor-general. Guernsey's States of Deliberation comprises the bailiff or deputy bailiff, 12 *conseillers*, 10 *douzaine* (parish council) representatives, 33 people's deputies, two Alderney representatives (since that island comes partly under Guernsey's administration), H.M. Procureur (attorney-general) and H.M. Comptroller (solicitor-general).

Call for abolition: Whereas Jersey's senators are elected by islandwide vote, Guernsey's *conseillers* are chosen by a 98-strong electoral college consisting of States members, *jurats* of the Royal Court, 34 parish representatives and the law officers. Many people in Guernsey think the island should either adopt Jersey's method or abolish the office of *conseiller* and create more people's deputies. However, the electoral college system is still strongly defended in political circles as a necessary safeguard to ensure that there is a bench of tried and

ers, it includes 12 people's deputies.

The atmosphere of the courtroom persists in the island parliaments, and this sets the tone of political life. Visitors find the debates remarkably disciplined compared with the barracking and background chatter of the House of Commons in London.

Proceedings in the States are opened in French—and a member could still address the House in French if he liked to risk not being understood by many of his present-day colleagues. As the Queen's representatives, the lieutenant-governors of Jersey and Guernsey normally attend States meetings (though with no vote), and in Guernsey, for example, an official is asked if "His Excel-

trusted members with the stature to head government departments. In 1986 the States came down firmly in favour of retaining the present system by 31 votes to 21.

Alderney and Sark have their own parliaments, and both make claims to be more "democratic" than the larger islands. Under a completely rewritten post-World War II constitution, the States of Alderney consists of a popularly elected president and 12 people's deputies. Sark's Chief Pleas, although historically a feudal body, provides more representatives per head for its 500 inhabitants than anywhere else in the British Isles, since, besides 40 *tenants* or landown-

lency" is present in the words: "*Monsieur Le Prévôt de la Reine, Son Excellence le Lieutenant-Gouverneur assistera-t-elle à la Séance d'aujourd'hui?*".

The courtroom antecedents of the States have left Jersey and Guernsey with a constitutional peculiarity that would never be tolerated in any newly independent country today. The civic head of the island, the bailiff, is both the chief judge and the president of parliament, apparently flying in the face of that sacred principle of democracy, a separate judiciary and legislature.

However, neither the Privy Council committee that proposed the post-war reforms, nor a Royal Commission on the Constitution that studied the islands' systems in the 1970s, saw any need for a change in the dual role of the bailiff, which was accepted as a time-honoured institution that had not been abused.

Hands-off policy: States meetings are like a mixture of a national parliament and a town council, as members have to deal both with weighty affairs and very parochial matters. There is no written agreement setting out the relationship between the Channel Islands and the U.K. Government, but by constitutional usage it is accepted that Britain is responsible for the islands' defence and international relations but does not interfere in

relationship has worked very amicably, partly because potential problems are quietly sorted out behind the scenes. Insular legislation is sent to the Home Office for comment before it goes before the States and, once passed, has to go back to the Privy Council for Royal assent.

The bailiff, deputy bailiff and law officers are appointed by the Crown, although their salaries are paid by the islands. The Home Office resisted a proposal from Jersey that the island should choose these officials itself on the grounds that this would not be consistent with the Crown's responsibility for its good government.

When a question was asked in the Jersey

their internal government. Whether the islands could take a major decision that conflicted with British policy is an open question. Guernsey abolished the death penalty before the United Kingdom did—but opinion in British government circles was already leaning that way.

The view of the 1973 Royal Commission was that the Westminster parliament "has, and should retain, the right in the last resort to legislate for the islands". By and large the

Left, in the U.K. fashion, riding to States of Jersey ceremonial. Above, the island's coat of arms, in St. Helier's market.

States as to who exactly "employs" the Crown officers, the answer was: no-one. This has led some people to wonder where legal accountability actually lies between Britain and the offshore archipelago, since complaints to the U.K. home secretary about legal decisions in the islands are invariably referred back to the "insular authorities".

The triennial general elections in the islands are like municipal contests in Britain before the town halls became a battleground for Left and Right. There are no political parties, and each candidate campaigns—very quietly—as an individual. There were lively political factions in Jersey a century ago, but in modern times party politics ended with the overwhelming defeat of the Jersey Democratic Movement by the "non-political" Progressive Party in the 1945 general election. The JDM (founded by a communist, Norman Le Brocq, who became—despite his unrepentant political leanings—a respected States member) still fields one or two candidates, but sees itself today primarily as a pressure group.

Lack of an official opposition has been held up by outside critics as evidence of political immaturity, but most islanders see it as just the reverse. At a Commonwealth Parliamentary Association conference in 1987, the Guernsey delegation posed the question: "Is party politics desirable in the government of small countries today?" The majority of Channel Islanders think not; they believe that non-party parliamentary debate enables MPs to get on with their job without wasting endless time in scoring off each other. Indeed, some islanders think there would have been far less trouble in the post-imperial Commonwealth if the former colonies had adopted the Channel Islands' system instead of Westminster's.

Non-party politics have certainly produced stability—a feature of the Channel Islands that the offshore financiers value as much as, or even more than, their low taxation. There is no risk of an election bringing a swing from Right to Left, let alone a drastic change of regime. The islands are virtually revolution-proof.

Not a penny: States members are unpaid (as MPs were in England at one time), bringing the inevitable criticism that running the community is the prerogative of the better-off. Voluntary public service is a tradition of which the islands are particularly proud, however, and it runs right through their institutions. Jersey still has honorary parish police forces operating alongside the States police, and Sark's law enforcement is done by unpaid feudal officers.

In practice, Jersey and Guernsey have compromised to some extent with their belief in honorary service, partly to enable the less well-off to enter parliament and partly because States work has become increasingly time-consuming. In Guernsey members can claim an allowance of up to £6,500 a year and in Jersey £6,000, although they have to start repaying it if their income from other sources exceeds a certain figure. A few members manage to live mainly on the allowance and are in effect full-time politicians. The majority (like many Westminster MPs) combine parliamentary duties with careers as lawyers, accountants, estate agents and farmers.

With the growing complexity of island affairs, and the increasing pressure on members' time, the hallowed tradition of honorary States service is beginning to be questioned. Equally on trial is the Channel Islands' system of government-by-committee, which is very similar to how local government operates in Britain. There is no central policymaking cabinet; the States comprises a number of committees, each responsible for a particular sector such as agriculture or tourism, which independently bring forward propositions to the House.

The system undoubtedly had its advantages in the past. It strengthened political stability by ensuring that no single States committee could push an unpopular policy through the House. And, under the honorary system, it rewarded those prepared to give their time to public service with their own little political empires. Today, however, it is being increasingly recognised that the lack of co-ordination has severe drawbacks when it comes to overall social and economic planning.

Even so, local politicians remain very suspicious of anything that looks like greater central control. When in 1987 the Jersey States commissioned a review of the island's government machinery from accountants Peat Marwick McLintock, the consultants were asked not to propose reforms that would undermine the committee system and introduce a cabinet. Nevertheless they concluded that the island's "cumbersome" system of government needed radical restructuring, and a new Policy and Resources Committee is being set up to provide greater coordination.

Present-day pressures certainly seem to be pointing towards change in both Jersey and Guernsey, and the days of "amateur" politicians and municipal-style government may be numbered.

Right, Alderney, resettled after the war, needs to cater for an increasing number of retired people from Britain.

THE TAX EXILES

The homes of the rich and famous are among the sights of Jersey. Coach drivers taking visitors on island tours will point out the clifftop house overlooking Bouley Bay where TV celebrity Alan Whicker has lived since 1973—or Villa Devereux, the £1.5 million high-tech house in St. Brelade built for inventor Ron Hickman, who made his fortune from the Black & Decker Workmate bench.

Sometimes it is the price paid for a property that is the guide's talking-point. Nowadays Jersey's wealthy settlers are not normally permitted to buy anything costing under £250,000 to £300,000, and £1 million is no longer exceptional. Lord Matthews, former deputy chairman of Britain's Trafalgar House group, paid nearly £1 million for his Jersey home in 1985.

Eagle's nest: No-one except the Comptroller of Income Tax knows exactly how many millionaires live in Jersey, but there are believed to be at least 250. The only statistic available is that quoted by economic adviser Colin Powell, who estimates that wealthy immigrants contribute 20 percent of the island's gross domestic income. Just one of them, best-selling author Jack Higgins (real name Harry Patterson), who moved to Jersey in 1976 after hitting the jackpot with his novel *The Eagle Has Landed* and now lives in a house with an indoor pool overlooking St. Aubin's Bay, paid about £500,000 in tax over a recent three-year period.

No-one can say, either, how rich you have to be to get accepted as a "K" resident in Jersey—a term taken from section 1(1) K of the island's housing law, which allows a newcomer to be admitted on "social or economic grounds" (the other main category is "J", which covers non-islanders who are taking up essential jobs).

Wealth is not the sole criterion for a "K" resident; someone with a dubious past would

be turned away, while former cricket star John Edrich got preferential treatment because he was ready to coach local youngsters. Basically, however, the would-be settler has to satisfy the economic adviser that he has sufficient safe assets to make a substantial tax contribution. The theoretical minimum is £10,000 a year, but over recent years the figure has gone up, requiring assets, it is said, of £1.5 million to £2 million. Among those who passed the financial

means test in the mid-1980s were racing driver Derek Warwick and the pop singer Gilbert O'Sullivan.

Until 1986 Jersey was allowing in 15 new wealthy immigrants a year. As part of a general tightening-up of controls to try to slow down the rate of immigration, the quota has been reduced to five a year. Local estate agents say this means that applicants will now have to show that they are worth at least £7 million to be considered.

To settle in Guernsey, you don't have to be a millionaire: it's enough to have £200,000 or so to buy an "open market" house and sufficient left over to live on. The island's

Preceding pages, tranquil escape in the lanes of Sark. Left, sun and sea attract the tax exile. Right, Oliver Reed, now a Guernsey resident.

system is to make available about 1,800 higher-priced properties (of which about 50 are usually on the market) for occupation without restriction by newcomers, and to reserve all the remaining houses and flats either for local people or for non-islanders granted an essential worker's licence.

Millionaires' row: Guernsey has a 50-acre (20-hectare) estate set aside for wealthy settlers—Fort George, above St. Peter Port, which was formerly the site of a 19th-century fortress once garrisoned by British redcoats. Known locally as "Millionaires' row", it comprises over 100 houses at prices running in the past year from £350,000 to £1 million.

the market. Two of Alderney's best-known tax exiles are Elizabeth Beresford, creator of The Wombles of Wimbledon and author of nearly 100 books, and cricket commentator and wine connoisseur John Arlott, whose hospitable island home is named The Vines. The former chairman of Lloyd's of London, Peter Miller, has property in Sark and often flies to Guernsey in his private plane.

The Channel Islands can boast a mini-Debrett of titled residents, although not all of them will be found in the local telephone books since the rich and famous tend to prefer ex-directory numbers. Lord Brownlow bought a six-bedroom house in Jersey for £225,000 in 1983 when he had to sell the

Guernsey's most famous recent arrival has been film star Oliver Reed. The hell-raising actor, who had already become a familiar local figure through the long breaks he took in the island, was not put off by being fined £100 in a Guernsey court in 1984 for disorderly behaviour. Oliver Reed likes Guernsey's sociable pub life, and when he married his young companion Josephine at a Surrey registry office in 1985, his best man was a Guernsey publican.

Alderney and Sark do not have the same housing restrictions as the larger islands, and the only real obstacle to settling there is the limited number of properties that come on

ancestral home, Belton House in Lincolnshire, because of death duties and rising costs. In the same year and for the same reasons, Lord Clifford of Chudleigh quit his family's 3,000-acre (1,200-hectare) estate at Ugbrooke House, near Exeter, for what he described as a "cottage"—a three-bedroom granite house—on the outskirts of St. Peter Port in Guernsey.

At one time the *rentiers*, as wealthy settlers are called in Guernsey, used to be mainly elderly, but nowadays they are often people in their forties and fifties who have sold their mainland businesses, or "semi-retired" from top jobs, and want a tax refuge not too far away from relations and friends.

One of Guernsey's recent comers has been Raymond Slater, who, at 51, sold much of his stake in a property and construction empire for an estimated £40 million and bought one of the island's grander homes for £1.2 million. A major Jersey-based trading and financial group is run by John Miller, who in 1973, when he was only 37, sold his English hypermarket to Finefare, retired to Jersey—and then got bored with doing nothing. Ray Allen, who made a fortune by introducing Kentucky Fried Chicken to Britain, now runs The Big Orange international franchise operation from Jersey.

While there are settlers who treat the is-

dent who put up the entire £750,000 needed to build a day hospital for the elderly.

Whicker's world: The famous among the *rentiers* help the islands by lending glamour to local events and promoting them in press interviews and TV appearances when they are travelling abroad. Alan Whicker opened one of the events in Jersey's 1987 Good Food Festival, and Cyril Fletcher presented a series of gardening programmes for Channel Television. And the resident authors, of course, tend to write about the islands; Jack Higgins's novel, *The Night of the Fox*, is set in Jersey during the German Occupation, and Elizabeth Beresford has used Alderney as a background for some recent stories.

lands just as a port of convenience, spending much of their time away and taking little interest in local affairs, many have become strongly attached to their adopted homelands. Newcomers are quickly recruited into the enormous amount of voluntary and charitable work that goes on in the archipelago—earning Jersey the reputation of being "a powerhouse of good".

There have also been notable individual donations, such as the wealthy Jersey resi-

Left, well away from the U.K. taxman: best-selling author Jack Higgins. Above, TV personality Alan Whicker.

In the anglicised Channel Islands the British tax exiles do not form any distinct expatriate set, and their presence provokes no noticeable resentment. Indeed, most islanders see them as a positive asset, adding colour and sophistication to local life, handsomely refurbishing old farmhouses that the natives no longer want, and providing welcome business for the shops, bars and restaurants. The ill-feeling is directed more towards the other end of the social spectrum, the so-called "illegal immigrants"—the seasonal workers and imported labourers who manage to stay on in defiance of the housing regulations.

Probably nowhere in the British Isles, outside the City of London, do financial activities loom so large in daily life as in the Channel Islands. Eavesdrop on a conversation in any upmarket bar or restaurant in St. Helier or St. Peter Port, and the chances are that the topic will be money dealings of some kind. The *Jersey Evening Post* and *Guernsey Evening Press* often make financial news their front-page story, and every day the papers carry columns of advertising for banking, accountancy and stockbroking jobs (local school-leavers are snapped up by the staff-hungry finance industry even before sitting for their final exams). Islanders are very conscious that the banks are now the power in the land, and anyone seeking sponsorship for a charitable cause or for a musical or sports event looks first in that direction.

Bank rate: Over the past 25 years and largely in the last decade, the Channel Islanders' life-style has become almost unrecognisably urban and affluent. In those simpler days of the 50s, the only banks were branches of Britain's high street clearers, along with the Jersey and Guernsey Trustee Savings Banks. Islanders would have laughed in disbelief if they had been told that by the 1980s their harbour capitals would be bristling with banks of every nationality and that finance business would be the mainstay of the economy.

Although Jersey's rate of income tax had been unchanged at four shillings (20p) in the £ since 1940, and Guernsey had reduced its rate from 5s. 2d. (26p) to the same level in 1960, the finance era was really ushered in by Jersey's decision in 1962 to abolish a usury law restricting interest rates to five percent. This was a calculated move by the then "chancellor", the late Senator Cyril Le Marquand, who is remembered today as the father of the islands' finance industry.

Merchant bankers looking for a low-tax base from which to service clients, espe-

cially excolonials and expatriates, began to see the potential of islands that were conveniently close to the City of London but outside U.K. jurisdiction and had a political system that ensured long-term stability. The first to move in were Kleinwort Benson, Hill Samuel and Royal Trust of Canada, followed not long afterwards by N.M. Rothschild and Hambros.

Even in the 1970s, however, offshore finance business was seen just as a useful extra

leg of the economy. No one foresaw how dominant it would become, outstripping traditional industries like horticulture and tourism as a source of States revenues. Today, as Channel Islanders are reminded every Budget day, it has grown into the golden egg that is largely paying for education, healthcare and other social services.

Over £25 billion of deposits are held by some 55 banks in Jersey, and nearly £10 billion by almost as many institutions in Guernsey. Many billions are invested in the hundreds of offshore funds run from the islands, and yet more billions are handled by local trust companies. There are branches or

Left, polishing up the nameplates of companies registered in the islands. Right, Reg Jeune, as president of Jersey's finance and economic committee, controls spending.

subsidiaries of most of the world's top banks—except, so far, the Japanese. As well as 12 U.S. and four Canadian banks, and others from all over Europe, you will find the Hongkong & Shanghai Banking Corporation, Bank of Bermuda, Bank of India and two Australasian banks.

None of them is just a nameplate; they occupy substantial, fully staffed buildings. Virtually all of the recent developments in St. Helier and St. Peter Port have been for banks and finance firms. Chase Manhattan Bank alone has spent £10 million on buying two new five-storey blocks in Jersey's capital, and the Bank of Bermuda and Royal Bank of Canada have been carrying out

always repudiated the description of "tax haven", arguing that their low-tax economies evolved naturally to serve the needs of small—and originally quite unsophisticated—communities, and that their tax structures have never been deliberately manipulated, as in some offshore centres, to attract financial business.

Such protestations have not saved the islands from repeated charges by certain Labour members of Parliament in London that they are leeches on the British economy, enjoying the advantages of U.K. citizenship without paying their share of taxation and then requiting this privilege by draining off untold millions of pounds from the British

major projects in Guernsey.

Shady dealings: In the early days, the prestigious names of merchant banking traded alongside a number of smaller so-called "banks", some of them shaky, one or two positively shady. There were financial scandals, such as those involving the Merchant Bank of Guernsey, linked with motor insurance fraud, and the notorious Bank of Sark, centre of a multi-million-dollar offshore swindle. Gradually, through protection of depositors' legislation and stricter vetting of would-be entrants, the islands were able to weed out the undesirables.

The Jersey and Guernsey authorities have

exchequer by providing a haven for tax-avoiders. The archipelago's image was not improved by the extensive use of Channel Islands companies made by the architects of the much-publicized Rossminster tax-avoidance schemes, or by the involvement of a Jersey company in the scandal surrounding Guinness's takeover of Distillers Company in 1986. The islands have also come under suspicion in connection with "insider trading" deals, and—particularly in America—as one of the offshore areas allegedly used by drug traffickers and other criminal organisations to launder their money.

Members of a House of Commons Select

Committee investigating drug abuse visited Guernsey and Jersey in 1985 and went away apparently satisfied that both the local law enforcement agencies and the banking community were as vigilant as their U.K. counterparts in the face of the growing threat from drug trafficking. Nevertheless no one pretends that "dirty" money does not find its way into the islands—if only because, as one Westminster M.P. put it, "if laundering is successful, you won't know it has been laundered, like a perfect murder."

The islands are following the United Kingdom by introducing legislation to empower courts to get more information from banks and to confiscate assets where

Islanders. The bonanza has brought prosperity, budget surpluses and full employment; parents see their children starting work at salaries they themselves never dreamed of—and without, as used to happen, having to move to the U.K. mainland to take up a professional career. But the boom has also brought big problems in the form of housing shortages, rapidly rising property prices, and inflated salary scales that other commercial sectors (and the local civil service) have great difficulty in matching.

Guilt complex: Some of the financiers complain that they are being made the whipping-boys for the islands' problems—and it is true that the average Jerseyman and

the handling of drug money is suspected, and are also taking steps to try to prevent local companies being used to cloak "insider trading" operations in the City of London. Officials admit that, in communities with limited policing resources, they have to rely primarily on the integrity of the professional community to protect the islands' good name.

Meanwhile, the sheer success of the finance industry has begun to alarm Channel

Left, a collection of imposing nameplates can glisten next door to a hamburger bar. Above, even tax exiles have to keep up with the *Financial Times*.

Guernseyman seems to have something of a love-hate attitude to the industry that has made his community rich. He knows that the islands cannot do without the massive tax revenues generated by the financiers and that it would be a disaster if ever they went away. At the same time, he laments the loss of the old, more innocent way of life and dislikes the idea that everything must now be done with one eye on the bankers. And perhaps, subconsciously, the traditionally hard-working, self-reliant Channel Islander feels a bit guilty that something as meretricious as dealing in money is now his main economic support.

Consider the judge's verdict: "The winning bull showed more maturity than the others, with an excellent front, wide chest and deep rib, but was not so well finished in the rear quarters, and a little weak on his legs. The second bull looked very stylish when walking, but was not so deep in the rib as the winner, and not so well-balanced. The third-place bull could have behaved better on the walk, but showed style, stretch and balance, with a good dairy bone."

The Miss World contest is amateur night compared with the intensity of a cattle show on the islands. The pedigree, pure-bred stars go by very strange names—Aimless Golden Dazzler and Design's Dreaming Boy were a couple of recent winners—but that's all part of their genetic lineage and enables the ancestry of individual cows or bulls to be traced back to the time when records were first kept in the late 19th century. More than 100 years of carefully controlled breeding have made Channel Islands cattle among the most genetically superior livestock to be found anywhere, and the main shows (held in May and October in Jersey; July and November in Guernsey) celebrate this heritage.

Animal exports: The breeding industry has played a vital role in ensuring the islands' continued prosperity. Animals were exported to the United Kingdom as early as 1700 and have since spread across all continents. One reason for their popularity is that they adapt easily to different climates, environments and conditions—whether the harsh winters of Canada and Scandinavia or the heat and diseases of the tropics. High shipping costs, however, mean that today most exports are sold to Britain or France, with an average price of about £1,000—though this could go as high as £3,000.

Wherever they have been sent, they have demonstrated their incomparable efficiency at producing milk with a high butterfat con-

Preceding pages, a farmhouse in Queen's Valley, Jersey. Left, a loving and lucrative relationship. Right, symbol of success in the St. Helier market.

centration. They have been crossed with scores of other different breeds; in India, for example, 25 million cows have been crossed with Jersey bulls. Channel Islands cattle are truly international and, in their own way, have acted as four-legged ambassadors, putting this small chain of islands firmly on the map.

There's no disputing the fact that they're thoroughbred. No live cattle have been allowed into Jersey for close to two centuries

and local farmers don't foresee this law being repealed. In Guernsey, legislation aimed at maintaining the purity of the breed has existed for almost as long, although recently some animals have been crossed with bulls from abroad in order to improve genetics in the island's herds.

What this means is that Channel Islands' cattle cannot be simply grouped together. Jersey and Guernsey, with their characteristic rivalry, have pursued entirely separate breeding programmes and, certainly for the past 100 years, have managed to keep the two bailiwicks' herds apart. Before that, there probably was some mixing. A Frenchman who bought a farm on the islands, for instance, could have quietly imported his own herd. More romantically, a Guernsey or Sark girl marrying a Jersey boy might have brought with her a calf given by her father as a wedding present to remind her of home. Evidence for such theories—pink noses, a tell-tale sign of Guernsey blood—still, sometimes, appear in Jerseys.

Records also show that in those early days thousands of cattle from Jersey and Guernsey were shipped to England via Alderney and became more commonly known as Alderneys when sold or exhibited at U.K. shows. Many French cattle coming into the islands at that time were re-exported to

spected by a panel of judges and awarded points. To begin with, most of the animals were without pedigree because few written records had been kept. In Jersey the honour of being the very first entry goes to a grey and white bull, "Dandy", owned by James Godfrey of the parish of St. Martin. The first cow, "Daisy", was light brown and white, and belonged to Mr. P. Paisnel of St. Clement. By August 1883, 448 bulls were entered as foundation stock in the Jersey herd book. Then the entries for bulls closed and no more have ever qualified. Today, a residual stock of no more than 200 are held at stud and the rest culled shortly after birth. The register of pedigree cows has never closed and, al-

England as Alderneys. The name was later dropped when the concept of individual breeds of domestic cattle was established.

The most important era began with the formation of agricultural improvement societies in Jersey in 1833 and in Guernsey in 1842, both of which received royal patronage. The Royal Jersey Agricultural and Horticultural Society and its equivalent on Guernsey introduced official herd book registers, the turning point in the creation of the two breeds.

Only cattle that conformed to an accepted general type, qualified for an entry into the herd books. Every cow that calved was in-

though the procedure for registration has now changed, to date 98,720 female animals were given herd book numbers in Jersey.

Colour, appearance, size and shape are considered in assessing a cow for admission to the herd book. The overall "look" is important and a complicated points system has evolved. Most people would rate Channel Islands cows "attractive" by bovine standards. They are fairly small in stature in comparison with other European breeds, such as the Holstein or Freisian, and are rather docile. The bulls, however, are said to be quite ferocious.

Both Channel Islands' breeds have in-ward-curving horns, but there the similarity ends. The accepted colour of the pure Guernsey cow is red and white—although, probably more for promotional purposes than anything else, she is known as the "Golden Guernsey". She has a narrow head and a long, straight muzzle tipped with a pink nose. Jerseys generally have fawn-coloured coats with white patches, are slightly smaller in frame than Guernseys, and are dish-faced with large, bright eyes and black noses sometimes ringed with a white band.

After setting up their herd books, both islands went through a series of export booms. Buyers had the assurance that animals were free of disease and were of pure

stock. Many animals were bought direct at island cattle shows, which became a magnet for breeders from around the world.

Thousands of cattle went to the U.S. and Canada. In 1919 a Jersey bull, "Sybil's Gamboge", one of the most prolific sires ever, was sold at public auction in the U.S., for $65,000—a record which has remained unequalled in real terms. It's the sort of price one would pay for a racehorse.

During the German Occupation of the

Left, shrewd judgements are made by farmers at a Guernsey cattle market. Above, the object of their appraisal.

islands from 1940 to 1945, hundreds of animals were requisitioned for slaughter in Jersey. Fortunately, slaughter was controlled by the island's agricultural society officials and mainly inferior animals were taken, leaving a nucleus of prime breeding stock at the end of the war.

Recently, the islands' burgeoning populations and the expansion of the tourism and finance industries have fuelled demand for milk and dairy products, and cattle are now raised more for milk production than for export. Butter, cream, milk in various butter-fat percentages, yoghurts and even cream liqueurs are now produced by the dairy boards in both islands.

Tomorrow's world: Although the true Channel Islander is a farmer, interested only in the land, many of the traditional methods of farming have begun to die out in the past 20 years. Today's farmer must be commercially-minded and understand the science of agriculture. Cattle breeding has changed too. No longer is it necessary to ship live animals all over the world. Instead, thanks to artificial insemination and embryo transplant techniques, cattle are effectively sent overseas, 600 at a time, on board an aircraft in a vacuum flask of liquid nitrogen. A shot of bull semen would cost a farmer overseas about £10. Live cattle are still sent to England and France, but the market has shrunk. The U.S. has its own herds of genetically superior Channel Islands cattle and doesn't have to import pedigree stock.

Thanks to a clever deal the islands did with the European Economic Community, their agricultural industry is still protected to a degree from outside competition. A main argument used in negotiating the islands' associated membership was that they should be allowed free movement of goods and livestock with the exception of cattle because of the importance of preserving the breeds' purity and disease-free record.

The States of both islands have been trying to halt the recent decline in the number of dairy holdings. Although total herd sizes—around 7,000 in Jersey and 4,000 in Guernsey—have remained roughly the same, the number of dairy farms has reduced considerably—as much as a 20 percent drop in three or four years. As elsewhere, larger herds and hard economics are now central to the farming way of life.

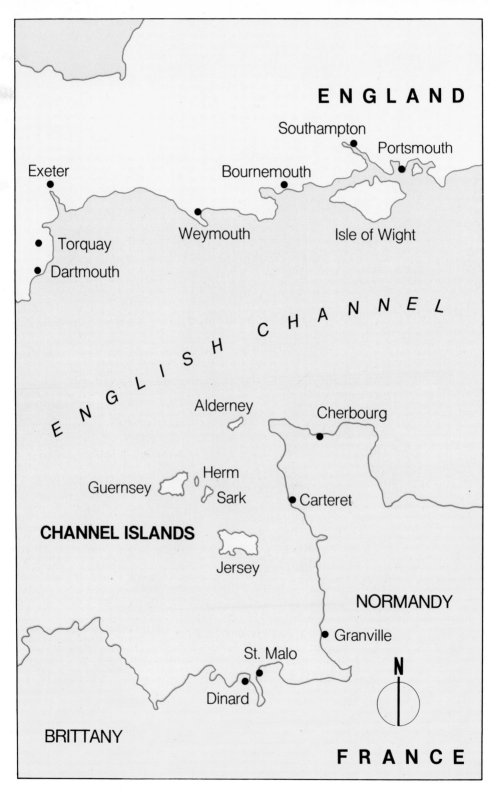

ENGLAND

Southampton

Portsmouth

Exeter

Bournemouth

Weymouth

Isle of Wight

Torquay

Dartmouth

ENGLISH CHANNEL

Alderney

Cherbourg

Herm

Guernsey

Sark

Carteret

CHANNEL ISLANDS

Jersey

NORMANDY

Granville

St. Malo

Dinard

BRITTANY

FRANCE

N

PLACES

Towering cliffs, Atlantic surf, solitary beaches, country walks, majestic castles, quaint cottages, fascinating wildlife, and an equable climate: the Channel Islands offer visitors a menu that's nothing if not varied.

Jersey, the self-styled "Queen of the Channel", combines a flourishing tourism industry with a traditional agricultural economy and, in St. Helier, a spectacularly successful offshore finance operation. Its symbol, Mont Orgueil Castle, has been defying France for seven centuries. Fort Regent is a truer sign of the times: an immense fortress built to resist Napoleon, it is now a Disney-like sports and entertainment centre.

While the newly rich go to Jersey, locals claim, the "old money" heads for **Guernsey**. The antagonism between the two islands is reflected in many small ways: in the different colour of telephone booths, the different helmets worn by the police, the different robes worn by the bailiffs, the different dialects. From the air, the island dazzles as the sun is reflected off thousands of greenhouses, in which the once dominant tomato is being augmented by such exotica as kiwi fruit. St. Peter Port, a jumble of narrow streets with a busy harbour, has an almost Swiss air of neatness.

Alderney, the least visited island, lies just eight miles (13 km) from France and the cobbled streets of its only town, St. Anne, have a very Gallic atmosphere. Somebody once described Alderney as a rock with 2,000 drunks clinging to it; certainly, the pubs are convivial places when the gales are blowing. The island was massively fortified by the Germans—12 forts ring its coast—and relics of the Occupation are all around. The adjacent **Burhou Island** has puffin colonies and a small bird sanctuary.

Sark, the dropout's last retreat, is just three miles (nearly five km) long and one-and-a-half (over two km) wide, and has the atmosphere of Victorian England. Cars are forbidden. The island is ruled in the manner of an independent feudal state by the Seigneur, who rides a bicycle and drives a tractor. The main settlement, "The Village", has the unreal air of a film set. Sark has no income tax, property tax, import duty, export duty or death duty; but it does have 30 species of butterfly, 170 species of bird, plus wild orchids and sea anemones—and the world's smallest jail.

You can walk round **Herm**, one of the quietest islands on earth, in an afternoon, enjoying its wild flowers and archaeological remains. On summer Sundays, though, it can become one of the world's most crowded islands as 2,000 day-trippers arrive by ferry from Guernsey. One beach has 200 varieties of shell.

Then there are the smaller islands—**Jethou, Brechou, Lihou**, the **Ecréhous**, the **Minquiers**—and, around them, reefs which, it's been said, can split a hull like a hacksaw slicing through melon.

That's the menu. As we mentioned, it's varied.

JERSEY

"A large harbour; a maze of streets, busy and prosperous, but noted for their cleanliness; a huge fort rising perpendicularly out of the town; good shops; numerous places of worship; a miscellaneous assortment of carriages and well-appointed 'Jersey cars' plus a general air of comfort..., are the prominent features of St. Helier."

Those words are from a guide published at the turn of the century. But, if you delete "a miscellaneous assortment of carriages and well-appointed Jersey cars" and substitute "a steady stream of hire-cars interrupted by the occasional tanned and carefree cyclist", you have a fair description of **St. Helier** today.

The original words described a relatively new community. In 1800 St. Helier had far fewer streets, no large harbour and no fort. It was less prosperous, too; tourism didn't get into gear until Queen Victoria's visit in 1846.

The name St. Helier has an ancient heritage; it commemorates the hermit Helerius, son of a Belgian nobleman who came to Jersey to seek an isolated spot where he could devote his life to prayer and fasting. He chose a place, today known as Heritage Rock, near the stone on which Elizabeth Castle stands, where he lived for 15 years in solitude and piety. In A.D. 555 he was murdered by axe-wielding pirates. As folklore has it, the hermit picked up his severed head and carried it for 200 yards, at which point the pirates "departed in great haste and fear". Helerius was later canonised—hence St. Helier's crest, two crossed axes that recall the hermit's death.

There are other pointers to St. Helier's past. Archaeologists have found evidence of habitation from the 12th century in the Old Street area of the town centre (near the Town Hall). Much of the Town Church dates from the 14th century. Elizabeth Castle pro-

vided an important focal point on Jersey's southern flank from the 16th century onwards. And there are buildings surviving from the 17th and 18th centuries. Growth was slow. In 1734, it is recorded, St. Helier still contained only 534 houses.

It was a long time before the town developed as a port. In the 17th century the main landing place was Havre Des Pas. Things improved a little after 1700 with the English Harbour and the French Harbour, though there were no major facilities until 1751, when George II gave the island £200 to help with the building of a new harbour. For a long time access was restricted by the tides. Even when Victoria Pier and Albert Pier were built in the middle of the 19th century, the harbour could really only function with continual dredging. Not until 1975 was substantial work undertaken. Existing piers were strengthened and widened and the yachting marina was built.

St. Helier's real expansion began with the French and American wars in

Preceding pages: St. Ouen's Pond and holiday-makers in St. Helier. Left, golf links at Gorey. Right, flesh and flora mingle in the annual Battle of Flowers.

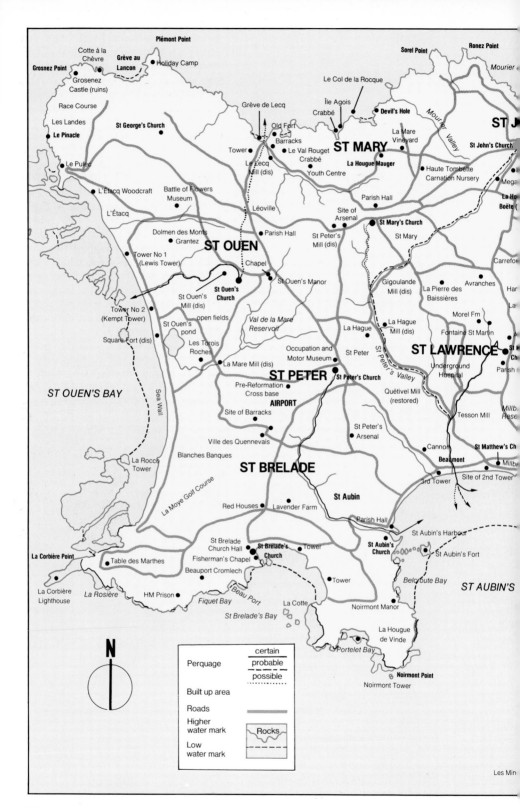

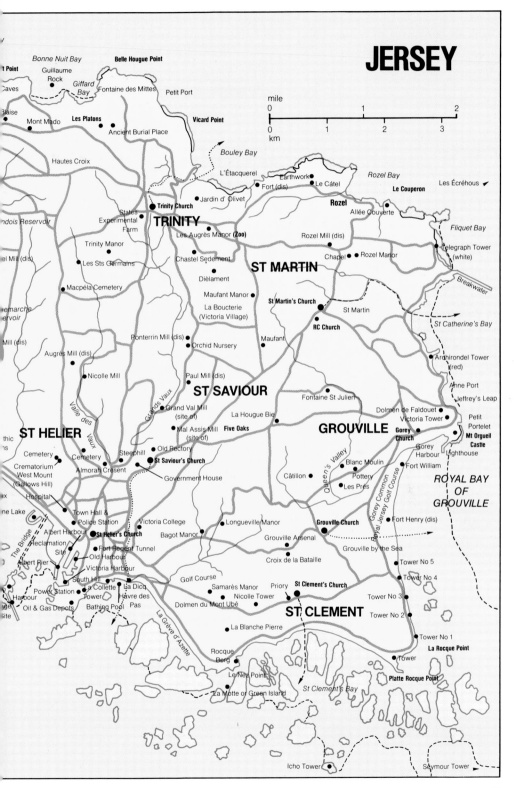

JERSEY

Bonne Nuit Bay
Belle Hougue Point
t Point
Guillaume
Rock
Giffard Bay
Caves
Fontaine des Mittes
Petit Port
Blaise
Mont Mado
Les Platons
Vicard Point
Ancient Burial Place
Hautes Croix
Bouley Bay
L'Étacquerel
ndois Reservoir
States Experimental Farm
Trinity Church
TRINITY
Trinity Manor
Les Augrès Manor **(Zoo)**
Les Sts Germains
Chastel Sedement
el Mill (dis)
Macpéla Cemetery
Dièlament
emarche ervoir
Maufant Manor
La Boucterie (Victoria Village)
Mill (dis)
Ponterrin Mill (dis)
Augrès Mill (dis)
Orchid Nursery
Maufant
Nicolle Mill
Paul Mill (dis)
ST SAVIOUR
Grands Vaux
Grand Val Mill (site of)
La Hougue Bie
ST HELIER
Mal Assis Mill (site of)
Five Oaks
thic ns
Cemetery
Steephill
Old Rectory
Cemetery
St Saviour's Church
Crematorium West Mount (Gallows Hill)
Almorah Cresent
Government House
Hospital
ne Lake
Town Hall & Police Station
Victoria College
Albert Harbour
St Helier's Church
Bagot Manor
ux
Reclamation Site
Fort Regent Tunnel
Old Harbour
Albert Pier
Victoria Harbour
South Hill
Golf Course
Harbour
Power Station
La Collette Tower
La Dico
Havre des Pas
Oil & Gas Depots
Bathing Pool
Dolmen du Mont Ubé
ST CLEMENT
La Grève d'Azette
La Blanche Pierre
Rocque Berg
Le Nez Point
La Motte or Green Island
St Clement's Bay

Earthwork
Le Cátel
Fort (dis)
Rozel Bay
Rozel
Le Couperon
Les Écréhous
Allée Couverte
Rozel Mill (dis)
Chapel
Rozel Manor
Fliquet Bay
Telegraph Tower (white)
ST MARTIN
Jardin d' Olivet
St Martin's Church
St Martin
Breakwater
RC Church
St Catherine's Bay
Archirondel Tower (red)
Anne Port
Fontaine St Julien
Jeffrey's Leap
Dolmen de Faldouet
Victoria Tower
Petit Portelet
GROUVILLE
Gorey Church
Mt Orgueil Castle
Gorey Harbour
Lighthouse
Blanc Moulin
Fort William
Câtillon
Pottery
Les Prés
ROYAL BAY OF GROUVILLE
Queen's Valley
Longueville Manor
Grouville Church
Fort Henry (dis)
Grouville Arsenal
Grouville by the Sea
Croix de la Bataille
Royal Jersey Golf Course
Gorey Common
Tower No 5
Samarès Manor
Priory
St Clement's Church
Nicolle Tower
Tower No 4
Tower No 3
Tower No 2
Tower No 1
La Rocque Point
Tower
Platte Rocque Point
Icho Tower
Seymour Tower

mile
0   1   2
km
0   1   2   3

the late 18th century when privateering (legalised plundering of enemy shipping) was a major and lucrative island industry. The French Revolution brought an influx of at least 4,000 refugees to the island. And during the Napoleonic wars, the population of St. Helier was swelled by the British garrison. Work on Fort Regent, begun in 1806, brought an influx of Irish workers too. Of the two Roman Catholic congregations in the town today, one is very Irish, the other very French.

The end of the Napoleonic wars saw military men and their families settle in Jersey. The climate was good, the living was inexpensive and the introduction of steamer services to England eased communication. Yet though the Regency and Victorian houses went up and the town grew, praise for the way St. Helier *looked* was guarded. An 1862 tourist guide stated: "The Town of St. Helier is altogether wanting both in architectural and picturesque effect."

Castle at sea: It's a criticism you can't make of **Elizabeth Castle.** At high tide, the sight of its turrets, towers and chimneys marooned on a rock nearly a mile out at sea is nothing if not picturesque.

At low tide, the visitor walking along the Esplanade can't help but notice the causeway tracing a beckoning track across the beach to the castle's outer gates.

Elizabeth Castle has been dubbed "one of the finest fortified sites in Western Europe". It's actually a castle "complex" comprising three distinct sections: the Upper Ward, built between 1594 and 1601; the Lower Ward, built between 1626 and 1636; and the Outer Ward, finished in 1668. And beyond that, along a 19th-century breakwater, is the **Hermitage**, built to commemorate St. Helier.

You can clamber in and around four centuries worth of fortifications, though when you tire of this there's plenty to learn about the castle's past. In the Lower Ward, the **Jersey Militia Museum** houses a display of military memorabilia stretching back several

Below, St. Helier has developed a busy marina. Right, floodlights turn Elizabeth Castle into a picture postcard.

ELIZABETH CASTLE

Until the 16th century, Mont Orgueil Castle at Gorey had been Jersey's principal stronghold; but improvements in the power of cannon meant that it was no longer impregnable. The islet of St. Helier was a natural choice for a new stronghold. Sir Walter Raleigh, one of Jersey's most distinguished governors, was involved in the construction, which began in 1594. It was he who diplomatically named the fortress "Fort Isabella Bellissima" (the most beautiful Elizabeth) after his Queen.

Elizabeth Castle didn't see any action until the English civil war. After Sir George Carteret, the Governor of Jersey, retreated to the castle, Charles II eventually paid his respects when Elizabeth Castle had become the last Royalist stronghold in Britain. His first visit was in April 1646, his second in November 1649. On this occasion he was proclaimed King in St. Helier's market-place by Sir George, even though the monarchy had been abolished.

In 1651, Parliamentary forces landed in St. Ouen's Bay and the castle was bombarded by mortars set up at the foot of Mont de la Ville. One bomb broke through the roof of a chapel built inside the ruins of the old chuch and penetrated the crypt where gunpowder and two-thirds of the castle's provisions were stored. The resulting explosion was catastrophic. It demolished the Abbey and forced Sir George Carteret to surrender. The Parliamentarians held Jersey for the next nine years. A cross in the Barrack Square marks the approximate site of the Abbey church.

During the 18th century, Elizabeth Castle was always ready for an attack from France, acquiring in the process a granite barracks and various moats, gates and look-outs. When the French finally arrrived in 1781 and entered St. Helier, the garrison at the castle was marooned. The French marched out to the castle with a copy of the surrender that the kidnapped Governor of Jersey, Moise Corbet, had been forced to sign. There followed a superb example of British insularity: when asked to surrender also, Captain Mulcaster, the senior officer in the castle, pocketed the documents without reading them and informed the enemy he did not understand French. It was left to troops under the command of Major Peirson to win the day in Royal Square.

hundred years, while the **Barracks** have a permanent artillery display that includes a short audio-visual show. In the Upper Ward, the **Governor's House** contains two elaborate tableaux depicting Sir Walter Raleigh and King Charles II.

Once back on dry land on the **Esplanade**, you aren't too far from what is usually known as the **Old Town**, though St. Helier's western boundary was actually taken to be at Charing Cross, much nearer today's town centre. A private house in Elizabeth Lane, called **Glen Rest** (Elizabeth Lane is to the north of Cheapside), is said to be St. Helier's oldest surviving dwelling. **Parade Garden**, a tidy arrangement of flowerbeds and trees that attracts strollers on summer evenings, was once a parade ground. It was built by General Don, a soldier known in Jersey for the island's "Routes Militaires". Close by, **West Park** and **People's Park** are two more open spaces with good views across St. Aubin's Bay.

Hustle and bustle: Don't hunt too hard for **The Weighbridge**: it doesn't exist. Once there was a weighbridge at this busy centre of town, but it disappeared long ago. The Western railway that ran along the Esplanade to St. Aubin and Corbière also went, but the railway station survived to house the **Tourist Office**. With the big ferries in the background and cars clogging the intersection between the Esplanade and the tunnel, the Weighbridge on a busy Saturday morning is a picture of boats, buses, bustle and bumper-to-bumper traffic.

A minute or two from all this is the **Occupation Museum**, the most central of a number of permanent Occupation exhibitions in Jersey. You can inspect a huge collection of German military hardware: guns, shells, range-finders, field medical supplies, a field kitchen, mannequins sporting Nazi uniforms and so on. Look closer at the several hundred items on display and you'll see a host of intriguing details of life in Occupied Jersey. The most fasci-

Jersey's tax-free status creates a "born to shop" atmosphere.

nating is a small bundle of blue toilet paper made from tomato tray-liners; the enterprising islander whose idea it was to provide for the convenience of others in this way is said to have made a fortune. All the items on display are placed in a serious and proper perspective in the video room where you can sit and watch an account of the invasion, the Occupation, the resistance and the eventual liberation. Interviews with Jerseymen who survived Nazi concentration camps provide a chilling reminder of how close Hitler came to the United Kingdom.

If the Weighbridge is a noisy focus of the town's energy, the shaded precinct of **Royal Square** is one place where you can escape it. Here many strands of Jersey's history come together—although, because the States Chamber (the seat of Jersey's government) and the Royal Court House overlook it, the square is the island's equivalent of London's Parliament Square and so is very much a part of the present. An administration building occupied this

site as far back as 1329. The first Court House was built in 1647 and rebuilt in 1764. The present buildings date from 1866. The Royal Court and the States Chamber are occasionally open to the public; the entrance to the public gallery of the States Chamber, open only when the States are in session, is in **Halkett Place**. At the western end of the square is the **Public Library**, an elegant place founded in 1736 by the Reverend Philip Falle, author of the respected *History of Jersey*, published in 1694.

St. Helier's Church, consecrated in 1341, is dedicated to the town's namesake, the hermit Helerius, commemorated by a statue above the north door. The chancel is said to be the remains of an 11th-century chantry erected near what was then the seashore, and the chapels to the north and south and the transept date from the 12th century; but the church took essentially its present form in the 14th century. Outside in Bond Street, the existing railings surrounding the church incorporate part of

Below right, Royal Square, a refuge from the bustle.

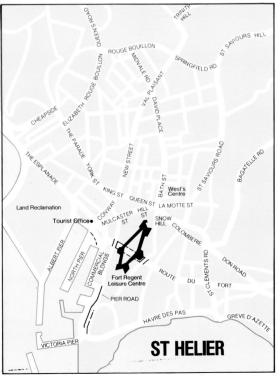

ST HELIER

ROYAL SQUARE

Royal Square started life as a market, though it doubled as a site for execution and incarceration. Records tell of two witches being strangled and burnt here in 1648. In the following century, prisoners being brought from Mont Orgueil Castle at Gorey were placed in an iron cage in the square to await trial. On market day, offenders were placed in the pillory (removed only in 1836) and exposed to the jeers and missiles of onlookers. Sentencing, performed in the Court House, could entail further drama. In 1787 an unfortunate named David Brouard and his wife were both whipped by the public executioner from the Court House, along the quarter-mile route to the prison at Charing Cross. The noise and commotion of market day caused real problems: Royal Square became so crowded that it was a constant source of complaint. The rolls of the Royal Court contain many references to the filthy conditions of Le Marché. A particular complaint was of desecration to the cemetery and the Town Church caused by wandering pigs and poultry. All this

prompted the decison to relocate the marketplace. In 1796 the States purchased a plot of marshy ground a short distance away (the site of today's Central Market) as a site for a future market. By 1800 market day was no longer held in Royal Square.

The glitzy golden statue at the eastern end of the square, depicting George II in the garb of Caesar, was unveiled on July 9, 1751, and it was in honour of this regal statue that Royal Square received its name. But by the middle of the 19th century the myth was firmly established that this was a figure of a Roman emperor salvaged from a stranded ship and renamed to suit the square. (The fact that this pseudo-Caesar was wearing the Order of the Garter was overlooked). Before this statue was erected, a market cross stood here, though it was lost without trace—probably in 1668, the same year that Royal Square was paved.

It's worth going into the National Westminster bank, a building occupying the site of the Cornmarket. The original granite arches of this open-air meeting place have been preserved in the banking hall.

Royal Square is best known as the site of the Battle of Jersey. Both Baron de Rullecourt and Major Francis Peirson died here in the battle between an invading expedition of French soldiers and the local militia. The French were defeated within 10 minutes of arriving at the square. As Balleine's *History of Jersey* tells it: "Peirson sent his main force up what is now Broad Street, while he himself led another party to the Rue de Derrière, which is now the King Street precinct, to burst into the square by the opening now known as Peirson Place." The Peirson Public House is said to have borne the brunt of the shooting.

Royal Square is a reminder that Jersey's next invaders stayed much longer. From a balcony in the States offices Alexander Moncrieff Coutanche, Bailiff of Jersey, announced that the island was to be liberated after five years of German military occupation. In 1985 the Duchess of Kent unveiled a plaque in commemoration.

Unknown to the Germans a stone-mason had already made his own discreet liberation proclamation just a few metres away. Having been given the job of relaying flagstones in Royal Square, he changed the position of stones to read "V" for victory and kept his efforts covered with sand. Today the sign reads "Vega 1945"; the additional letters were added to commemorate the arrival in 1944 of the Swedish ship *Vega* with urgent Red Cross supplies.

the chapel screen used to separate male and female prisoners attending services at Jersey's now-demolished Newgate Prison.

Glimpses of the past: If you pass through Pier Road, the western approach for Fort Regent, on your way from the Town Church, don't miss out the **Jersey Museum** at the lower end of Pier Road. It occupies a magnificent four-storey house and knits together threads from Jersey's past. A period bedroom and kitchen reproduce domestic scenes from the last century. An ornate Victorian pharmarcy that once stood in the town's Halkett Place is also reconstructed for posterity. Rooms are devoted to Jersey's natural, maritime and postal history. Of special interest is a basement room which provides an insight into law and order in the island. The main exhibit is an enormous 12-person treadmill installed in 1836 in Jersey's Newgate Prison. While you ponder the hardship and tedium that must have produced for past inmates, look down at the sandstone slabs on the floor; these too are taken from the Newgate Prison and bear inscriptions carved by prisoners from the last century.

The star attraction of the museum is Emilie Charlotte Le Breton—better known as Lillie Langtry or "Jersey Lily". An entire room is given over to memorabilia of her life. When she arrived in London as a newly-married 21-year-old, she mixed in fashionable circles and became famous as a society beauty. Eventually she numbered among her friends and admirers the Prince of Wales (later King Edward VII), whose intimate relationship with her provoked much gossip. One exhibit, a quote taken from a certain Lord Carrington, concerns the dubious reputation Lillie Langtry's beauty had earned her. On hearing that her parrot was missing, he remarked: "I didn't know she had a parrot, though I'd heard she'd had a cockatoo."

In its own way, **Fort Regent** has just as much to say about the island's past as Jersey Museum. But, once you've

FORT REGENT

The Battle of Jersey in 1781 concentrated the Jerseyman's mind on the island's vulnerability. Invasion, however, wasn't a new theme. The French threat to all the Channel Islands was perceived way back when King John lost Normandy in the 13th century. In 1550, King Edward VI identified the strategic location of what was to become Fort Regent. He said: "Because on occasion of foreign invasion we be informed you have no place to retire unto, we require you to convey your Town unto the hill above the same, which we be informed may with little charge be made strong and defensible."

More than 250 years later the fear had surfaced again. In 1806, when the Napoleonic Wars had entered their 13th year, Sir George Don, the Lieutenant-Governor, expressed his fear of imminent invasion. He said: "From the great progress of the enemy on the Continent, I must expect to be attacked in the spring." Mont Orgueil, Jersey's great castle at Gorey on the east coast, had earlier been superseded by Eliza-beth Castle. Now it was the turn of Sir Walter Raleigh's fortress to fall foul of changing military capabilities. Jersey was about to embark on the third of its great trio of fortifications.

It was John Hambly Humfrey, Commanding Royal Engineer, who drew up plans for this fort. But, when the scheme was finally agreed on, work could not start for 18 months. The delay was caused by a fierce argument over the money due in payment for the site of Mont de la Ville. The colossal sum of £11,280 was eventually settled on. The British Government then spent over £1 million on making Fort Regent (named after the Prince Regent, later George IV), well-nigh impregnable.

This fortification was the hub of a wide network of defences that General Don and Royal Engineer Humfrey had conceived. This comprised barracks, arsenals, martello towers, batteries, and General Don's celebrated "Routes Militaires" that were built to move soldiers around quickly. Fort Regent was completed in 1814. With Waterloo just a year away, the reason for its construction, Napoleon Bonaparte, was about to disappear. Nevertheless, this lofty outpost was home to the British garrison until 1927.

bought your ticket and stepped into the fort's dazzling modern interior, history is the last thing you'll be concerned with. Today it's a bastion of sport and leisure, a mega-facility just dying to involve you in something. With a swimming pool, squash courts, pool and snooker tables, badminton courts, plus facilities for gymnastics and table tennis, it's an indoor sporting oasis. At the centre is the chameleon-like Gloucester Hall, purpose-built to serve either as a sports arena or be converted into a 2,000-seat auditorium.

A haphazard succession of bars, restaurants, self-styled piazzas and a beer-garden still leaves room for a Wild West Games Room, mini-golf, 'Fort Fun', an aviary, toy shops, an aquarium and an exploratorium. And (under-fives please note) just a stone's throw from Humfrey's Magic Music Hall there's a corner where you can pose with lifestyle cardboard cutouts of BJ from *The A-Team*, pop star George Michael and a generous profile of topless pin-up Samantha Fox. A signboard

nearby confidently assures you that a photograph taken here "fools the experts". Whatever you make of Fort Regent, nobody can deny that it really does provide "something for all the family", rainy days or not.

The centre's greatest asset owes nothing to Jersey's leisure planners, however. Its view over St. Aubin's Bay and much of St. Helier is the best on the island and a trip to Fort Regent is worthwhile for this alone.

By leaving Fort Regent on its eastern side (you can enter this way, too) you can take a short cable-car ride down to some steps leading to the heart of Jersey's shopping area. **King Street** is the main pedestrian thoroughfare, though it connects with **Queen Street**, **Don Street** and several others (the map issued by the States of Jersey Tourism Committee shows this central cluster of pedestrianised shopping streets in mauve).

There's much fruitier shopping in the **Central Market**, at the junction of Beresford Street and Halkett Place. In

Below, promenading is pleasant in St. Helier— it's parking the car that's impossible.

fact, fruit and vegetables are only half the story as the 34 stalls sell a wide variety of fare. Whether you are purchasing or not, the Central Market is one of St. Helier's shopping landmarks. The Victorian building is an ornate structure of iron columns and slatted window panes, the sort of architectural features that went hand in hand with the coming of the railway. Its centrepiece is still the towering 15-foot (five-metre), four-tier fountain. It was the disturbance caused by Market Day to Royal Square that led to this site being purchased for a market. The original building, erected in 1803, was a grand affair, closely modelled on the City of Bath market and was hailed as "one of the finest in Europe". In 1881, it was decided to build a new market to celebrate the centenary of the Battle of Jersey. The building was completed in 1882, though two of the seven entrances have elaborately adorned gates dating back to 1803.

Beresford Market, running betwen Beresford Street and Minden Place,

grew out of the Central Market. Established as a fish market in 1841, it is the best place in St. Helier for fresh fish and offers lobster, squid, scallops, crab and much more.

Low-down on St. Clement: The road passing through the tunnel under Fort Regent leads along the south coast into the parish of **St. Clement**. St. Clement's Road, just over a quarter-mile along the way, marks both the western edge of **Howard Davis Park** and the parish border. A local philanthropist, Thomas Davis, dedicated the park in 1939 to his son Howard, who was killed in World War I.

On the coast just south of the park, a slipway called **Le Dicq** was a favourite haunt of Victor Hugo, St. Clement's best-known resident. By a large rock here (le Rocher des Proscrits) Hugo and his compatriots gathered in the evening to make plans against Napoleon III, 'the Sawdust Corporal'. A commemorative tablet was inserted in the rock.

Hugo lived nearby at 3 Marine Terrace (his house unfortunately was

St. Helier market: fresh produce and freshly painted.

108

demolished) and established his mistress, Juliette Drouais, at Harve des Pas. He spent three years in Jersey before his recriminations against Queen Victoria forced him to depart for Guernsey. Much as he is said (by natives of Guernsey, at least) to have maligned Jersey, his tributes to the island were lyrical. To Hugo, Jersey was *"un bouquet grand comme la ville de Londres"*. There were, of course, features of Jersey life he didn't care for: having to keep his shutters closed when he held Sunday billiard parties, for instance.

A good part of St. Clement lies below high-tide level, making it prone to flooding. The worst inundation, in 1811, prompted the States of Jersey to build a seawall. But the parish long made good use of the low-lying land. For several centuries, St. Clement was dominated by the **Manor of Samares**, a name derived from the French for "salt marsh". The ancient way of making salt was to let the sea flood low-lying land, block the channel, and then let the sun evaporate the water. The land between Samares Manor and the sea was certainly put to profitable use and is still known as Samares Marsh.

Until 1763, all who held land on the Manor had to make the seigneur's hay, to fetch his wood and wine, and even to clean out his pigeon-house. Today the Manor is the best place to visit in this parish. When the garden was extensively developed in 1924, with 40 gardeners and at a cost of £100,000, it quickly earned the reputation of being the most beautiful of its kind in Britain.

A short distance from Nicolle Tower on the A5, near Samares Manor, is a Neolithic passage-grave called **Mont Ube**. Discovered in 1848 by quarrymen, this is the most ancient site in St. Clement and is believed to be around 4,800 years old.

Directly south of Samares Manor, the island just a few hundred metres off the coast, **Green Island**, is the most southerly in the British Isles—though it is only an island approaching full tide. Early this century, some rectangular "cist" graves were discovered here;

Elegance lingers on in Samares Manor.

THE MIGHT OF MONT ORGUEIL

When King John lost Normandy to France in 1204, work started on the castle at Gorey as a bastion against possible French invasion. Just how far-sighted this plan was may be judged from the fact that, between 1204 and 1600, the French made no fewer than 15 attacks on Jersey.

Mont Orgueil, meaning "Mount Pride", was named by Henry V's brother, the Duke of Clarence. In the middle ward, the uncovering of a huge rampart indicates that an Iron Age "hill fort" existed on this site long before this first part of the castle was built.

Mont Orgueil is built on the concentric principle, employing a series of defences each independent of the other. Wherever possible, the walls grow straight out of the rock so that together they are a formidable obstacle to would-be attackers.

The defenders of this castle in the 14th century had every reason for strengthening Mont Orgueil. In 1338, Sir Nicholas Behuchet, a French admiral, had successfully invaded Jersey, though he was

forced to retire when his siege of Mont Orgueil failed. In 1339, a seaborne force of 52 vessels was unable to take the castle. Another French attempt in 1374 also failed. Mont Orgueil did fall victim to a betrayal brought about by the Wars of the Roses. In 1461, Margaret of Anjou (the wife of Henry VI) sought the help of her cousin Pierre de Breze in the failing Lancastrian cause. De Breze obliged in the form of an invasion that resulted in a seven-year French occupation. In 1468, Sir Richard Harliston regained the castle after a siege.

Without treachery Mont Orgueil was invincible—but only as long as armies consisted of archers and armour-suited knights. The castle's defences were laid bare with the advent of the cannon. The round towers which had ringed the castle were too lightly constructed to withstand being shot at, and even displayed an unfortunate tendency to collapse when big guns were installed. The last effort to strengthen the castle was the massive Somerset Tower. This, however, couldn't defeat Mont Orgueil's proximity to Mont St. Nicholas: this neighbouring hillside provided an ideal position for enemy cannon.

Although defeated at this point in history, Mont Orgueil still has a colourful story to tell. In the 17th century it served as a prison. You can still see the chamber in which William Prynne, whose writings incurred the censure of Charles I, began his sentence. Not only incarcerated, Prynne was also fined £10,000, had his ears cut off and his face branded with the initials S.L. ("seditious libeller").

In 1660, when the English monarchy had been restored, two leading parliamentarians of Jersey, Dean Bandinel and his son, were imprisoned. Their celebrated attempt to escape by tying bedclothes together and climbing out of a castle window is recalled in one of four tableaux.

By the 18th century Mont Orgueil was no longer a prison. In 1789, it regained briefly some of its former splendour as a refuge for aristocratic families fleeing the Reign of Terror and the guillotine in France.

Afterwards it faded into virtual obscurity until the early part of this century when the stronghold was formally handed over by the Crown to the States of Jersey. The last thread was woven by the Germans who incorporated it into their fortifications during World War II.

they are exhibited in **La Hougue Bie Museum**.

Inland again, along the A5, is **St. Clement's Church**, from which the parish takes its name. The earliest reference to this church is from 1067. St. Clement's has some of Jersey's few remaining medieval frescoes (wall paintings). These were found in 1879 by workmen employed in an extensive 19th-century restoration. Before their discovery, they had been hidden by plaster and were already damaged and defaced.

The east coast: Plat Rocque Point, in Grouville Parish, marks the easternmost point of St. Clement's Bay. It was here on January 5, 1781, that Rullecourt landed the invasion force that was to be defeated a few hours later at the Battle of Jersey.

Rounding Plat Rocque Point, you get your first view of the east coast and the Royal Bay of Grouville to Gorey and Mont Orgueil Castle beyond. Halfway round the bay is **Grouville Common**, part of which is used by the **Royal Jersey Golf Club**. This is regarded as *the* golf course on the island. If you've already been to the Jersey Museum you'll have heard the name of one man who played here: Harry Vardon, five times winner of the British Open Championship. And, if you and a partner get the opportunity to battle it out here, spare a thought for past losers: Gorey Common used to be a duelling ground where disputes could be settled with pistols at 20 paces.

Grouville Church was established as a parish church before 1035, though the nave is said to be over 1,000 years old. The date of consecration, 1322, applies merely to the completion of the Chancel and the Tower. The font is a curious survivor of the Reformation. Originally part of the Town Church of St. Helier, it was later recovered from a farmyard where it had been playing the undignified role of a pig trough.

Gorey's giant: Those who find such antiquarian anecdotes tedious might argue that Jersey would be little worse off for the loss of a medieval font. They

Left, inside Mont Orgueil Castle. Below, the castle towers over Gorey.

might have a point—but the loss of an entire castle is a different matter. When plans for Elizabeth Castle were begun at the end of the 16th century the intention was to demolish **Gorey Castle**. Walter Raleigh recommended to Queen Elizabeth I that it should stay since it was a "stately Fort of great capacytye" which he considered "were a pity to cast down".

Sir Walter Raleigh wasn't the first to show concern over the fate of the castle at Mont Orgueil. Governors of Jersey continually sought money from England to maintain the castle. Some even had to dip into their own pockets.

Mont Orgueil dominates the village of Gorey and the entire Royal Bay of Grouville. And many would say it has greater prowess than the two fortifications that were to follow: Elizabeth Castle and Fort Regent. They would say also that it is the most cherished of Jersey's monuments. With more than 100,000 visitors a year, it certainly gets its fair share of the tourist trade. If you visit during the day, make sure you return to Gorey after dark: Mont Orgueil, when floodlit, is even more picturesque, even more dramatic and even more memorable. Whoever decided the castle should be illuminated created the ultimate picture postcard.

The castle has undergone many modifications over nearly eight centuries. Inside, the best insight into who did what, where, when, why and how is provided by four tableaux, each accompanied by a lengthy commentary. Once you've negotiated the ancient passages and stairways to arrive at the highest point, the views all around are, not surprisingly, stunning.

Gorey's bright lights: Sitting in the shadow of this great castle is the small, picturesque and unassuming town of **Gorey**, the southernmost community in the parish of St. Martin. Quaint and quiet, Gorey isn't much more than a line of tidy shops and pubs ringing the small harbour. But that isn't to belittle it: Gorey was once a "pearl of the east". A thriving oyster industry was the main reason behind the construction of

Gorey, though a port, is a sleepy place.

Gorey's harbour and church. Oysters were so plentiful, it is said that restaurants supplied them free to customers, though the practice doesn't survive today.

Gorey Pier was built in 1820, though there must have been an earlier structure of some kind as there is a 17th-century reference to Gorey having "the most ancient harbour of all in the island". Today, Gorey is the only official port for Jersey after St. Helier.

The Jersey Eastern Railway ensured Gorey was very much in the swing of things when tourism began to develop, late last century. The present car park and bus-stand mark the site of the old railway station. The flowerbed running along Gorey's long promenade marks the site of the old railway track.

If you can't find **Jersey Pottery** when you're in Gorey, just follow the tourist coaches. No self-respecting tourist economy would be without its pottery, and the Jersey Pottery puts the craft very clearly and very professionally on display. You can visit only on weekdays and during normal working hours because the pottery is an authentic, profit-making enterprise. There are no guided tours here, though there are plenty of tourists. Modern, clean and spacious, the premises are laid out so that you can hover just a few feet away from the staff as they create their pottery. They use liquid clay, a mixture of sodium silicate, clay, soda ash and water and import the raw materials from Devon and Cornwall. In each department are large signboards describing processes such as "fettling" and "casting" and revealing the function of a machine called a "blunger". Once you tire of peering at the unself-conscious potters, you can shop in the showroom. Even if you aren't tempted by the wide range of pottery, you shouldn't resist the garden restaurant, where a combination of good food, good wine and the shade of willow trees makes Jersey Pottery all the more worthwhile.

Leapers, lepers, legends: On the seaward side, the parish of St. Martin's

Creating that Riviera look: top tans get top priority.

stretches all the way from Gorey up to Rozel Bay and includes what many consider to be Jersey's most beautiful coastline.

On the coast road out of Gorey, just a few hundred metres beyond Mont Orgueil, is a site known as **Le Saut Geffroy** (Geoffrey's Leap). The name refers to the antics of a convicted criminal who survived his sentence of being thrown over the cliff. Not satisfied with one miraculous escape, he leapt over the cliff once more. This time he was killed. Some say this story is a romantic retelling of what really happened. The "truth" has Geoffrey showing less bravado. In the Middle Ages, condemned men were pushed off the rock with their hands and feet bound. When Geoffrey was pushed, he managed somehow to free himself and swim ashore. Everyone regarded this as a miracle and he was pardoned. A short time later, when he was again convicted of a crime, he asked for the same punishment but was unable to repeat his escape and died.

This promontory, made famous by a medieval leaper, was also home to medieval lepers: records show that there was once a leperhouse in this locality.

Near Gorey Church, a site of even more ancient interest is **Faldouet Dolmen** (also known as La Pouquelaye de Faldouet). This passage grave, said to date from 2,500 B.C., is 45 feet (15 metres) long, 17 feet (six metres) high and has a capstone whose weight has been estimated at 24 tons. One of Jersey's more dramatic Neolithic dolmens, it is well worth seeing.

Less than two miles (three km) away from Dolmen de Faldouet along the B28 into the parish of St. Saviour is Jersey's most famous ancient site, **La Hougue Bie**. This 33-foot (11-metre) long Neolithic passage-grave is topped by a mound 40 feet (13 metres) high. The whole structure dates from about 3,000 B.C. That's the easy part of the story. The origins of the mound and the larger of the two chapels above it are less certain. One legend, first found in a manuscript of 1734, provides an expla-

Left, contemplating the options at Geoffrey's Leap. Right, the mound at La Hougue Bie.

nation for the name Hougue Bie at least.

The word "Hougue" refers quite simply to a burial mound. The word "Bie" might come from the family name of "Hambye". The legend says that Lord Hambye of Normandy crossed to Jersey to slay a dragon in the vicinity. Lord Hambye's servant, hoping that he would gain credit for this feat, murdered his master and buried him. When the servant arrived back in Normandy he induced Lady Hambye to believe that the dragon had killed her lord and that he had killed the dragon to avenge his master's death. He also duped her into believing that it was his master's dying wish she should marry him. The wedding followed, though the servant was eventually unmasked. As a memorial to her murdered husband Lady Hambye had a mound built on high ground where he had been buried. It was named La Hougue Hambye.

A chronicle of 1585 is said to record this event, saying that the Lady of Hambye erected a mound in a conspicuous place to enable her to view her husband's burial place from the castle-keep at Hambye (in Normandy). She also built a small chapel. All that can be said in support is that on the opposite coast of Normandy, a few miles from Coutanche, on the heights above the village of Hambye, are the ruins of the castle which once belonged to the Seigneur of Hambye.

This account refers to the larger of the two chapels, **Notre Dame de la Carte**. There is at least one other legend accounting for its construction. Archaeological and historical sources say that the simple design and primitive masonry do indeed show it to date from no later that the 12th or 13th centuries.

The origins of the smaller **Jerusalem Chapel** are more certain. It was built by Dean Mabon around 1520, shortly after his return from the Holy Land. Until 1924 another structure stood on the mound as well. **La Tour d'Auvergne** was a mock medieval structure attached to the western end of the building by James d'Auvergne shortly before 1780.

La Hougue Bie is more than just an

Ancient passage grave at La Hogue Bie.

ancient site. There is a good archaeological museum in the grounds as well as permanent exhibitions on geology and agriculture. You can even learn the full story of Jersey's railways here in an old surviving guard's van.

Given the number of military towers along the road approaching Gorey from the south, you might find the sight of one more as you leave Gorey to the north less than inspiring. But **Archirondel Tower**, set in the little bay of Havre de Fer and built between 1793 and 1794, has the distinction of being the prototype for what is probably the best known tower in Jersey: **La Rocco Tower** in St. Ouen.

A problematic pier: At Verclut Point, **St. Catherine's Breakwater** is nothing less than a Victorian military folly. It forms the northern arm of what was to be one of two Channel Island naval bases (the other site is in Alderney). The southern arm was to reach out from Archirondel Tower. The perceived threat was once again the French, who around 1840 had strengthened Cherbourg and a number of other ports. A British Navy admiral warned that the site was ill-chosen because it would quickly silt up. Work started in 1847 nevertheless. The building programme succeeded in doing little more than absorbing £250,000 of taxpayers' money. The Archirondel arm was abandoned in 1849. When St. Catherine's Breakwater was completed in 1855 to a length of half-a-mile, it did indeed emerge that the "harbour" was too shallow for British warships.

From grave mistake to another ancient grave: **Le Couperon Dolmen** at Saie harbour. You can reach this site either by walking back from Rozel or by following the B91. Le Couperon is a "gallery grave", designed for collective burial.

Rozel and its bay make for another of Jersey's picture-postcard locations. One of the best views of the village is had from the slopes of **Rue Fontenell** which leads in from the south. Rozel, small and unspoilt, nestles in a cove with a wooded hillside rising behind it.

St. Catherine's Breakwater: it seems to go on and on.

A single street of houses and seaside stalls fronts the promenade. You could walk from one end to the other in about as many minutes as it takes Rozel's curiously unperturbed resident flock of geese to saunter across the rocky beach at low tide. The harbour here was built in 1829 and shared some of the spoils of Gorey's 19th-century oyster trade. Some barracks, built in 1809, now form part of the upmarket hotel, **Le Couperon de Rozelle**.

The lush **Rozel Valley** can be approached from behind the village. It owes some of its flora to a 19th-century naturalist, Samuel Curtis, who planted a variety of subtropical trees and shrubs, many of which can be seen today.

An important part of Rozel's history, though sadly not open to the public, is the Manor south of Rozel, less than a mile from the Parish Church of St. Martin. A seigneur from Normandy, where the original "Rozel" is, owned land in Jersey and lent the locality this Norman name. The Lempière family,

Waiting for the tide at Rozel Harbour.

one of Jersey's oldest, bought the Manor in 1360. Though the family was displaced from ownership at one time, it is today in the possession of descendants of that line. The Lord of Rozel (together with the Lord of Augrès Manor) holds the hereditary title of Royal Butler, which gives them positions of honour when there is a royal visit to the island.

The steep slopes leading out of Rozel make up part of **Le Catel Rozel**, an Iron Age earthwork fortification. Coins from Gaul and Rome found in the vicinity suggest this must have been an important strategic site in the past.

Cliffs and climbers: Bouley Bay contrasts strongly with Rozel Bay. Here there's no picturesque village, though the cliff slopes are higher and the landscape is altogether more grand. Not surprisingly, perhaps, the British Hill Climbing Association has adopted Bouley Bay for its annual championships. As long as you are a paid-up member of the BHCA equipped with either a motorcycle, saloon car, racing

car, sports car, or even just a bicycle, you can join in the fray.

A more peaceful location is the **Jardin d'Olivet**, a flat common popular for walks and picnics. This was a battleground in 1547 when a French invasion force, having already seized Sark, confronted the Jersey Militia. Bouley Bay has seen no other struggles since then, though this might be due in part to 18th-century fortifications to the west and east: **Les Hurets** and **L'Etacquerel**.

The star of Trinity Parish is undoubtedly **Jersey Zoo and Wildlife Park**. Make no mistake, though, about *this* family of animals; this is not the "jungle top-40" approach to zookeeping—no chimpanzee tea parties here, no dolphin antics, no polar bears to be gawped at, no elephants at which you can throw bread rolls. Gerald Durrell, the zoo's director, founded it with the serious intention of building up, under controlled conditions, breeding colonies of animal species threatened with extinction. But don't be put off by the scientific approach: the grounds,

spaciously laid out, are a clear invitation to amble and take time to look, listen and learn. Cheetahs, spectacled bears, Cuban boas, Sumatran orangutans, lemurs, flamingoes and gorillas are among a cast of creatures that is sometimes feathered, now and then hairy, possibly carnivorous, occasionally venomous, but invariably endangered. (See feature on pages 224-229.)

About a mile to the south of Jersey Zoo, near Victoria Village, is the **Eric Young Orchid Foundation**. Here you can see the fruits of a lifelong passion for orchids. Eric Young, the founder, came to Jersey after World War II and set up the basis of his collection in 1958. In the same year he bought the stock from a local orchid nursery that was about to close down. He transferred his newly acquired orchids to a run-down market garden near Howard Davis Park purchased around the same time. Less than a decade later this growing collection of orchids was described as "the finest private collection of orchids in Europe, possibly the world". Eric Young's ambition was to have his extensive collection housed in a suitable location and opened to the public, but he died before the project was completed. It's a haven for would-be photographers armed with tripods, and its refusal to "go commercial" has endeared it to many visitors—the Duke and Duchess of York included—since it opened in 1986.

The highest point on Jersey is nearly three miles (five km) away back up near the coastline at **Les Platons**, where, at 435 feet (133 metres) above sea level, there is a small cist grave. This ancient monument is set amid modern radio transmitter masts, which at least make Les Platons easy to find.

Anyone with passions for rock-climbing, caves and prehistoric deer might wish to go out to the end of this particular headland. At the bottom of the steep cliffs (do not attempt the descent without ropes and a guide) is the cave at **La Belle Hougue**. This site is of limited archaeological interest— the only remains ever found here were of a previously unknown type of an-

Orchids attract a swarm of photographers.

cient deer—but the 100-foot (30-metre) deep cave will reward the efforts of any dedicated speleologist.

Goodnight, badnight: The fetching name of **Bonne Nuit Bay** comes from a chapel built by this stretch of Jersey's rugged northern coastline in 1150—the Chapel of Ste. Maria de Bona Nochte. The name wasn't passed down the centuries in its original form, though; the chapel is referred to once in ancient records as the Chapel de Mala Nocte. Goodnight or Badnight, it doesn't really matter; Bonne Nuit Bay is scenic, secluded and peaceful. It's rocky too, and the inevitable stories of smuggling are easy to believe. The bay was fortified in the 18th and 19th centuries, although the only remaining structure is **La Crete**, built in 1835 on the eastern headland of Bonne Nuit Bay.

The rock in the middle of the bay, **Le Cheval Guillaume**, is named after Guillaume de Vauville, who gave the Chapel of Ste. Maria to the Abbey of St. Saveur de Vicomte in the 12th century. In centuries past, it was considered a protection against bad luck to row around it on Midsummer's Day.

There is little else on the coast of St. John's Parish to entice you other than the **Wolf Caves** and **Sorel Point**. The Wolf Caves are accessible only at low tide. You have to pay to make the 400-foot (120-metre) descent, though your efforts are at least rewarded by a "diploma" to prove you made it down and back up.

The road leading north out of St. John's Village, the **Route du Nord**, was built during the German Occupation to provide employment for those who wouldn't work for the Germans. In a public car park there is a memorial with the following inscription: "This road is dedicated to the men and women of Jersey who suffered in the World War 1939-1945."

Depending on which way you look at things, Sorel Point can be something of a sorry sight. True, the views out to sea from this windswept promontory can be magnificent—weather conditions permitting, you can see Alderney, France, Guernsey and Sark—but turn your back to the sea and look eastward to **Ronez Point** and you'll see some ugly cliff slopes quarried and scarred to provide raw material for a cement works nearby.

Bacchus and Blayney: If you don't find the sight of Jersey's cement industry refreshing, make your way to **La Mare Vineyards** in St. Mary's Parish and enjoy the fruits of Jersey's first step into viticulture and winemaking.

La Mare Vineyards were established in 1969 by Robert Blayney. A fifth-generation member of a family of Northumberland wine merchants, he was able to call on more than a little expertise when he arrived in Jersey. That was just as well, for while grapes had been grown in abundance last century there was no record of a vineyard here and certainly no local experience to draw on. How the Blayneys fared from 1969 onwards is explained in a video that greets you at the entrance to this 12-acre (5-hectare) site. When you emerge from the viticultural film show, the neat lanes of vines (well over 1,000

at the last count) and the many *miles* of wire supporting them is proof of how successful they've been. Wine is not the only liquid refreshment to flow forth from La Mare. The Blayneys are also Jersey's largest cider producers, though here they are not breaking new ground: cider has been a tradition on the island since Tudor times.

Once you've viewed the vines, there's a modest but nicely put-together exhibition on the history of wine, the Blayney family and of the 18th-century farmhouse in which they live. The displays include a range of fermentation paraphernalia old and new, a 2,300-year-old amphora (wine jar) and a letter from Buckingham Palace acknowledging receipt of a bottle or two sent to the Queen. So what does it taste like? Choose between Clos de Seyval and Clos de la Mare and you won't be disappointed.

The natural archway cut into the rocks on the coast to the north of La Mare Vineyards, the Creux de Vis, is better known as the **Devil's Hole**, though you'd do well to resist the temptation to visit it. The present pathway, which starts discreetly in the Priory car park, stops about 100 feet (30 metres) above the sea and allows for only a rather disappointing view. An older stairway, which has either collapsed or been demolished, once led much lower and clearly provided a better vantage point. The "devil" in question stays well away in any case. Marooned in a murky pond at the start of the cliffpath, the devil is the menacing figurehead (limbs and body added at a later stage) of a ship wrecked here in 1851.

To the south of La Mare Vineyards, La Haute Tombette Farm is home to the **Jersey Butterfly Farm**. This started life as a carnation greenhouse. Only later was one glasshouse set aside for a colourful collection of butterflies. The idea wasn't original, for Guernsey lays claim to the first "butterfly farm". Indeed, the man who got Guernsey's version off the ground advised on the setting up of this one.

Sunbeds and Caesar: If Rozel is the

Left, raw materials for the wine trade at Val de la Mare. Right, taking to the water at Plémont.

most picturesque bay on Jersey's north coast, then **Grève de Lecq** is the most popular. Perhaps, a little too popular.

Grève de Lecq was attractive to ancient strategists, too. Overlooking the bay to the east, **Castel de Lecq** is an Iron Age mound on which a hill fort is said to have stood. Not quite so ancient, but certainly more attractive, is **Le Moulin de Lecq**, a restored mill (now a pub/restaurant) whose origins can be traced back to the 14th century. It was last used for grinding in 1929, though the wheel still turns. Inside, the huge, creaking wood-varnished cog—bottles of spirits sitting precariously near it— forms an impressive backdrop to the bar.

Just a short distance away are the **Grève de Lecq Barracks**. Built in 1810 as part of the web of military roads and installations surrounding Fort Regent, these neat granite buildings are in an excellent state of repair. Inside, (they are open only two days a week) there are displays illustrating what life was like in these barrack-houses. The

only other military remnant is a round tower dating from 1780, which today keeps company with a crowded carpark.

Grève de Lecq has all the trappings of a lively English tourist resort: a big seaside cafeteria; another big carpark; even a **Caesar's Palace** which lurks less than a minute's walk from the old mill.

On to St. Ouen: Le Moulin de Lecq marks another parish boundary, that between St. Mary and St. Ouen. The largest of Jersey's parishes, St. Ouen has a reputation for being windswept and at times remote. However, this ruggedness didn't stop the builders of **Plémont Holiday Village** to the east of **Grève au Lanchon**.

The best known site in St. Ouen, amid the barren heathland of **Les Landes**, is **Grosnez Castle**. This lonely outpost certainly doesn't compare with Jersey's other great castles. Little is known about it either. References on 16th-century maps show that it was already in ruins more than 400 years

Safety-net for inexperienced swimmers at St. Brelade's Bay.

ago. An account of Bertrand du Guesclin's invasion of the late 14th century mentions two castles. One was certainly Mont Orgueil and it is possible the other was Grosnez.

Less than half-a-mile to the south of Grosnez Castle is a lofty concrete **German observation post**, one of the island's largest fortifications. You can inspect the interior if you like—damp, derelict and empty though it is. The cliffs here are steep and provided the final resting place for a number of heavy guns that were dismantled at the end of World War II. When the tide is right, you can see a cluster of rusting German gun barrels lying heaped and forgotten in a tangle of rocks and surf at the base of the cliffs.

About two miles (three km) southeast of Les Landes you can make the transition from this scenic promontory of gorse and heather to flowers of quite another kind at the **Battle of Flowers Museum**. If you don't get to see the Battle of Flowers itself, the museum is the next best thing. Founded in 1971 by

Miss Florence Bechelet, a Jersey resident who has built and entered a number of exhibits for the Battle of Flowers, the museum houses more than a dozen of the floats that have made their way down Victoria Avenue in years gone by. Exhibits such as "Arctic Scene," "Dovecote" and "Monarchs of the Prairie" are accompanied by some evocative black-and-white photographs of the event.

When the weather is bad, the wide sweep of St. Ouen's Bay is far from welcoming. Not that this put off Sir Admiral Blake in 1651: his fleet conveyed the Parliamentary forces that subsequently landed here and repulsed the disunited Jersey royalist factions during the English Civil War. These days, the bay's invaders are usually surfers competing in local, national and international competitions. And they are seldom at a loss for a wave or two; at times the surf is fine even by Bondi Beach standards. There's a remarkable contrast between this section of Jersey's coast and a small sheltered bay like that at Rozel, given that they are separated by only a few miles.

Wild, sparse and windswept though St. Ouen and its bay area, there's plenty to see and do here. Running along the bay's edge is the misleadingly named **Five Mile Road**. If you walk its length it may feel like five miles (eight km), though it's a little over three miles (five km). Walk along the beach from the northern edge of the bay by the headland rock of **Grand Etaquerel** down to the slipway near **L'Oeillère** and you'll do a little better at four miles (6.5 km). After a walk like that, you'll appreciate just how large St. Ouen's Bay is. Look at the map and you'll see it marks the western edge of no less than three of Jersey's parishes: St. Ouen, St. Peter and St. Brelade.

Nurturing nature: In an area as empty and open as this, it's the flora and fauna that command most attention. Much of the land is now a protected environment. Towards the north, La Mielles de Morville is a park and nature reserve. To the south, Les Blanches Banques, an extensive network of sand-dunes, has

A German observation post near Grosnez, an immovable reminder of the Occupation.

also been protected.

Les Mielles de Morville were designated a "special place" in 1978 in recognition of the high wildlife and landscape value of St. Ouen's Bay. More than 400 species of plant life have been identified in this small area. **St. Ouen's Pond**, an important part of this nature reserve, is a well-established bird-ringing station. Since it was decided to conserve Les Mielles de Morville, the area has lost much of its unkempt appearance. It was formerly a landscape of disused sheds, broken fences, derelict dwellings and dumped rubbish. Perhaps the Germans can take the blame for originally setting the dereliction in motion: their fortifications were preceded by the demolition of all the houses along this Sunset Strip. But the landscape helped the residents in one way: when fuel began to run low, peat was cut and dried here.

The full conservation story is told at **Kempt Tower Interpretation Centre**, another of the defences built during the Napoleonic Wars. Here the National Trust for Jersey has laid on a permanent exhibition covering the related subjects of wildlife, geology and history. The best view of St. Ouen's Bay can be had from the top of this tower.

The dune plain of **Les Blanches Banques**, among the 10 largest in the British Isles and one of the most important systems in Europe, is thought to have existed for more than 3,000 years. Neolithic tombs and flint tools found on the dune plateau of **Les Ouennevais** are said to be even older. There are likely to be more ancient artefacts buried beneath the sandwaves since there are a number of past references to the area being engulfed by sandstorms. It's a hazard you won't face today: the dunes have been made stable by vegetation, so much so that their southern edge is taken up by **La Moye Golf Course.**

Crafty woodcraft: While sand buried things in the south, the sea did the same in the north. An entire forest near L'Etacq was submerged when the sea level rose after the Ice Age. According

A wild and windswept walk at St. Ouen's sand dunes.

to legend, more than a forest was lost: the drowned village of Le Brecquelle is believed to be located close by.

A highly visible landmark northwards along the coast beyond Grande Etaquerel is **La Pinacle**, once an object of worship. Archaeological evidence of settlement from the Neolithic and Bronze Ages as well as the Iron Age and Roman Empire has been found here.

Modern-day **L'Etacq** is a small community just a few hundred metres inland. **L'Etacq Woodcrafts** has made a rather forlorn attempt to shape the story of the lost forest to its advantage. Make no mistake, when you pay your money to enter L'Etacq Woodcrafts, you are buying your way into the woodcraft store at the end of the building. True, there is a half-hearted recreation of the lost forest, but anybody who knows what any other forest looks like will be unimpressed. True, there is a short video pontificating on the role of wood in ancient folklore and ritual. True, you get to see the woodworking staff chiselling, sawing and generally behaving like craftsmen. But when you get to the other end, to what is after all a shop selling woodcraft, you'd be forgiven for asking yourself if you've had value for money. More's the pity, because some of the woodcraft for sale is fine. Why, you ask, do they bother with the tacky "theme-park"? Wouldn't they be better off just selling their creations?

Golden opportunity: It may or may not be a case of "look, don't touch" if you visit **Jersey Goldsmiths** at the northern end of Five Mile Road. The emphasis is on selling gold, not on making it. You can choose from a breathtaking range of gold jewellery— some affordable, some less so. By the entrance is a pile of gold to show what £1 million-worth would look like: it is a surprisingly modest bulk and would fit snugly into a good-sized sports bag.

If you enjoy tracking down traces of prehistory, finding **Dolmen du Mont Grantez** will present a worthwhile challenge. There's a distinct lack of signs pointing the way and maps seem to indicate little more than its being

L'Etacq: the name is Old Norse, dating from when the Vikings roamed these waters.

located somewhere or other in the meadows overlooking St. Ouen's Bay. If and when you do find it—it's about 600 feet (200 metres) from a roadside near St. Anne's Church, cunningly concealed by a stone wall which is itself obscured by ferns—the setting and the accompanying view repay your efforts. This is a passage-grave where skeletons dating back 5,000 years were found in 1912. Of the 10 Jersey dolmens, this is the second oldest site. Seven burials were found together with limpets, animal bones, pebbles and pottery.

One place not worth looking for is **St. Ouen's Mill**, known as Le Moulin de la Campagne. There are references to a mill on this site dating back to the 14th century, but the present mill was built in the 19th century and is used by the local Sea Scouts troop.

Enquire before you visit **St. Ouen's Manor**; its opening times are restricted. The magnificent stately building figures prominently in this parish's history. The de Carteret family have owned land here since before 1066,

though the first mention of a manor is in 1135. The oldest part of the building is the south tower, built in 1380. The west and north wings followed in the 16th century and the south and east wings in the 17th. At one time, when the Manor passed into the hands of four female members of the de Carteret family, it looked as if the traditional line of possession would come to an end; but in 1880 it was inherited by Edward Charles Malet de Carteret.

Inside the grounds, the **Chapel of St. Anne**, constructed at either the same time or earlier than the oldest part of the Manor proper, has served as a barn in past centuries of neglect and during the German Occupation as a storehouse and butchery. After François Scornet, a French patriot fleeing his homeland, was forced to land in Guernsey, he was sentenced to death, then executed at the Manor.

The **Shire Horse Farm** has assembled a collection of horse-drawn carriages and farm implements that provide a vivid and absorbing retelling

St. Ouen's Manor: historic seat of the de Carterets, a prominent Norman family.

of Jersey's agricultural history. But the shire horses played no part in that history; they were imported from England to work on the farm and to provide rides for tourists. A more authentic feature here is the farmhouse kitchen where you can choose from hearty fare that includes ploughman's lunches and cream teas.

Making Tracks: St. Brelade is Jersey's second largest parish. Its southwestern corner is marked by **Corbière Lighthouse** standing more than 100 feet (30 metres) above sea-level. It derives its name from *corbeau*, French for crow, a bird traditionally taken to be an ill omen. This part of the coastline has indeed wrecked a number of ships. Marine traffic navigated these waters unaided by a lighthouse until 1874 when Corbière Lighthouse, the first in Britain to be built in concrete, was completed.

At full tide the lighthouse is cut off from the land. You can walk down to it at half-tide, though you should keep an eye on the water-level. An inscription along the pathway reads "Take heed all ye that pass by," and recalls the fate of assistant lighthouse-keeper Peter Larbalestier who lost his life trying to rescue a visitor cut off by the incoming tide.

In 1943, **La Rocco Tower** in St. Ouen's Bay was used by German guns at Corbière for target practice. Until then the tower had been in good shape, but the Germans breached its ramparts and damaged the main structure.

Until 1936, Jersey Railways and Tramways ran a train service from St. Helier to St. Aubin and Corbière, between which there were four stations: Pont Marquet, Don Bridge, Blanches Banques and La Moye. The line fell on hard times, but you can still follow the route of the track along **Corbière Walk** right through to St. Aubin.

St. Brelade's Bay is wide, sandy, peaceful and made all the more picturesque by the wooded slopes stretching back from the promenade. John Keble, a 19th-century writer and theologian, wrote on visiting St. Brelade's Bay that

A passenger steamer passes Corbière Lighthouse.

126

such locations should be kept secret and that "it would soon be spoiled if the pleasure-seekers got hold of it". Pleasure-seekers certainly have got hold of it, but it hasn't been spoiled and is unlikely to be. The **Winston Churchill Memorial Park**, with its tidy lawns and trim flowerbeds, typifies the care that goes into St. Brelade's upkeep. While this mini-resort does have its fair share of guesthouses and hotels, it's generally a peaceful, quiet place.

At the western end of the bay is **St. Brelade's Church** and its neighbouring **Fisherman's Chapel**. The nave and chancel of the church date from before 1066. It was named after Bren Gwaladr, a companion of St. Sampson who came to Jersey in the sixth century. The older parts of the church have been added at various (mostly unknown) times. One recorded date is 1537 when the church was enlarged. The north aisle was constructed at this time.

It was once a convention that criminals could take sanctuary in parish churches such as St. Brelade's on the condition that they fled the island soon after. A perquage path was provided to ensure direct access to the sea. St. Brelade's has the shortest such escape route in Jersey. Its perquage path leads out from the southeast corner of the churchyard down a flight of steps to the beach.

The Fisherman's Chapel is of much greater interest than the church. The exact date of its construction is uncertain, though recent excavations have suggested it is late 12th century. There was possibly a chapel on this site before then. The Fisherman's Chapel is known for its medieval wall paintings which, despite long neglect and damage from the sea air, retain their faint pastel-coloured outlines.

The church and chapel are set in austere grounds with tall oaks, ancient cedars and neat rows of gravestones. Locals would certainly recognise some of the island's better known family names. Another tomb, a short distance along the road leading between the church and the cemetery, houses **Jesse Boot**, founder of Boots, the UK chain of chemists. His family has long been an important benefactor to Jersey.

Many would say St. Brelade's Bay (at low tide it forms a long continuous stretch of sand with **Ouaisne Bay**) is the island's best beach. If you prefer more secluded locations, **Beau Port** and **Belcroute Bay** provide equally attractive alternatives.

Ouaisne Bay leads onto the quiet and undisturbed stretches of heathland of **Ouaisne Common** and **Portelet Common**. In **Portelet Bay** is the **Ile au Guerdain**, the last resting place of Philippe Janvrin. In 1721 this sea captain died of plague while on his ship anchored in Belcroute Bay. His body was not permitted to be brought ashore so his wife and a party of mourners attended his funeral service from a distance, watching from the beach.

Further south still, **Noirmont Point** is the site of a major German naval artillery installation. A four-storey emplacement, it was the command post for a number of gun positions on this

Get up and go at St. Ouen's Beach.

headland. Although the bunker is only occasionally open to the public, it has been carefully restored by the Channel Islands Occupation Society.

Pirates' haunt: The town of **St. Aubin**, on the opposite side of St. Aubin's Bay from St. Helier, is another of Jersey's "picture-postcard" communities. It takes its name from a sixth-century Bishop of Angers, patron saint of those seeking protection against pirates. It was an ironic choice. For the town, a thriving commercial centre long before St. Helier came to the fore, owed at least part of its wealth to piracy. The more polite term of "privateering" is preferred by historians who point out that confiscation of seaborne goods was once a legalised activity.

St. Aubin's first pier—the southern arm—was built in 1675 (the south pier you see today dates from 1754) in St. Aubin's privateering heyday. Shortly after 1675, the diarist Dumaresq wrote: "The conveniency of the pier has occasioned a small town to be built, consisting of about fourscore houses." The Bulwarks, the houses beside the harbour, were built in 1790, while the pier was added in 1817.

St. Aubin was never able to keep up with the growth of St. Helier. At one time the only route to its "new" neighbour was across the beach of St. Aubin's Bay at low tide. General Don's military road didn't reach all the way to St. Aubin until 1844. It was the coming of the railway in 1870 that put the town on the map; the present Parish Hall, on the northern pier, was once the station.

Right from its early days, St. Aubin was more popular than St. Helier. A guidebook first published in 1911 paints an especially rosy picture:

"For convenient and prompt access to beautiful scenery and lovely walks, St. Aubin has the advantage over St. Helier. The little town is in the very heart and centre of the best the Island has to offer... leading up from the town is a valleyroad beside the railway, with thickly wooded hills on either side, and cottages in picturesque untidiness smothered in a careless growth of roses, honey-suckle and greenery."

There is little to "see" as such in St. Aubin other than take time to walk the back streets by the Royal Channel Islands Yacht Club and enjoy the relaxed atmosphere of the harbour setting. **St. Aubin's Fort** is accessible only at certain times owing to the tide and is really worth visiting only for the view it provides of St. Aubin itself. It's not open to the public. This building's long history of renovation and refortification since its original construction in 1542 hardly stands up to the glittering past of Elizabeth Castle less than two miles (three km) across the water.

One place difficult to miss is the **Shell House** on the steep hill leading out of St. Aubin to St. Brelade's. The sloping garden outside this small bungalow has been decorated with a variety of seashells by its owner for over 30 years.

Valley excursions: St. Peter's Valley is Jersey at its rural best. It always has been. When Queen Victoria asked to see the most beautiful spot on the

St. Aubin's Bay, where pirates once took refuge.

island, she was taken on a tour of the valley. A convenient starting point for several of Jersey's most popular inland locations is **St. Matthew's Church**, in the parish of St. Lawrence, popularly known as "the Glass Church". The original was built in the mid-19th century so that people living in this neighbourhood didn't have to walk more than a mile (one-and-a-half km) inland to the Parish Church of St. Lawrence. In 1934, the church was renovated by Lady Trent in memory of her husband Jesse Boot, the chainstore founder. The main feature of this renovation was the art deco glasswork of René Lalique, a celebrated craftsman of the time. Windows, door panels, screens to either side of the altar, the font, a 12-foot (four-metre) cross and even the altar rail are all made from a frosted opaque glass. This was the only church Lalique decorated in its entirety with glass.

St. Matthew's is adjacent to **Coronation Park**, also the result of Lady Trent's generosity. She gave it to the island in 1937 on the understanding that

it would be maintained as a place for the aged and the young.

At different times the stream running down through St. Peter's Valley served eight mills. **Moulin de Quétivel** is a fully restored example of how these would have looked. References to Quétivel Mill have been traced back as far as 1309, when it was a Crown Mill. The tenants of the king living in St. Brelade had to supply the heavy timber, while the King provided iron, masonry, carpentry and the main sluice-gates. The mill's name derives from a now extinct family. Records dating back to 1307 refer to Rauf and William de Keytovel and other bakers having been fined without full adjudication. By 1934, however, little of the machinery remained. It was left to the Germans to rescue it from oblivion when they decided during wartime food shortages to grind local-grown corn. In 1969, the National Trust of Jersey stepped in to preserve the mill. Today it is in full working order and with its detailed exhibition panels and carefully restored interior, is well worth a visit.

Heaven to hell: A right fork before Moulin de Quétivel leads you to an altogether different side of the island's history. If St. Matthew's Church makes you feel closer to heaven, then the **German Underground Military Hospital** will make you feel that much closer to hell. This extensive subterranean complex was built with the aid of forced labour and slave workers, all of whom lived and many of whom died under inhumane conditions.

Intricately renovated and meticulously researched, the hospital has been turned into a huge and impressive museum. Even though coachloads of visitors disembark at Meadowbank to queue at the entrance to the tunnel, this site loses none of its dignity as a memorial. A plaque sums up the intention in three simple sentences: "Under these conditions men of many nations laboured to construct this hospital. Those who survived will never forget; those who did not will never be forgotten. This exhibition is a reminder of the five years of Occupation and is dedi-

St. Matthew's, known as the Glass Church because of René Lalique's superb glass.

cated to all who suffered the hardship of that time."

The tunnel complex was originally intended as an artillery barracks. At first, no forced labour was used; the 319 Infantry Division set to work in 1941 excavating and drilling. When it became apparent that there weren't enough Germans to complete the job, the infamous Organisation Todt became responsible for the works and it wasn't long before Spanish Republicans (captured in France), North Africans, Alsace Jews, Poles and French were press-ganged into service. In late 1942 Russian prisoners-of-war were also put to work here. In 1944 the would-be barracks were converted to a military hospital. When the liberation came the tunnels exceeded about half-a-mile (one km) in length. In addition there were nearly 1,600 feet (500 metres) of unfinished tunnels.

Walking around the "hospital" today, even in the company of a continuous stream of tourists, is an eerie experience. A map detailing the planned extent of the tunnel complex shows that only about half of it was ever completed and is a reminder that the Germans intended the Channel Islands to be permanently fortified outposts of the Third Reich.

A copious cocktail of medical and military paraphernalia not only vividly illustrates what the hospital looked like but paints a broader canvas of the history of the Occupation. The German Underground Hospital is therefore the telling of two related stories. On the one hand there are the hospital wards, operating theatre, Kommandant's office, radio room and officer's mess. On the other hand several displays show what life was like under the Germans. Near the exit the two themes are brought poignantly together. A collection of photographs, documents and other items tells the story of some of the slave workers who lived and died in the service of the military hospital *and* the story of the Jersey citizens sent away to concentration camps in France and Germany.

Painful memories, kept alive in the German Underground Military Hospital.

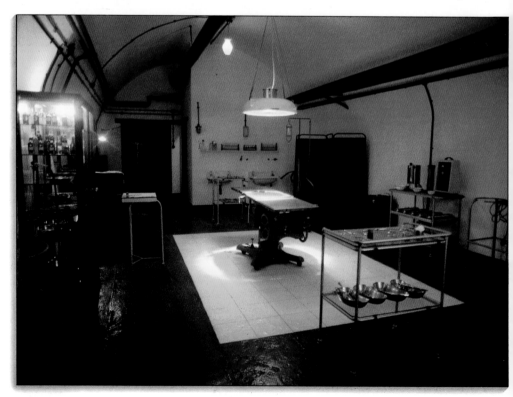

If Jersey is at times inclined to induce a feeling of war-weariness in the visitor, don't expect St. Peter's Valley to provide more than a partial escape. Just over a mile from the German Underground Hospital is **Strawberry Farm**. The name sounds tranquil enough, though a main attraction is the **Fortress Commander's Bunker**—the HQ of a network of six widely dispersed similar fortifications. The bunker is now a small military museum with much of the original equipment and fittings still intact. Strawberries are the big draw, however, and a large open-air restaurant lets you choose from a sparkling menu that includes lobster and a good selection of wines. There's a model village depicting Jersey's history in miniature and a craft centre.

Fun with flowers: Near the top of St. Peter's Valley, meditations on war are interrupted by the **Fantastic Tropical Gardens**. Aimed at those who like their horticulture served up with extra spice and colour, the gardens are a theme-park, a journey through miniature "countries". The first is Spain: the entrance is no mere entrance but the Jersey-Spain border and you get a passport rather than an admission ticket. If you lose your way once inside, you can ask directions from the park ranger (he's the one wearing a khaki uniform, riding boots and carrying a revolver).

As the garden trail leads into each new country you are greeted with appropriate music and passport official. Turn one corner and there's a seven-foot Buddha statue squatting contentedly next to oriental foliage. Turn another and you encounter Pancho, a mechanical parrot who sings to the tune of *The Mexicans Dance On Their Hats*. Elsewhere the *"African Queen"* floats on a duckpond traversed by a wobbly rope-bridge.

The Fantastic Tropical Gardens is way, way over the top, but good fun. As a tourist attraction with "something for all the family" they cunningly kill two birds with one stone. Parents can enjoy the tropical flora while children can ponder why the crocodiles beneath the

rope-bridge in Africa don't seem to move. St. Peter's Village is at the centre of the parish of the same name, less than a mile (about one km) from Jersey's airport. **St. Peter's Church** is sometimes known as St. Pierre dans le Désert, a reference to the sand-dunes of Les Mielles close by to the west.

The earliest recorded mention of this church dates from 1053, though much of the present structure was built in the 12th and 13th centuries. Its bell, cast in Normandy in 1649, is inscribed *"Mon nom est Elizabeth la belle"*—which may be simply a pun on "bell" or, alternatively, a diplomatic compliment to Elizabeth, the wife of Sir George Carteret, whos was closely connected with the parish.

But few visitors come to St. Peter's Village to see the church. Attention is focused instead on the **Jersey Motor Museum** and **Occupation Museum**. The former, also known as the Car Museum, exhibits more than cars. There's a carriage from Jersey's first railway as well as a collection of motor-

bikes, miniature cars and U.S. and German military vehicles from World War II. Cars take pride of place: Jaguars, Fords, MGs, Rolls-Royces, Bentleys and other classic makes stand gleaming and sleek, often with their original price tags on display (a new 1936 MG Midget could have been yours for just £222). It's a collection guaranteed to evoke nostalgia and convince you that driving today isn't as much fun as it used to be.

The six-room **Occupation Museum**, better known as St. Peter's Bunker, is said to house the largest collection of Nazi memorabilia in the Channel Islands. If you've been to the Occupation Museum in St. Helier, the Underground Hospital and the bunker at Strawberry Farm, you'll probably leave not remembering which sten gun was in which location. The fact is that these six tiny rooms are packed as tightly as they could be. It's the only place in the islands where you'll see one of the few remaining Enigma cipher machines. But the personal artefacts say much more than do the guns and hardware.

One display case states: "War Does This To People" and contains anonymous letters telling the Gestapo and the Field Commandant which neighbours were selling goods on the black market, using home made radio sets or stocking secret supplies of food. The penalty for each of those "crimes" was inevitably severe.

An alternative, or additional, valley route from St. Matthew's Church takes you directly north, up through **Waterworks Valley**. More secluded than St. Peter's Valley, Waterworks Valley at one time had as many watermills as St. Peter's. But the growth of St. Helier in the last century meant that the water supply had to be more extensively utilised. **Millbrook Reservoir** was built in 1898, **Dannemarche Reservoir** in 1909 and **Handois Reservoir** in 1932. A shady country lane takes you past the first two of these; the last is easily reached on foot. They're a reminder that, on islands, water can be a precious commodity.

Left, summer mowing at a St. Peter's residence. Right, taking the sun at La Maison de Garde, built in 1765 and now a National Trust Property.

GUERNSEY

However hard you compare the merits of Jersey with those of its largest neighbour, there's one category in which Guernsey will always win: its capital. **St. Peter Port**, hugging the slopes that rise back from the sea, has managed to preserve a mixture of elegance and charm that St. Helier could never pretend to match. In fact, you'd have to go much further afield than St. Helier to find a town as endearingly quaint, tidy and well-preserved as St. Peter Port. The neat lines of Regency and Victorian buildings, the numerous cobbled streets, the steep stairways and alleyways weaving their way up and down between houses, a forest of boat masts jostling for attention just a few metres from the buildings overlooking the harbour—all this gives St. Peter Port a charisma that most would associate more with the Mediterranean than the Gulf of St. Malo.

The town has succeeded in fighting off many of the exterior signs of modernity. This doesn't mean it lags behind. Whichever historic buildings are occupied by the offshore banks and investment houses, a crucial part of the island's economy, they no doubt do business aided by the latest technology. Outside in many of the streets you get the refreshing feeling that time has stood still. In some areas around Hauteville and Clifton, and elsewhere, the street scene occasionally looks as if it's a film set.

There's more than tradition in St. Peter Port. Much is made of the Frenchness of some parts of the Channel Islands, though all too often it's a quality that disappears behind crowds of unmistakably British holidaymakers. In St. Peter Port, while the holidaymakers are very much evident, the Frenchness, the cosmopolitanism, is more discernible. And it's not just the street names that suggest you've left Britain.

Perhaps St. Peter Port's greatest asset is that it makes you *want* to explore it.

Walk along its streets and alleyways and you can't help feeling that something interesting *will* appear around the next corner. Visit the "tourist sites" such as Castle Cornet, the Museum, Hauteville House—all well worth seeing—and you'll still feel inclined to stroll around the town afterwards just for curiosity's sake. And, after you've done all that, look back at the town's wide skyline from a vantage point like Castle Cornet and you'll get the feeling there's yet a bit you "missed".

A sense of history: Above all, it's St. Peter Port's past that gives the town its enduring strength. For this is the oldest community in the Channel Islands. And it shows. The splendid Regency and Victorian dwellings hide much earlier chapters that go back to as early as the 13th century.

Little is known about earlier periods, though the discovery of a Roman ship in the harbour in 1982 showed that this part of Guernsey's coastline was a refuge for seamen even in ancient times. So before you set foot in St. Peter Port

Preceding pages: St. Peter Port's harbour; a Guernsey garden at Le Fariouf. Left, the British Bobby at work. Right, traditional Guernsey costume.

today, it's useful to know something of what has gone before.

While it's known that the Town Church existed as early as 1048, one of the most important early developments was the construction of **Castle Cornet**, which started in 1206. A few decades later, in 1275, King Edward I ordered a new pier to be built (this was destroyed when the French attacked less than 20 years later) between the castle and the town. Guernsey, and St. Peter Port, didn't wane in strategic importance: in the following century, King Edward III ordered that St. Peter Port should be enclosed by a wall.

Some defence works were definitely built, the most notable of these being La Tour Beauregard—though, despite a second order from the King, it seems unlikely that St. Peter Port's wall was ever erected. Local archaeologists, at least, have found no evidence of such a structure. There are clear markers, however, of the full extent of the medieval town; the small standing stones, or *barrières de la ville*, are alleged to have marked the sites of the gates in the "town wall". These stones don't date from medieval times. The one inserted in the wall near the Hansa Health Food shop, on the south side of Fountain Street, bears the date 1700.

Guernsey's early growth owed much to its position as a landmark to sailors. In an 11-month period in 1329, for example, it's recorded that 487 foreign ships called at St. Peter Port. From the 12th to the 16th century fishing was of prime importance, though the town remained compact. By the middle of the 16th century, St. Peter Port consisted of little more than Cornet Street, Fountain Street, La Grande Rue (today's High Street), La Rue des Forges (today's Smith Street) and The Pollet.

It was the practice of privateering, which began in the later part of the 18th century, that really saw St. Peter Port grow in size and wealth. This was a form of legalised piracy by which privately owned vessels were licensed by the British government to seize and plunder enemy ships. The pickings were phenomenal: in 1778 alone local

GUERNSEY

mile						
0	0,5		1		1,5	2
0	0.5	1	1.5	2	2.5	3
km						

Martello Towers	♜
Car Park	O
Border	
Road	
High Water Mark	
Low Water Mark	- - - -

Rocks

Fort Hommet

Vaz

Fort le Crocq

Perelle Bay

Chapelle Dom Hue

Priory

La Catioroc

Fort Richmond

Perelle

St Apolline Chapel

Lihou Island

Fort Saumarez

Trépied Dolmen

KING

L'Erée Aerodrome

PERELLE RD

GRANDE RUE

RD

M

DES

L'Erée

FELCONTE RD

RUE DES

Creux-ès-Faies Dolmen

Les Adams

L'EREE RD

RUE BATON

Reservoir

ROUTE DES

NEUF

Rocquaine Bay

La Longue Rocque Menhir

CLOS LANDAIS

ROUTE DES PAYSANS RD

Sous L'Eglis

Fort Grey (Maritime Museum)

ST PIERRE

Les Islets Arsenal

ROCQUAINE RD

DOMAINES RD

RO

Fort Pezeries

Zig-Zag

Portelet

COUDRE RD

LES SAGES RD

St Peter's Church

PLAIS

Table des Pions

Vau de Monel (NT)

RUE DE LA LAGUE

Colombier

DU BOIS

TORTEVAL (det)

Torteval Church

TORTEVAL

TV aerials

Pleinmont Point

Mont Hérault Watch House

PLEINMONT RD

Les Tielles

F

Wate

Le Creux Mahié

Havre de bon Rep

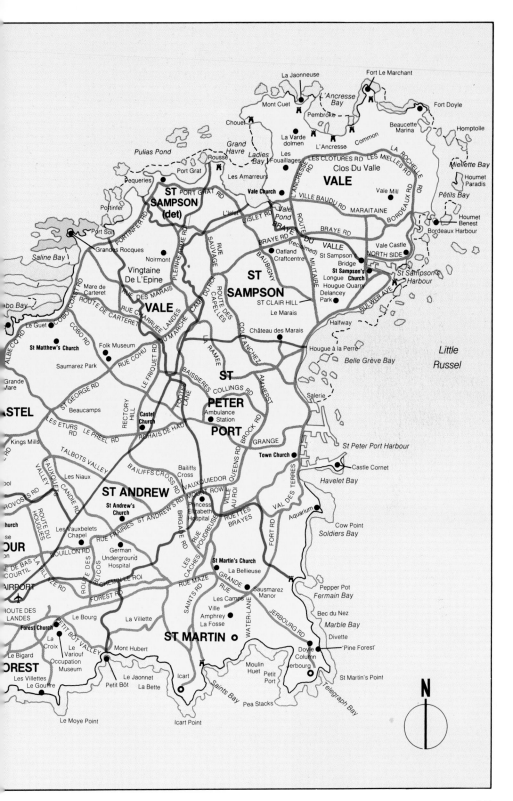

privateers brought in a total of £343,500 in prizes.

By 1800, St. Peter Port had grown from a small quayside settlement into a town of wealthy merchants. Many of the medieval buildings were beginning to disappear. St. Peter Port's new-found wealth manifested itself in the form of fine Georgian and Regency buildings: **Elizabeth College** (1826); **Bonamy House** (1820); **the Church of St. James the Less** (1818); **La Parte** (1801); **Lukis House** (1840); and the **Constables' Offices** (1787). The growth wasn't just in grand public buildings like these. As in Jersey, the Napoleonic Wars brought an influx of new residents. There was such a demand for houses that new buildings spread up the slopes around the town and onto the plateau above.

The harbour was unable to keep pace with these new developments. By 1750 there were two small jetties enclosing an area roughly the size of today's Victoria Marina. But ships were frequently damaged in bad weather and there was no low-water landing place. When the steamship service between Guernsey and England started, the need for better facilities became even more pressing. In 1853, new jetties were begun and the area of the harbour grew from four acres (1.6 hectares) to more than 80 acres (32 hectares). By 1865, the two long breakwaters you see today had been completed.

Castle Cornet: After the Town Church, this fortress sitting on an islet at the end of the southern pier is the oldest site in St. Peter Port and makes a good place to start exploring. Less than half-a-mile (one km) from St. Peter Port, there are close to eight centuries' worth of fortifications here. The buildings that remain are in excellent condition. It's only an accident of history that prevents it competing, visually at least, with Elizabeth Castle in Jersey. In the 17th century Castle Cornet wore a lofty and majestic crown in the form of Donjon Tower. When lightning struck it in 1672, it ignited gunpowder stored at its base. Donjon Tower, not to mention a number of important people and buildings, disappeared forever. There's more to Castle Cornet than attempting an assault on the remaining fortifications. Within the castle wall the **Armoury**, the **Military Museum**, the **Maritime Museum** and the **RAF Museum** between them tell many a tale about the history of Castle Cornet and of St. Peter Port.

The heart of things: The best-known thoroughfare in St. Peter Port is the narrow pedestrian way of the **High Street**. It's also one of the oldest. Always busy during the day, the High Street is walled in by tall, elegant buildings to either side. Walk south down this ancient way and an even taller and more elegant building dominates the view ahead: the **Town Church**, more correctly known as the Parish Church of St. Peter Port but also dubbed "the Cathedral of the Channel Islands". The first reference to this building was made by William the Conqueror in 1048. Subsequent extensions and renovations make it more modern than that. Some parts may date from the 12th

Left, indignity for Prince Albert. Right, the noonday gun is fired at Castle Cornet.

CORNET CASTLE

When King John lost Normandy to the French in 1204, Guernsey felt just as threatened as Jersey and Castle Cornet was built. The fear was well-founded, though it was more than a century later that France succeeded in breaching the castle's defences. In 1338, shortly after the start of the Hundred Years War, the French invaded the Channel Islands twice. On the second attempt they captured Castle Cornet and became masters of Guernsey, Alderney and Sark. Their occupation was shortlived: the castle was recaptured in 1345 after three days of fighting. The French recaptured it in 1356, but only held it a few months.

Two periods of rebuilding saw Castle Cornet evolve into essentially its present form. The Tudors undertook extensive renovation between 1545 and 1558. During Henry VIII's reign, a prominent military engineer of the day, John Rogers, strengthened the castle's defences by building the Mewtis Bulwark on its southeast side. During Elizabeth's reign, under the Governorship of Sir Thomas Leighton, the castle took on an entirely new appearance; Paul Ivy, who drew up the plans for Jersey's Elizabeth Castle, was involved in the redesign. The key consideration was that advances in artillery brought the castle's walls within range of enemy ships in the harbour.

During the English Civil War, Guernsey's Governor, Sir Peter Osborne, retreated to Castle Cornet in defiance of the rest of the island, which took parliament's side. The castle came under siege for nine years, during which time its garrison received supplies by sea from royalists in Jersey. The castle made a tempting target for the cannon in St. Peter Port. Resistance eventually proved futile. When the castle surrendered in 1651, it was the last part of the British Isles to fall.

One of Guernsey's prominent landowners at the time, the Seigneur of Sausmarez, Sir Amyas Andros, played an important role by liaising between the King's forces which controlled Jersey and the loyalist garrison at Castle Cornet. After the restoration, Charles II made him Bailiff. He was one of only two prominent Guernseymen who were not obliged to seek pardon from the King for their conduct during the Civil War.

century, though the earliest reliable record of construction is an inscription of 1466 relating to the south transept. The full history of this great granite building at the harbour's edge is uncertain, though two events are well-recorded. In 1721 the present steeple was built and in 1886 the church underwent a significant restoration.

However long you spend in St. Peter Port, you won't tire of walking up and down the High Street and on into **The Pollet**, another narrow lane with the same old-world air about it. The High Street and The Pollet combined run for a little over half-a-mile. This route is marked by two *barrières de la ville*, one by the northeast corner of the Town Church in the High Street, another opposite Moore's Hotel. Important people made this thoroughfare their home. Moore's Hotel was a residence of the de Sausmarez family.

An archway opens up off High Street, just before the junction with Smith Street, to Lefebvre Street and the **Constables' Offices**, one of those grand

buildings built at a time of new-found wealth in the 18th century. This Georgian mansion was once the property of the distinguished Le Marchant family. Near the top of Lefebvre Street, in Rue de Manoir, is the **Royal Court House**, built in 1799. This replaced a more ancient building called La Plaiderie, which was situated near Moore's Hotel and was demolished in 1929. Guernsey's parliament, the Assembly of the States, holds its debates here. The public is invited to watch the proceedings from a public gallery whenever the States are in session.

Medieval St. Peter Port was little more than a clutch of thatched buildings to the north and west of the Town Church, though little of the medieval town survives today. The High Street was its constricted main artery. The Town Church marked the focus of much of the town's energies for this was where St. Peter Port's markets set up shop. One pointer to the kind of produce that was sold takes the form of a street name. Just a short distance from the Town Church is a small lane called **Rue des Vaches**. When there was no proper harbour cows brought for slaughter were driven out of boats at low tide, forced to swim ashore, and herded together in "Cow Street".

Today's **Market Halls**, to the west of the Town Church, are all more than a century old. The Fish Market was completed in 1875, the Meat Market was designed in 1822 and the Vegetable Market was built in 1879. Across from the lowest exit on the north side of the Market Halls, an even older building is the **French Halles**. This market hall was completed in 1782. John Wesley preached here in 1787 in the Assembly Rooms in what is now the Guille-Allès Library.

In medieval times, **Fountain Street** was remarkably narrow. With the buildings on either side projecting progressively at each storey, it is said that people could lean out of the windows and shake hands with their neighbours. The Fountain Street of today was laid out by architect John Wilson in 1833. This was originally a cobbled street.

Patriotism and purchasing power in St. Peter Port.

144

The Georgian elegance of **Barclay's Bank** gives you a good idea of how this sloping road beside the Market Halls once looked before modern alterations were made to some shopfronts.

Beauregard Tower, built in 1357 on the orders of Edward III, is thought to have stood on the site of **St. Barnabas' Church**, at the top of Cornet Street. The church was erected as a memorial to the Reverend Charles Guille, a former rector of St. Peter Port. Before the Guernsey Art Gallery and Museum was built, it housed the Lukis and Island Museum.

Victor's view: At the junction of Cornet Street, Tower Hill and Cliff Street, Hauteville does exactly as its name promises: it goes up to the top of the town—or at least to one of St. Peter Port's "summits". One of the best vantage points is to be had from the top of **Victor Hugo's house**, itself one of Guernsey's star attractions.

Hauteville House, also known as Maison Victor Hugo, is not so much a memorial to an exile and writer as a museum to an eccentric but nevertheless inspired interior decorator. Some knowledge of the man makes a tour of his house all the more meaningful.

Victor Hugo was just one of over 200 political refugees who fled to the Channel Islands in 1851 following the coup of Louis Napoleon in France. He started his exile in Jersey and might never even have made it to Guernsey had not that same defiant spirit so boisterously expressed in his house led to his expulsion from Jersey. In 1855 the newspaper for the exile community, *L'Homme*, criticised Queen Victoria for having made a state visit to Paris. The people of Jersey, more than a little angered at this defamation of their sovereign, succeeded in getting the newspaper closed down and three of its senior staff expelled from the island. Victor Hugo led a petition signed by himself and 35 fellow refugees in protest. The petition ended: "And now expel us!" The lieutenant-governor of Jersey obliged and all the signatories were hustled off the island with remarkable speed.

Hugo's single-mindedness is all around you when you take a tour of Hauteville House. He lived here from 1856 until 1870. During that time he created an interior that is nothing less than a triumph of the imagination. Here are just a few of his furniture innovations: ornate wooden chests and commodes dismantled and turned into wall panels; backs of chairs turned upside down and used as curtain pelmets; tapestries cut up and rearranged to line high and broad ceilings; and an enormous stately bed (intended for an expected visit by Garibaldi) made out of 25 other pieces of furniture.

The catalogue of eccentricities extends beyond the decor. Hugo's personal habits are just as revealing. He was, for example, fond of hanging a small flag outside his bedroom whenever he'd slept well so that his mistress, installed in a street nearby, could rejoice at his restful night. The guided tour finishes in Hugo's study where, aided by a panoramic view over St. Peter Port, he wrote his prodigious output of novels, poems and essays while standing.

Victor Hugo slept here.

Despite its quirkiness, Hauteville House is stately and grand. You can only view the building on a conducted tour, though the eminently knowledgeable guides who lead the way make this one of the best places you can visit anywhere in the Channel Islands.

Old Town to New Town: When you walk back down Hauteville you have by no means tackled the most difficult of St. Peter Port's slopes. There are plenty more to test you. One of the few "flat" streets in town is the square formed by the **Commercial Arcade**, behind the Town Church. This elegant and stylish 19th-century shopping mall, which attracts a steady stream of window-shopping tourists, would have been even more elegant and stylish had its developers not run out of cash: the original idea was to provide a glass roof to the arcades. The two Jerseymen who conceived the expensive scheme went bankrupt in 1833.

You can give your stamina a tough test by ascending **Arcade Steps**—all 111 of them. This stairway, which opens out on the western side of the arcade, climbs the steep cliff which was created when Commercial Arcade itself was excavated. As you go up, it's not too long before you are forced to stop for breath. That's just as well, for once you are above the level of the rooftops you can enjoy an uninterrupted view of St. Peter Port's picturesque harbour.

At the top you are in **Clifton**, the border line of an important area of growth for the town in the 18th and 19th centuries. Before you turn left or right, take a look at the building nearly facing you. This is **Clifton Court** and dates from 1825. It started life as a Wesleyan chapel and later became Guernsey's first telephone exchange. Further along the road to your left is the **Salvation Army Hall**, dating from 1831.

There are two more heart-pounding flights of steps leading off Clifton: **Clifton Steps** and **Constitution Steps** (also known as Les Escaliers de Mont Gibel). At this point the strong may be tempted to go down one set and ascend

In order to enjoy the harbour view, Victor Hugo used to write while standing by this window.

146

the other. The weak will shun such bravado and head straight for the neat streets of Regency houses nearby that mark the **New Town** proper.

Havilland Street, **St. John Street**, **Sausmarez Street** and **Union Street** boast some of the finest Regency buildings in St. Peter Port. This small oasis of Georgian architecture makes for a landscape of white stucco, classical columns, cast-iron railings and wide sash windows. A minor landmark in Union Street has become something of a celebrity. A small plaque behind it states why: Victorian Pillar Box. The British Post Office installed its earliest roadside posting boxes in the Channel Islands in 1852-53, and this box is the oldest survivor still in daily use in the British Isles. It has been restored to what is believed to be the original livery of the past era.

The New Town wasn't the only part of St. Peter Port to be identified with this new era of growth. The notion of "new" seems to have gripped other parts of the town. In 1780, the Assembly Rooms, above the central French Halles, were at first referred to as the "New Rooms" in order to distinguish them from the Old Assembly Rooms in The Pollet. Earlier, in 1764, the parish of St. Peter Port purchased L'Hyvreuse as a military parade ground. Before it assumed the name of Cambridge Park (adjacent to Beau Séjour Leisure Centre) it was called the New Ground.

Two of the most visible points on St. Peter Port's skyline are in the vicinity of the New Town. In College Street is the imposing building of **Elizabeth College**. Though founded in 1563 and named after Queen Elizabeth I, today's edifice dates from 1829. The college's first headmaster, Adrian Saravia, was one of the first translators responsible for the Authorised Version of the Bible. Less than a quarter-mile away is **Victoria Tower.** This heavily crenellated tower was built in 1848 on the site of an old windmill to mark Queen Victoria's first visit to the island in 1846.

Visitors looking for views and versions of Guernsey's past and its people

Candie Gardens in St. Peter Port.

should spend time in the **Priaulx Library**, in Candie House, and the **Guernsey Museum and Art Gallery**. When the island's thoroughly modern museum was opened in 1978, it made a successful debut by winning the British Museum of the Year Award a year later. But its modernity hides some real historical pedigree. Many of the exhibits here were collected by F.C. Lukis, Guernsey's pioneering 19th-century archaeologist, more than a century ago.

The open-plan design of the exhibition area gives Guernsey some exhaustive but easily digestible coverage. Geology, archaeology, horticulture, agriculture, industry and history are mixed and matched to good effect. There's also an audio-visual show to take you further into the island's heritage and traditions.

When history palls, the Art Gallery may beckon. There are no Renoirs here, though one or two examples of his work wouldn't be out of place. The great French Impressionist visited the island in 1883 and found inspiration for 18 paintings. The small collection of oils and watercolours you can view comprises work by a mixture of local and visiting artists. Much of the work on display is by Peter Le Lièvre, a Guernseyman whose paintings provide a valuable portrait of island life during Queen Victoria's reign.

Outside in the grounds you can't help noticing that the museum's tearoom has an uncanny resemblance to a bandstand. Don't be surprised: that's indeed what it was. In fact, the museum's design, a cluster of octagonal pavilions, takes its inspiration from the Victorian bandstand. The building diplomatically separates a **statue of Queen Victoria** from one of her critic, **Victor Hugo.** From the time of his banishment, Hugo had little to say in praise of Jersey and saved his eulogies instead for the people of Guernsey. Words inscribed on the statue are from the dedication of his novel, *The Toilers of the Sea*:

"Au rocher d'hospitalité et de liberté,
à ce coin de vieille terre

Queen Victoria was not amused by Victor Hugo; now both stare stonily.

148

Normande
où vit le noble petit peuple de la mer
à l'Ile de Guernsey, sévère et
douce."

Translated, this reads: "To the rock of hospitality and liberty, to his corner of ancient Norman soil, where live the noble little people of the sea, to the island of Guernsey, stern and gentle."

One of the town's most modern facilities, **Beau Séjour Leisure Centre** and its grounds, occupy about as much space as medieval St. Peter Port once did. This clean and forward-looking building stands in stark contrast to the centuries of history in the centre of town. Nevertheless, since its opening in 1976, it has proved increasingly popular to both visitors and residents. You can play badminton, table-tennis and squash here, as well as swim. Beau Séjour also houses Guernsey's largest theatre and concert hall.

Parish without: Including the Parish of St. Peter Port, Guernsey is divided into 10 parishes. It's an easier administrative arrangement than was the case in the past. At one time there were more than 70 fiefs in Guernsey—each presided over by a seigneur.

To the west of St. Peter Port, **St. Andrew** is the only one of Guernsey's 10 parishes that has no coastline. Its western boundary is one of the oldest in the island. It marks a dividing line drawn in the 11th century by Duke Richard II of Normandy who created the boundry by separating Guernsey feudal landholdings into two.

Just a mile-and-a-half out of St. Peter Port, the main road into St. Andrew passes **The Hangman's Inn**; a site nearby was for many centuries a place of execution. The best-known victim of the hangman's noose was a certain Gaultier de la Salle. Two stories account for his fate on the gallows. One tells how he illegally executed a fellow official (who had already received a royal pardon) and was hanged for his crime. Another tells of an attempt by Gaultier de la Salle to "frame" a neighbour for theft in order to gain the upper hand in a dispute over rights to the use

The shopfronts have stayed traditional; the price-tags haven't.

of a water well. He almost succeeded in his deception but was exposed and hanged in place of the innocent man. Near The Hangman's Inn is **Bailiff's Cross**, a small commemorative stone incised with a cross marking the spot where the condemned man is said to have halted to take Holy Communion on his way to the gibbet.

Men were condemned to death elsewhere in St. Andrew's. Many of the slave workers who died building Guernsey's **German Underground Hospital** are said to have been buried in the concrete. It's a suitably unnerving thought to ponder, for while Jersey's subterranean hospital has been extensively renovated, the one here in St. Andrew's, Guernsey, has been little altered since the end of World War II. It saw action in 1944 when it received soldiers wounded during fighting in the D-day landings.

Nearly all the military medical equipment has since been removed and as a result, the German Underground Hospital is sombre and cavernous, echoing a network of tunnels with only a handful of unintrusive displays to set things in perspective. The dim lighting, the wet concrete floors and the very emptiness of the place all help to make this a chilling experience indeed. You somehow feel closer to the past here, making it an entirely different proposition to Jersey's counterpart; if you've seen one underground hospital, don't assume you've seen the other. These tunnels in St. Andrew's took more than three-and-a-half years to build but were operational for only nine months. Today, renovated or not, this particular Nazi nest can still serve as an appropriately solemn memorial to the slave workers who died here.

Les Vauxbelets College was founded in 1904 by a 17th-century French religious order "The Brothers of the Christia Schools". It's not the college that the people come to see but the famous **Little Chapel** built in its grounds. This miniature church is largely the work of a monk, Déodat, who had the novel idea of decorating his creation with thousands of pieces of broken china. The result is one of the most outlandish mosaics you are ever likely to see. Modelled on the grotto in the Church of Lourdes, the Little Chapel is barely 16 feet (five metres) long and has difficulty accommodating even a dozen people. The chapel standing today is the last in a sequence of three. Déodat started work on a smaller first version in March 1914 but demolished it immediately after it was built. The second one stood until 1923; it was in that same year he started the present building. In 1939, when he returned to France due to ill health, the care of the chapel was entrusted to a fellow monk, Brother Cephas, who continued with the decoration until he retired in 1965.

Just beyond the chapel, some of the farm buildings on the estate are used by **Guernsey Clockmakers**, who make and sell a collection of clocks and barometers many of which easily match Déodat's creation for novelty value.

A short distance to the north of the Little Chapel is another of the island's horticultural landmarks, the **Rose**

China revisited at the Little Chapel.

Centre. Here you can learn about some real state-of-the-art rose cultivation: the humidity and temperature of the greenhouses are controlled by computer. In the entrance area, a rather ponderous video traces the life of a Rose Centre rose all the way from the early stages of its cultivation to New Covent Garden Market in London, where many of them are sold.

As you walk around the growing areas you can sniff your way from one type to another, taking in the florid list of names as you go: Sterling Silver, Jaguar, Champagne, Golden Times, Gabrielle, Jacaranda and so on. The most scented varieties, incidentally, have the shortest life. Before leaving, you can read the "thank you" letters written on behalf of the Queen, the Queen Mother, and the Duke and Duchess of York, all of whom have been sent consignments in the past. And you can surprise somebody by making your own selection, which will be sent, with an appropriate message, on your behalf.

Right in the southwestern corner of

St. Andrew's parish, in the direction of the airport, is the **Guernsey Zoo.** Working as a charity, it's a modest collection that concentrates deliberately on smaller species such as servals (a small member of the cat family), the Parma wallaby, the Lar gibbon, pygmy goats, squirrel monkeys and other mammals and birds.

To the manor born: The boundary of **St. Martin's Parish** lies less than half-a-mile to the south of St. Peter Port. The tricky and winding road of Val des Terres takes you to the **Aquarium,** still in the parish of St. Peter Port. This started life in 1861 as a tunnel that was supposed to extend the road along La Vallette into Fermain Bay. The Aquarium has two sections: one for fish found in European waters, the other for tropical varieties. Despite the inclusion of oddities such as a fish found off Mexico whose name translates as "the fish that carries a needle and grunts like a pig", it's uninspiring.

Once you've climbed the steep hill of Val des Terres you'll pass the site of

Imported sport: American football has caught on in Guernsey.

Fort George. Constructed between 1780 and 1812, it was used by the Germans in World War II and was bombed by Allied planes in 1944 in preparation for D-day.

Fort George is still in the parish of St. Peter Port. Go to **Sausmarez Manor** and you'll cross the parish boundary into St. Martin's. The de Sausmarez family has for centuries been one of Guernsey's most distinguished dynasties. Over the years its sons have served as bailiffs, governors, naval officers and in the Foreign Office. There are recorded references, as long ago as 1254, to a forebear by the name of William de Saumareis, who was Seigneur of Samares in St. Clement, Jersey. It is not known when he acquired his new fief in St. Martin's parish in Guernsey, though it's likely its manor house occupied much the same site as today's.

Sausmarez Manor retains only a fragment of the ancient building in the form of an outhouse containing stonework that dates from the mid-13th century. Since then, the manor house has been added to many times. Its most distinguishing feature is the Queen Anne facade, which was erected between 1714 and 1718, and replaced an earlier Tudor building.

The de Sausmarez family didn't always live here. In 1557, Seigneur George de Sausmarez died without an heir and the manor passed into the hands of John Andros. In all, six members of the Andros family became Seigneur, after which, in 1748, the manor came back into the hands of the original owners.

Sausmarez Manor is one of the best-preserved 18th-century buildings in the Channel Islands and the organised tours around the grounds and the house are well worth taking. The refreshing lack of austerity is due to the fact that the manor is still lived-in. In fact, it's one of the most hospitable museums you're ever likely to come across. Though it is still eminently stately, with tapestries, paintings and a wealth of magnificent antique furniture and effects to fill you with envy. It was a refusal on the part of

Sir Havilland de Sausmarez to keep up with the times that saved much of this heritage from the Nazis. In 1940, the Germans were intending to use Sausmarez Manor as a hospital but decided not to go ahead with their plans because the house did not yet have electric lighting.

St. Martin's Parish Church is best known for the engaging and much-photographed menhir which stands outside it. The statue, most of which was carved around 2,500 B.C., originally stood in the churchyard and was named **La Grandmère du Chimquière** (the Old Lady of the Cemetery). It later served as the left pillar of the churchyard gate. It is believed the crack through its torso was the result of an attack by a churchwarden who was angry over the worshipping of stone idols.

Hugging the coast: Guernseymen acknowledge 30 bays around the island, but there are others they keep to themselves. The finest are along the southeastern and southern coasts. They

Unicorn rampant at Sausmarez Manor.

are a challenge to find and sometimes even more of a challenge to climb down to. But then that's half the fun.

Partly in the parish of St. Peter Port and partly in the parish of St. Martin is **Fermain Bay**, one of the island's most popular summer haunts as well as the starting point of a long cliff walk that will take you right along the south coast to Pleinmont. In the summer, Fermain Bay is served by a ferry service from St. Peter Port, though you can walk down from several other directions.

Like Fort George, **Doyle's Monument**, a short walk beyond Fermain Bay, was a victim of World War II, though this time it was the Germans who were responsible for its removal. You pass the site of this erstwhile 100-foot (30-metre) tower on your way to **Telegraph Bay**. Today the memorial that has taken its place provides good views out to the Normandy coast.

Lieutenant-General Sir John Doyle (1750-1834) was to Guernsey what General Don was to Jersey. Doyle directed the building of Fort George and

urged the States to reclaim Braye du Valle, the low-lying land in the north of the island which flooded at high tide and daily turned Clos du Valle into an island. The sale of the land that was gained paid for the construction of Guernsey's military roads. Doyle was also responsible for three Martello towers—Fort Grey, Fort Sausmarez and Fort Hommet—which were built after a number of smaller towers erected more than 20 years earlier had been criticised for being too small to provide effective firepower.

Before Doyle arrived on the scene, the peninsula on which Doyle's Monument stood had already been fortified. You can still make out the three parallel lines of ramparts and trenches running to the cliff edge to either side of the site of the monument. These were originally thought to be Roman but are in fact part of an Iron Age fortification. The stone-walling west of the monument is the only remnant of **Château de Jerbourg**, a medieval castle much mentioned in ancient documents.

The next three coves along this stretch of coast, **Petit Port**, **Moulin Huet** and **Saint's Bay**, are all still within the parish of St. Martin. A steep path near Doyle's Monument leads down to the first of these. Roads go down close to the other two and the cliff path also provides access.

Whether you are walking, cycling or driving around, the lanes weaving their way down near the coast are like a maze. As each lane leads into another, there's a signpost to **Moulin Huet Pottery**. If you can't find it at first, don't give up. It's a small, unassuming workshop turning out a tasteful selection of wares. You can watch the pottery being made at the back of the building and there's no pressure on you to buy.

Petit Bôt is one of the island's smallest beaches. A one-way road leads down from Forest Church and up again into St. Martin. Petit Bôt attracts its fair share of visitors when the weather is good. With the Martello tower, and a tearoom occupying what was once an old mill, this tiny opening onto the sea is inclined to get crowded.

Napoleonic tower at Petit Bot.

Not far from Route de Petit Bôt is the **German Occupation Museum.** Guernsey figured just as prominently as Jersey in Hitler's fortification of the Channel Islands (more than 66,000 mines were laid around Guernsey alone) and this museum has assembled an exhaustive collection of Nazi memorabilia. Its especially detailed collection of documents provides a welcome change from the sight of guns, shells and all the paraphernalia of combat. The permits, orders and censored newspapers on display give you a good idea of what the day-to-day life of ordinary islanders was like. One exhibit, an excerpt from the States Memoranda to the German authorities, dramatically underlines the food and fuel shortage that gripped the island after the Allies had landed in Normandy.

The museum is also good on Guernsey's wartime domestic lifestyle. An "Occupation Kitchen" sets the scene in late 1944, curtains drawn for curfew at 9 o'clock and a crystal set brought out for the British Broadcasting Corporation news. In another room the reconstruction of an entire street depicts a number of sites—a bicycle store, a shop, a café and several other buildings—in St. Peter Port. The recreation shows how they would have looked during the Occupation.

Near to the Occupation Museum, the **Parish Church of Ste. Marguérite de la Forêt** is thought to have been built on the site of a dolmen. The oldest part of the church, the southeast corner of the present building, rests on a series of boulders that seem to have formed part of a pagan burial chamber. The circular churchyard suggests that it does trace the shape of an ancient burial mound.

If you follow the road to the right of the Forest Church and turn left at a crossroads further on, you'll reach a mini-waterfall at the cliff edge called the **Gouffre**. The wife of Mr. Guille, co-founder of the Guille-Allès Library, fell to her death here. There's an observation platform to protect you these days; you can walk beyond it to the end of La Moye Point right down to a small harbour at the end.

Western wrecks: Your first glimpse of **Rocquaine Bay** as you cross Guernsey's southwestern corner is dramatic. At low tide it stretches more than two miles (three km) to the tip of Lihou Island. Towards the southern end of the bay, sitting squat against a flat rocky shore, is **Fort Grey**, one of the island's three "true" Martello towers. Fort Grey's location, situated on a small islet and connected to the shore tower on the wide battlements, has earned it the nickname of "the Cup and Saucer".

Like all of the Martello towers in the Channel Islands, Fort Grey was built as a defence against French invasion: it was erected in 1804. There was, however a much earlier stronghold here. From the 17th century onwards there are references to a small castle known as Château de Rocquaine having stood on this site.

Today Fort Grey is Guernsey's **Maritime Museum**; and there could be no better site for it. The sea surrounding the island's western tip is a ship's graveyard which has seen countless

It's yesterday once more at Guernsey's German Occupation Museum.

vessels founder on the notoriously dangerous rocks of Les Hanois. Victor Hugo said of them: "These rocks—these midnight assassins—have filled the cemeteries of Torteval and Rocquaine." The earliest reference to them, however, concerns a wreck described more than six centuries ago in an Assize Roll dated 1309. When you stand behind the walls of Fort Grey today it's a sobering thought to ponder the loss of life that has taken place less than two miles away from you. There's a gun pointing out to Hanois Lighthouse that was salvaged from HMS *Boreas*, which sank in 1807. On that occasion alone 195 lives were lost. Local researchers have managed to locate and name over 100 shipwrecks in the vicinity between 1734 and 1974.

Guernsey was for a long time the cornerstone of two very important sea routes: the transatlantic run to the United States, and the southerly run from Britain and northern Europe down into the Mediterranean. Most disasters occurred in the 19th century when traf-

fic on these trade routes had reached a peak and was as yet unaided by the Hanois Lighthouse, which wasn't completed until 1862. Fort Grey's museum tells the shipwreck story in detail. The upper floor traces the history of navigation while the lower floor displays the finds of Guernsey's underwater archaeologists. It's a diverse display that features a whole range of finds from elegant silver candelabra that once graced the table of a naval captain serving in the reign of George III to a porthole whose smashed glass illustrates how forceful the sea can be.

The promontory of **L'Erée** forms the northern arm of Rocquaine Bay. **Fort Sausmarez** recalls Lord James Sausmarez, one navigator who was unhindered by the hidden rocks in this bay. In 1794 he defeated five attacking French frigates with his ship HMS *Crescent*. During World War II, the Germans crowned Fort Sausmarez with a four-storey observation tower. Today this curious hybrid is on private land and is not open to the public.

While you are in this area you can visit **Le Creux ès Faies**, Guernsey's third largest megalithic tomb, if you can find it. Find L'Erée Hotel and you're about 1,000 feet (300 metres) away.

Pagan worshippers had also been busy on **Lihou Island**. When a handful of Benedictine monks arrived from the Abbey of Mont St. Michel, probably in 1114, they found three dolmens and seven menhirs and used the stones as foundations for their chapel Notre Dame de la Roche. Catholicism was the order of the day from there on until the Reformation, when the chapel fell into ruins, some of which remain today. Apart from a solitary farmhouse, the island is windswept and barren, though this is due in part to its role as a target for German gunners practising their skills. You can walk over to Lihou Island from L'Erée twice a day at low tide.

Less than a mile inland the prospect at the **Tropical Vinery** is decidedly less bleak. The contents of this row of greenhouses are far from mundane. You can view the Citrus Houses, the Mediterranean House, the Madeira House and the Desert/Oasis House. Quite literally, there's a whole world of blooms here. Avid horticulturalists will certainly be impressed.

Follow Les Paysans Road southward and you come to the **Coach House Gallery**, where there's a tasteful selection of painting and ceramics from Guernsey and farther afield displayed for sale. The Coach House is a sympathetically restored complex of old farm buildings. The gallery was started in 1975 at Braye du Valle, in the north of Guernsey, by a group of practising artists and enthusiasts. The Coach House Gallery has established a good reputation; past exhibitors here include Sir Hugh Casson.

St. Saviour: The **Parish of St. Saviour** is roughly rectangular in shape. It has the airport on its southeastern edge and a coastline that takes in all of **Perelle Bay**. "Perelle" is derived from the Celtic word for rock and at low tide the bay is a lunar landscape of rocks. This bay was always a good location for

Lihou Island, as seen from Guernsey.

collecting ormers. Duncan's *History of Guernsey* quotes one observer who estimated that a crowd of 200 people on March 9, 1841, gathered an amazing 20,000 in three hours.

When the tide is out and the rocks emerge Perelle Bay looks rather desolate and uninviting. Fort Richmond, a curious looking barrack house that seems to have been dropped into a large hole so that its roof is not much higher than ground level, and **Fort Le Crocq** hardly compensate. Both of these fortifications were built in the 19th century and have long been neglected. At the southern end of Perelle Bay, on Le Catioroc Point, is **Le Trépied Dolmen**. Less than 20 feet (six metres) long, this dolmen, like many others in Guernsey, was excavated by F.C. Lukis in the last century, and is said to have been the scene for witches' sabbaths in the 16th and 17th centuries.

A much earlier and fortunately less neglected building lies a few hundred metres inland from the centre of Perelle Bay. **St. Apolline's Chapel**, which dates from the end of the 14th century, is the only medieval chapel surviving in Guernsey. Dedicated to a deaconess who was burnt alive by the Romans in the third century, it's just 27 feet long and 13 feet wide (nine by four metres), and contains some restored frescoes. Before the Reformation this would have been one of many similar chapels in Guernsey. When it was acquired by the States last century it was being used as a stable.

There are references to the original Parish Church of St. Saviour as early as 1030. The building you see today is the usual story of additions and renovations though much of it dates from the 14th and 15th centuries and from rebuilding that was done in the 17th century after lightning struck the tower.

One of the most interesting sites you can visit in St. Saviour's is also the dampest, the darkest, the dingiest and the dirtiest. But don't let that put you off: at **St. Saviour's German Tunnel** you have the opportunity to see some of Guernsey's German past "in the raw". Had this dank and gloomy nest of tunnels ever been completed, it would have served as a munitions store. When the British Army arrived in 1945, they decided it would make a good place to dump some of the German military hardware that was fast accumulating as the island returned to normality. The tunnel running under St. Saviour's Church was filled with everything from helmets to ammunition cases, from field kitchens to tanks.

This hardware graveyard wasn't opened again until 1969. Some of the equipment was retrieved for the Occupation Museum; a small portion of it was left behind. To the strains of wartime music you can inspect the few hundred metres of tunnelling and see some of this military paraphernalia as it would have appeared after 25 years underground. Apart from two 400-lb (180-kg) roll bombs (which would have been hung from the cliffs ready to be dropped in the event of an enemy landing), the "exhibits" are generally such mundane objects as boots, gas masks and water bottles. All are rusty, dirty and haphazardly laid out on makeshift shelves. Yet it's this very informality that somehow conveys a more immediate sense of the Nazi presence, as if you had discovered them yourself just months after the Germans had departed. Water drips from the rock ceilings and, when you enter, the cold assaults you within minutes. This is a uncomfortably authentic experience, but perhaps it's more valuable for being so. Walking around these inhospitable, tomb-like passages, you can begin to appreciate just how miserable the conditions were in which the wartime slave labourers had to work.

There's light relief to be had from all this just half-a-mile away at the **Strawberry Farm**. The greenhouses here have been turned over to some really intensive strawberry-growing. Before you sit down and feast on the fruits of the Strawberry Farm's labour, you can wander round and take a close look at how it's all done. Once you've polished off a bowl of strawberries, drowned in fresh Guernsey cream, there's plenty more to whet your appetite for amusement: an aviary, a "Nature Wonderland", a woodcarving shop, a pottery shop, Crazy Golf and a good restaurant. If the summer crowds are anything to go by, the Strawberry Farm has concocted the kind of menu designed to please all the family.

The **Bruce Russell Goldsmith, Silversmith and Jewellery Shop** feeds an entirely different appetite. When the Huguenots sought refuge in the Channel Islands in the 16th century they brought with them considerable expertise in silver and gold. Bruce Russell makes no attempt to link himself with that tradition, though his family has been engaged in this craft for two generations. You don't have to satisfy yourself with just watching people at work here; there's a wide enough selection of wares on sale to suit most people's pockets.

Tomatoes and telephones: Guernsey's largest parish is **Castel**. Right at the centre of the island's northern coastline, it takes in Vazon Bay, Cobo Bay, Saline Bay and Port Soif.

The beach of **Vazon Bay** is a wide expanse of firm sand. Beneath it are the remains of a submerged forest, evidence of which is exposed periodically by storms. As well as being a good windsurfing bay, the wide flat beach is used in summer for motorbike racing. On the northern headland of Vazon Bay is the partly restored Martello tower of **Fort Hommet**. It still has German pillboxes and gun positions which can be seen clinging to its stonework.

Near the village of Kings Mills, one popular spot for tourists, is living proof that you can take just about any subject and build a museum around it. Visit the **Guernsey Tomato Centre** and never again will you munch a tomato in ignorance of the kind of expertise that went into growing it. This is a permanent exhibition of the history of tomato-growing in Guernsey. Greenhouses were originally constructed on the island to cultivate grapes in 1805. By 1830, it is said, a gentleman just wasn't a gentleman if he didn't have a vinery in his garden. Tomatoes, long thought to be poisonous, were declared to be good for health midway through the 19th century. The Channel Islands were ideally situated to help supply the demand. In Guernsey, most of the greenhouses had been turned over to tomato cultivation by the end of the century. The Tomato Centre shows how the industry adapted its methods. Greenhouses from 1899 and 1920 have been set up, and taped commentaries explain what's going on in them. There's also a section that shows early cultivation techniques and traces the development of the greenhouses.

The story of the tomato, in Guernsey at least, is one of decline. In 1957, more than nine million 12-lb (five-kg) trays were exported, while in 1986 just one-and-a-half million left the island. The Tomato Centre, though, is a thriving concern, an example of just how ingenious you can get when it comes to exploiting tomatoes. Tomato aficionados can even buy a bottle or two of tomato wine here.

By far the best museum in Castel Parish is the **Guernsey Folk Museum**,

A local butterfly takes a close look at a migratory species.

set up by the Guernsey National Trust in Sausmarez Park off Cobo Road. (Don't confuse Sausmarez Park in Castel with Sausmarez Manor in St. Martin). The original part of the house was built in the early 18th century by William Le Marchant before it came, through marriage, into the hands of the de Sausmarez family. The main building, which belongs to the States of Guernsey, is a hostel for elderly people, though the grounds are open to all. The stables house the Folk Museum, a thorough exhibition of Guernsey's rural memorabilia. Founded in 1968, it is based on a collection of agricultural implements collected by one of the Langlois family.

The museum recreates a number of period rooms such as a kitchen, a bedroom, a wash-house dairy, a cider barn and a cartroom. Many of the costumes and pieces of furniture are more than 100 years old and in excellent condition. With sepia-tone photographs of thick-whiskered farmers dressed in smocks and clutching hay forks helping to tell the story of Guernsey's rural life in the last century, the Folk Museum oozes rural nostalgia.

If the Folk Museum is the best museum in the parish, then the **Telephone Museum**, just a few hundred metres away, is certainly the smallest. Housed in an unassuming suburban house on a one-way system that means many visitors would pass nearby without ever noticing it, this is one display that seems bent on anonymity. Its restricted opening hours don't help either. The Telephone Museum is for confirmed phonophiles only. If you want to pay a call, you'd do well to check with Guernsey Tourism first.

The correct name of **Castel Church** is Ste. Marie du Castel. It's said the church was built on the site of a Viking fort, Le Château du Grand Sarazin, from which the parish takes its strategic name. The view today's church commands over the sea to Alderney, Herm and even the French coast suggests it would have been a strategically valuable site. There are references to Castel

All you ever wanted to know (and more) about the tomato.

Church from 1155 in a document confirming that it was then under the patronage of Mont St. Michel. The Neolithic statue in the churchyard was excavated from under the chancel in 1878 during restoration work.

Le Friquet Butterfly Centre is an even more peaceful place. This is a working nursery growing carnations, gerbera, chrysanthemums, ferns and many other varieties of plants. There are more than two acres (one hectare) of flower houses to explore. At the centre is a greenhouse that is home to an equally dazzling variety of butterflies. Once inside you find yourself in a setting of domestic and semi-tropical plants that forms the habitat for a host of flutterers that originate from Central and South America and Europe. If the idea of walking among butterflies doesn't at first strike you as being worthwhile, try it all the same. But remember that, because these creatures are cold-blooded and therefore only active on bright warm days, you're unlikely to enjoy the full effect of their frenetic activity if you visit when it's wet and dull.

The sight of so much delicate motion going on around you and the near silence that accompanies it is surprisingly therapeutic. Many of the butterflies are just as surprising; some are as many as eight inches (20 cms) across. As an added diversion there is a Mexican red-legged tarantula and a pink-toed bird-eating spider behind glass. Once outside again, you might like to play a little croquet on the wide lawns, or watch the ducks on the pond, or have a gentle putt. At Le Friquet the emphasis is firmly on keeping things peaceful and quiet.

Follow the Cobo Road coastwards and you'll reach **Cobo Bay**. If you recognise the distinctive pink-red hue of the rocks along the coast here and in Albecq Bay you should award yourself full marks for observation. This stone known as Cobo granite has long been a source of stone for buildings on the west side of the island; **St. Matthew's Church**, at the southern end of the bay, is a striking exampl of its use.

One of the oldest dwellings discovered in the Channel Islands was excavated at **Ruette de la Tour**. The earliest of several houses, all built on the same foundation, was a longhouse dating from the 10th century.

Cobo Bay itself is sandy and safe and with its windsurfing school attracts both the sedentary and the energetic. Here, as in several of the west coast bays, the slipway extends as a paved or cobbled path onto the beach. These were built for seaweed gatherers to bring their horse-drawn carts right down to the beach. The seaweed, known as *vraic*, has long been used as a fertiliser on the island.

Hidden tombs: Guernsey's second largest parish is **Vale**, though you have to include both parts of it. Look at the map and you'll see that the northern part of Guernsey comprises two parts of Vale and two parts of St. Sampson. There's little to see as such in the southern **Vingtaine de L'Epine**, but there's lots to keep you occupied in the northern **Clos du Valle**.

A reminder that the local currents must be taken seriously.

On or near slipway

Cobo

ull to release

Until 1806, Clos du Valle wasn't even part of the mainland. La Braye du Valle was flooded daily at high water, making this northern extremity of Guernsey an island only reached by a bridge at St. Sampson's. The reclamation of 300 acres (120 hectares) of land in La Braye du Valle was engineered by the building of an embankment at the head of Grand Havre in the north.

The clearest landmark you'll see as you approach La Braye du Valle around Grand Havre is **Vale Church**. More properly known as St. Michel du Valle, the church was consecrated in 1117. Spare a thought for ancient worshippers ordinarily resident in Vingtaine de L'Epine who, before Doyle's intervention in La Braye du Valle, were no doubt obliged frequently to negotiate the incoming or outgoing tide before they were able to enter God's house.

At Vale Church you are right on the edge of **L'Ancresse Common**, where golf reigns supreme. Your view across the common is barely interrupted by the gently undulating landscape—a mix-

When the shortest distance between two points is across the beach.

ture of common, rocky outcrops, pine trees, gorse, heather and numerous "Martello towers" dotted across the horizon. When you look at this, at times, rather bleak scene it's a little difficult to believe that you are just six or seven miles (10 or 11 km) from the steep, craggy and beautiful cliff walks on the south coast of the island.

A Channel Islands travel guide published in 1911 made much out of L'Ancresse Common: "It is usual for visitors to pay one visit to L'Ancresse and to dispose of the district in an afternoon's ramble. So much the worse for the visitor. Many days can be well and profitably spent in exploring this out-of-the-way part of Guernsey."

Precisely *how many* days you spend up here on L'Ancresse Common will depend entirely on how successful you are in searching out some of the cunningly hidden ancient remains that lurk here. A few hundred metres north of Vale Church (ask any golfer for directions to the fifth hole) **Les Fouaillages** were discovered in 1978. These small burial chambers set within a large triangle of stones in the ground have excited much archaeological interest. The layman is likely to be more impressed to discover that pottery found near this site is believed to date as far back as 4,500 B.C. A few hundred metres further to the north, **La Varde Dolmen** is much easier to find. And so it should be, for it is the largest megalithic structure in Guernsey. This passage grave, running more than 40 feet (12 metres) into a high mound, is covered by six enormous capstones, one of which is over 16 feet (five metres) long. The tomb was discovered in 1811 by soldiers during military exercises. The event was doubly significant for among those who came to have a look was F.C. Lukis, Guernsey's best-known archaeologist. It is said that the young Lukis went home with a skull under his arm— a prize that went to form the nucleus of the future Lukis Museum.

Rounding the tip: A perfect place enjoy a lofty view of Guernsey's north shore is from the roof of the restaurant overlooking **Beaucette Marina**. As

you approach, all you'll see will be the tops of masts bobbing about. The marina was originally a quarry until somebody decided it was a good place to park an ocean-going yacht or two.

The restaurant here combines first-class seafood with surprisingly modest prices. After all, most of the clientele could no doubt afford much more. If you wonder where some of the tax exiles in the Channel Islands hang out, Beaucette Marina must surely be one of their haunts. On a good day the car park boasts more than its fair share of Porsches, Mercedes and other sleek cars, though the yachts in the marina put the motor cars to shame.

Fort Doyle is at the end of this promontory. Named after Guernsey's military road builder, the modifications made by the Germans mean there's little to see here.

Two other locations between Beaucette and St. Sampson each recall famous Guernsey names. A few hundred metres offshore is an unassuming island called Hommet Paradis,

made famous by Victor Hugo as the home of a character in his book *The Toilers of the Sea*. A short distance before you reach Vale Castle is another of the megalithic finds excavated by F.C. Lukis in the 19th century, **Déhus Dolmen**. This passage grave is the second largest on the island. More than 60 years before Lukis attended to this tomb's history, a resident of Guernsey bought the site for £4 10s (£4.50) to prevent it from being broken up and destroyed by quarrymen.

Another site of considerable antiquity is **Vale Castle**. It's unfortunate that so little of this fortress remains. The ramparts are solid enough, though the rest of the fortress doesn't live up to the promise it seems to hold you as you first approach. When Clos du Valle was effectively a separate island it would no doubt have been a strategic site; but now that the waters have been forced to recede, Vale Castle looks rather forlorn, like a stranded whale.

The earliest occupation of the hill on which the castle stands is said to date

Dining out at Beaucette Marina.

162

from the Iron Age, when, around 600 B.C., a double-banked hill-fort is believed to have stood here. Excavations in 1980 revealed that the first medieval fortification was erected around the year 1400, when a number of buildings were constructed close to the existing walls. There are further references to the castle in the 16th and 17th centuries. During the French Wars in the late 18th century barracks were built; these were demolished in 1945 by the Germans and the miniature "street pattern" of cobblestones you can see today is all that remains.

St. Sampson: One of the clearest views to be had from Vale Castle is of the town of St. Sampson—though it's something not to be envied. It's difficult to believe that barely two miles (three km) to the south is one of the most elegant and attractive townscapes in Europe. St. Sampson, sad to say, pales in comparison. The landscape is uncompromisingly industrial whichever way you turn. From Vale Castle the view is filled with cranes, warehouses, scrapyards and oil storage tanks.

In all fairness to the town, St. Sampson never set out to be good-looking; it was always working too hard. As the harbour from which Guernsey's granite was exported, it made a massive contribution to the island's wealth. In the mid-19th century the industry entered an unparalleled boom and St. Sampson began to earn its reputation as the industrial north of Guernsey. It still plays that role. Today, most of the cargo coming into the island is off-loaded in St. Sampson's harbour.

The name of the town has charismatic origins at least. St. Sampson crossed over to the Channel Islands from Brittany, where he was Bishop of Dol, in about A.D. 550 and is said to have landed on the shore of the natural harbour—which subsequently took his name. St. Sampson, generally held to be the first to preach Christianity in Guernsey, is said to have built a chapel or oratory on the spot where the church stands today.

There's no reliable record of its construction, though it is referred to in a document of 1054. The church you see today originally stood practically on the seashore, in the same way as St. Brelade's in Jersey. The most popular date claimed for the construction of this building is 1111.

The thoroughfare known as the Bridge, bordering the innermost part of the harbour, marks the spot where there was once a bridge connecting the mainland to Clos du Valle; reference to it is made in court records in 1204.

One other place to visit in St. Sampson is the **Gun Museum**. This is a compact but impressive display of weaponry dating from the American Civil War onwards. German guns from World War II are inevitably well represented, though the collection runs from curious home-made firearms from Indonesia and northern India to some impossible miniature pistols and a number of highly elegant and obviously very valuable antique pieces.

There are really only two or three places you are likely to want to visit in the **Parish of St. Sampson**. Not much

Roadside shopping in the Guernsey valleys.

more than half-a-mile from the Beau Séjour Leisure Centre, and almost in the Parish of St. Peter Port, **Château des Marais** is arguably Guernsey's most curious site. Also known as Ivy Castle, this is a remarkably preserved small medieval structure. There's nothing especially curious about that, however, but to get there you have to make your way straight through a run-down and drab housing estate. When you find the castle, sitting in a field littered with small heaps of rubbish and the remains of abandoned cars, you suddenly realise you've stumbled across a remarkably unaffluent corner of Guernsey.

The surrounding houses make for a very sorry sight—a street scene that those familiar with Britain's much talked about "inner cities" will recognise. The wealthy types patronising places like Beaucette Marina suddenly seem a million miles away.

The castle itself was built shortly after the loss of France by England in 1204 and is surrounded by a small moat. Late in the 18th century, during the Napoleonic Wars, the castle was refortified. The magazine and much of the existing stonework date from that period. Archaeologists believe that the mound on which Ivy Castle is built was part of a much earlier site, possibly dating from the Bronze Age.

The **Oatlands Craft Centre**, occupying what was once a brickworks, is a much more colourful alternative to St. Sampson. Here you have the chance not only to acquire craftswork—glass and pottery mainly—but also have a chance to watch it being made from close quarters. The potting seems tame in comparison to the glassblowing, where you can step right inside the workshop and feel the full force of the glowing red furnace fires.

The glassblowers perform their delicate and practised task with a skill bordering on nonchalance. You can do little more than stand and stare at them work, wondering how they can take the brunt of the heat *and* suffer the deafening roar of the fans that feed the flames with oxygen. Sweated forced labour indeed, you might think—but you'd be wrong: the craftsmen you see here are their own bosses.

The glassblowers and the potters set up Oatlands Craft Centre themselves and invited glass engravers, a silversmith and the proprietor of the patchwork shop to join them. Everybody involved expects to make a living through their wares. The absence of any entrance fee is no guarantee you won't dip into your pocket, however: the quality of goods in the main shop is high and there are bargains and opportunities galore to spend.

There's a further chance to indulge your taste for craftswork at **Guernsey Candles**, located a few minutes down the road from Oatlands. While the candles here assume all kinds of extravagant, decorous and impressive configurations, there's little sense of this being a craft workshop in the same way that Oatlands is. But that doesn't matter: Guernsey Candles gets its fair share of the island's tourist traffic and the souvenir hunter could do worse than light a candle for Guernsey.

Left, the Guernsey vegetable you can't avoid. Right, farmers waiting for a cattle auction to start.

ALDERNEY

Alderney, the saying goes, is inhabited by 2,000 drunks clinging to a rock in the English Channel and its only export is empty bottles floating away on the tide.

There is more than a grain of envy in the voices of Guernsey or Jersey people who purvey the drunken image of Alderney. Sour grapes make bad wine and it is their loss of a slow and peaceful way of life, Alderney's lack of bureaucracy and her relaxed attitude to visitors who drink too much, that prompt the saying. More birds than bottles will be seen when bobbing on the sea in a boat, and the great demand to live on the island is the only reason Alderney's residents cling to the rock.

It is a retreat for islanders from Guernsey and Jersey, and many other places too; they leave families behind and flock to spend a few days fishing, playing golf, or enjoying a party. Spirits and glasses are raised and the tone of the place is lowered. Alderney people accept the fact with equanimity; indeed they seem to become more welcoming every time the "I must get away from it all" ploy is used.

Pub scene: Walking the island's wind blasted-cliffs in a squall, you may decide that sitting in a warm pub is the only thing worth doing. It's hard to avoid drink in Alderney. **Braye Street's** welcoming pubs are the first—and often only—sight visiting boat people see after they leave the Yacht Club bar. The pubs are more like clubs than conventional watering holes—full of character and characters, they seem the natural place to be on an island which offers few places of entertainment to visitor or resident.

Take the **Divers**, for instance—and many do. A huge old copper diving helmet hangs over the door, as if just raised from the shoulders of the person who preceded you. Warm chatter flows out of the bar as the next step is taken to enter the inner portal. Smiles on faces

turned doorwards to greet the casual customer and a grey granite slab floor sprinkled with fine sand give a momentary shock. It's said the sand softens the fall when so much has crossed the bar that the swaying woodwork fails to support the drinkers; bar staff boast that the Divers is the only pub in Britain to have a new carpet daily.

Half hidden in the sand is a coin, cemented to a granite slab; unwary drinkers who try to retrieve it are pounced upon for a contribution to a charity aiding shipwrecked mariners. More than £450 raised testifies to the popularity of both the bar and the joke. A warm fire burns in a corner and the landlord is hospitable without grovelling. If you are in a party the chat flows naturally, but the lone visitor is welcomed and taken in by the assembled patrons. The island's bars are pleasant places.

John Arlott, well-known wine buff and His Master's Voice of BBC cricket commentaries, retired to Alderney to preside over one of the island's few

Preceding pages, Alderney's wide-open spaces. Left, the sign of a celebrated pub. Right, beach picnic on the edge of Braye Bay.

cellars (the granite nature of the island makes them difficult to dig). Retiring to the rock realized ambitions nurtured by his many holidays on the island: Arlott started visiting in 1951 and spent whole summer holidays with his family there, commuting to the UK for cricket matches. When he retired in 1981 there was little adjustment to be made: it was a "desperately easy" place to live in, with a "pleasant absence of bores".

"I am stimulated by islands," Arlott said. "I tried to buy Fort Raz—to have an island off an island. Now I spend my time reading and writing. The great thing is the privacy of the island, a personal privacy which is accepted by islanders." Don't people gawp through the gate? "Very few—certainly not as much as the mainland." According to Arlott, there are "settlers", as locals call the newcomers, who clearly will not get on with the island way of life, whose departure is predictable even before they have unpacked a suitcase. Their characteristics? "Usually pomposity and a determination to change the is-

land on sight," says Arlott.

Settlers receive a letter of welcome from the island's "Chancellor of the Exchequer" when they buy a house in Alderney. The population has more immigrants than locally born people, a fact which is reflected in the make-up of the States of Alderney, the island's parliament. There are enthusiastic people who stand for election on the "I am locally born and proud of it" ticket, but it is the people who retire to the islands who usually make the best politicians. They have made at least one success to be able to move "offshore" and know how to arrange their lives to find the time and organise the administration to get things done.

The traditional ex-colonial, former civil servant settlers have ceased to find the island attractive in recent years and more people are pulling successful businesses across the water. Media people, writers and broadcasters, many with teenage families, are more common these days.

Like everyone in small communities

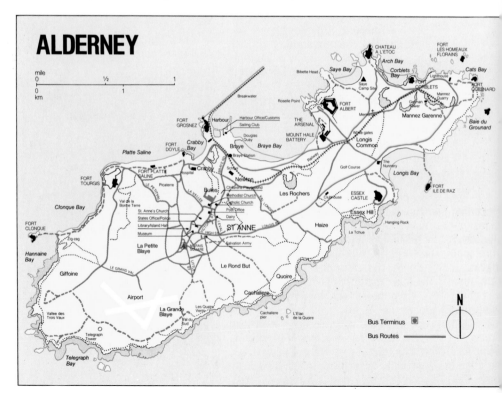

they have to make their own entertainment. The island's 2,200 residents have clubs, choirs, theatrical groups and sports teams. Their footballers have not won the tripartite inter-island Muratti Cup for many years but the squad is strong enough to take on teams of a semi-professional standard from Jersey and Guernsey. John Arlott is chairman of the thriving Alderney Cricket Club which provides the click of leather on willow at **Les Butes**—a spectacular pitch where you might expect a well-hit ball to reach the harbour half a mile below. The island has a thriving society which runs and maintains Alderney Museum and the recently reconstituted lifeboat crew already have several rescues to their credit.

But in common with most small communities the activities always seem to be achieved despite some disaster. Take the sign which remained through a summer season at the Alderney Arts Centre and Cinema window in Victoria Street: *'The following films, postponed because of the projector breakdown,*

St. Anne: you can stroll to it from the airport.

will be screened in OCTOBER with <u>*new*</u> *equipment.'* It must be said that the films which followed were the very latest releases.

The upper parts of Alderney are an ancient network of fields which have been farmed in strip fashion through to modern times while the lower areas serve a thriving harbour. Land and sea are connected by a long steep road which runs from the high parts of the island to the pub-lined Braye Street.

St. Anne, a town built on the hillside connecting the farmers with the fishermen, is the capital. It is split by a cobbled road which drops from the High Street to the hipped-roofed Wesleyan Methodist Chapel—Victoria Street links the upper town with shops at Les Rocquettes and the cricket green on Les Butes. The hill continues steeply to the hotels and bars in Braye Street, and the harbour.

Old times: Much of Alderney is an agricultural wasteland; indeed it is so poor that a strip farming technique, widespread in Europe during the

Middle Ages, was employed to make best use of the 450 acres (180 hectares) of good land; there were no hedges or banks. It supported 700 people in the days of Queen Elizabeth I. Farm houses and buildings were clustered on poor soil around the top of St. Anne, giving that part of town a rustic, rural look. The fields were separated into rectangular blocks called riages, each about 14.5 acres (5.9 hectares), across the end of which ran *vaindifs* where the ox-team turned when pulling a plough. The *riages* were sub-divided into parallel strips, some running north and south, others east to west. Strips belonging to a family were scattered among the *riages* so that everyone had a share of good and poorer land. They have been split and amalgamated many times since then and now vary in size.

Modern life, of a sort, hit the ancient strip farming on the Blaye more than 50 years ago when the first Channel Island airport was opened. It has changed little since. A few prefabricated huts and a hangar surround the tiny airport in which departures are announced in a loud voice and arrivals are marked by the shouts of greeting as some island family is reunited. The island's lifeline routes are operated by one of the world's smallest and most successful airlines, **Aurigny Air Services**, which flies 17-seater Trislander aircraft from Guernsey and Jersey, Cherbourg and Southampton all year round.

Both the Devoniun, a small car-ferry linking Alderney to Torquay, and Condor Hydrofoils, which bring passengers from Guernsey and Jersey, are summer services. The island's heavy goods are carried from Guernsey in small freighters operated by the Alderney Shipping Company.

One benefit of the island's compactness is that you can easily walk into St. Anne from the airport. The farming influence dominates as you enter **Marais Square**. This was the centre of life for the farming folk—roads radiate from the square past old farmhouses, the architecture filled in with Georgian and Victorian dwellings. Alderney

Getting to Alderney in an Aurigny Trislander is an experience in itself.

people maintain that, until the deportation during the German Occupation, they had their own breed of Channel Island cattle. They say that the Alderney cow was smaller than the Guernsey but it is doubtful if they ever existed as a separate breed. Undaunted, their story is told on the side of the Marais Hotel. "The legendary Alderney cow, now extinct, attracted buyers to the auctions held in this square from all over the world," says the sign next to a picture of a dairy maid and the island's Dodo. A sadly unused but beautiful granite trough occupies center stage in the cobbled square.

Here, perhaps more than anywhere on the island, the vast number of cars can be best judged—almost every adult member of the population has one. It is impossible to get good pictures of the town anywhere between the Marais Square cow trough and the beautiful house-line of Braye Street as so many cars clutter the views.

Parts of the island have a strange feel. A regular visitor complained that the area around **Le Grande Blaye**, at the back of the airport, seemed always "to be quiet and spooky". It is where one of the island's four concentration camps was built during the last war, he was told chillingly. Many of Alderney's small community were evacuated to Britain before the German forces landed in 1940. Many of them joined up—some died fighting with the British—but the people who remained in Alderney were taken to Guernsey where they spent the Occupation. All livestock and possessions were left behind. One family and a couple of labourers stayed but they were whisked away sharply after liberation leaving accusations of collaboration. Islanders are reluctant to talk about their black sheep. "It's too soon yet," they say.

While residents were in exile atrocities of a fashion, now well-known, went on in secret. Russians, Poles and many French Jews from German concentration camps were imported to labor as slaves, under the notorious Operation Todt. They worked on the brooding fortifications which were built as part of Hitler's Atlantic Wall—the massive concrete structures became tombs for many of the detainees who died of starvation, and stand as a lasting memorial. Other Todt workers were buried in unmarked graves around the island.

They are not forgotten. The **Hammond Memorial** stands above **Longis Common**, the site of hundreds of unmarked graves, and the place where visiting delegations from the Polish and Russian embassies in London attend services held there every year. It is said that the island was silent of birdsong when the Alderney people returned after liberation. But while they were away gannets had colonised Les Etacs rock to circle Alderney evermore, like the souls of the Todt workers they are supposed to represent.

History on show: The first steps of visiting natural historians should be to Le Huret, at the top of High Street, where the island's story is explained in the **Alderney Museum**. The setting is old fashioned with huge glass cabinets housing the last public remains of

Quenching
a thirst for
history.

Alderney men from the time of neolithic settlers to the folk who returned after the Germans left. The collections are housed in the Old School which was opened as a museum by the Lieutenant-Governor of Guernsey, Sir Charles Mills, in 1972. It was, almost inevitably, too small and the Queen Mother opened a new extension in May 1984. On show are the crafts and trades of Alderney, its natural history, the misery of the Organisation Todt slave workers—illustrated with the blue and white striped shift worn by one wretched prisoner or more—a 4,000 year-old spear and the latest island stamps.

Washed-up whales have appeared on Alderney's beaches and their pitiful pictures immortalise the poor beasts. The photographs include some of a sei whale, thought to have become confused by French warships' sonar. Kept alive by water spraying over its body, the anxious islanders waited for the tide to rise so the whale could return to sea. As the creature made grunts, pops and whistles, its school of relatives swam offshore until it was liberated and they all went out to sea together.

Alderney's court sat outside the Old School in Le Huret until modern times; even today royal proclamations are read out there. It now sits a short distance away in the **Court House** which can be visited during office hours. The court room doubles as the meeting place for the States of Alderney, the island's 12-seat legislative assembly.

This curious body is neither town council nor parliament as they are governed by the States of Guernsey who extend legislation to the island, when appropriate, and administer her health, postal and social services, police and education. This causes great resentment in Alderney whose population would prefer to be autonomous and control their own destiny.

After the war: The Occupation and deportation of Alderney families was the greatest instigator of change the island has ever seen. Residents returned in November 1945 to find many of their houses destroyed, the island in ruin, fields overgrown, the breakwater smashed by the sea in several places and breached across a 50-metre section. Their economy was nonexistent and the island had no money.

The U.K. Labour Government, which swept into power under Clement Attlee in 1945, stepped in to help "our dear Channel Islands", as Churchill referred to them in his end-of-war speech. But a farming cooperative failed, the penalty for putting the airport on the fertile fields of the Blaye, and Alderney people were given the choice to become part of the county of Hampshire or to have their island administered by Guernsey. They chose the latter in an arrangement described by John Arlott as a "shotgun wedding".

It has given rise to the resentment felt by islanders for their southern administrators—nobody enjoys a shotgun wedding. Islanders grudgingly put up with the interference of a distant and, as it is seen, rather out-of-touch administration. Alderney has two seats in Guernsey's parliament and is able to influence those areas of budgeting and

The island's *jurats* carry on ancient traditions of government.

policy-making which affect the island. But because all Channel Island politicians are amateur and the island is far removed from Guernsey, the representatives visit the seat of their administration for the monthly meetings of the States, and only occasionally in between times.

The **States of Alderney** meet in the Court House opposite the administrative offices in Queen Elizabeth II Street. They sometimes discuss street names—Queen Elizabeth II Street was New Street, renamed after a visit by the Queen in 1978 and now known as QEII. Victoria Street was changed from Rue de Grosnez for a similar reason in 1854, but Route de Braye, Grande Rue and La Petit Rue have become Braye Road, High Street and Little Street due to a general anglicising of the island.

St. Anne's Church, which has entrances from both Victoria and QEII Street, is one of the few architect designed places of worship in the Channel Islands. Luckily the later and better known Gothic architecture of Sir George Scott—London's St. Pancras Station Hotel and the Albert Memorial—cannot be guessed from the design of the church which is noble and has a Norman influence. Completed in 1850 to accommodate the billeted garrison and large population of Irish labourers, it is dignified, light and spacious, with a pyramidal tower which acts as a landmark from the sea.

An unusual feature of the church is the Caen stone imported as a building material; most Channel Island churches make use of local stone only. St. Anne's was built as a memorial to his parents by the last hereditary Governor of Alderney, Rev. John Le Mesurier. It became the centre of controversy during the Occupation. Some of the bells were shipped to France, where they were to be melted down to make munitions, and the church was used as a store and wine cellar giving rise to accusations of sacrilege. Four of the six bells were recovered outside Cherbourg after the war and the other two were found in Alderney. All six were sent to the

United Kingdom where they were recast to hang in the refurbished church.

Labourers for the building industry arrived in the late 1840s to produce materials for and work on the ring of forts built to protect the anchorage which was to mirror Portland Harbour on the other side of the Channel. Many Irish immigrants were fleeing the potato crop failure and the horrors of famine and the number of workers trebled the local population. The Rue Neuve project to provide houses for the new residents was started—with it went a new Court House and prison cells to accommodate those with high spirits and a taste for the Alderney hooch.

The cruel sea: Planners designing the **breakwater** never consulted local fishermen who predicted that storms and winter gales would smash even the greatest structure built in that position. The prediction proved correct and the problem gives island authorities their biggest worry to this day—a continual maintenance programme is needed to keep the breakwater intact as gales push waves from America to rip into it each winter. Half the 4,680 feet (1,430 metres) length was abandoned many years ago and the resulting 600-metre reef remains a hazard to shipping entering the anchorage.

But it provides valuable shelter for hundreds of French and British yachts which visit the island each year. Their crews and skippers spend heavily on provisions and in the bars, often taking the opportunity to sleep ashore, filling the occasional gaps which occur in every hotel booking chart. Island fishermen take advantage of the shelter and the sand of Braye beach is protected from erosion by the breakwater. It is the island's most valuable asset.

Within six months of its completion in 1864, two huge breaches were torn in the wall of the breakwater. The U.K. Treasury became increasingly worried: not only had the cost of building gone way over budget but the running expenditure was also horrendous. A committee of inquiry was held in London eight years later to consider whether to de-

The seas around Alderney aren't always so calm.

stroy the structure, let the sea take it or continue maintaining the breakwater. A deputation from Alderney argued that the U.K. Government built it for their own advantage, destroying the former safe anchorage used by fishermen. It had to be maintained or the island would be ruined, they said, and the committee agreed.

Upkeep of the breakwater remained the U.K. Government's responsibility for more than 100 years. Relevant documents were found after the Occupation and the wartime breaches were repaired at great expense as part of the 10-year rehabilitation programme for the island. The Treasury continued to pay until after the Falklands Conflict when an extraordinary event sent a shock wave through the Alderney community. The States of Jersey, in a spontaneous act of charity to people who had suffered a similar occupation to that of the Channel Islands in World War II, immediately sent £5 million to the Falkland Islands Fund and Guernsey followed with a contribution of £100,000 towards sheltered accommodation for the elderly. Within weeks both islands were formally asked for a contribution towards the United Kingdom defence bill.

Similar requests had been batted off with ease in the past but this time the demand was definite: the islands would be protected in the same way as the Falklands, an act generously acknowledged by Guernsey and Jersey, and the contribution had to be paid. Having let the cat out of the bag, there was no catching it. A number of methods of payment were considered but eventually Guernsey said that they would make no contribution. The independence and constitution of the bailiwick was clearly laid down in ancient royal charters and would not be jeopardised. Instead they would take over the running and maintenance of Alderney's breakwater.

This was a body blow to Alderney. Their economy booming, offshore finance bringing in money, full employment and Alderney's accounts with

In rough seas, the Quesnard Point lighthouse becomes a life-saving beacon.

Guernsey showing a surplus led the politicians to hope for independence. But the "Falklands factor", which added the cost of maintaining the breakwater to the annual budget, dealt those hopes a severe blow.

Fears of yomping French troops marching across Alderney so worried the early Victorians that every good beach is guarded by a fort. Built to create "the Gibraltar of the Channel", the 12 forts were a panic measure to counter and blockade the strongly fortified French naval base at Cherbourg. They were built rapidly between 1845 and 1861, but within a few months of completion the forts and breakwater were obsolete. Steam ships, better explosives and a rifled gun which brought Alderney within range of heavy artillery on the French coast, turned forts into follies.

Fort patrol: The forts form a basis for an excellent walk. Designed by young engineer Captain William Jervois, the plans were clearly drawn by a person with a strong aesthetic sense. They fit smoothly into the landscape and incorporate not only the functions of Victorian military defence but also embellishments such as medieval machicolations and arrow slits.

Geographically, the first and possibly most striking is at **Clonque Bay** where a spectacular path, which runs from **Fort Essex** three miles (5 km) away along 300 foot (100 metre) cliffs, zigzags down to sea level. The path from Clonque passes **Fort Tourgis**, a huge barrack block on the hillside, before joining the main road which runs to the harbour.

Fort Platte Saline was a small battery built to protect the bay of that name from attack. It has been swamped by the sand and gravel works which exploit the tidal deposits on the beach.

The breakwater is protected by **Fort Gronez** at its base while **Fort Albert**, the biggest, squats on the hillside overlooking the habour and Braye Bay. **Château à L'Etoc,** between Saye and Corblets Bay, where a tunnel helped *vraic tcherieux* (seaweed gatherers) to

Fort Clonque's bulk is a reminder of Alderney's historical importance to naval strategists.

leave the beach with their ox-drawn carts, has been converted into flats—**Fort Corblets** on the next headland is also a private dwelling.

Three small abandoned defences protect the rocky east coast. **Fort Hommeaux Florains** is on an islet off the lighthouse, **Fort Quesnard** makes the headland while **Houmet Herbé** looks out over the Race towards Cap de la Hague. A fort on **Raz** island, connected to the mainland by a causeway, houses a collection of moth-eaten stuffed birds while **Fort Essex**, high on the cliffs above, guards Longis Bay.

One way to get a good view of the forts, and of the island as a whole, is to take the spectacular boat trip around Alderney on the Hull—registered "Beverley Rose". She calls at the low-lying island of **Burhou**, where puffins nest, and noses close under 2,000 pairs of gannets on the Garden Rocks. The trip is a birdwatcher's delight, but holds a great deal of interest to the casual visitor. There are several rocks around the island which have folk tales associated with them. The stories of the boatman give an insight to island life and people that live there.

When the breakwater was being built the couple who lived in the lighthouse decided to send their teenaged girl to main.land Alderney to broaden her education. She was not a worldly lass, having been born in the Casquets. Within days of her arrival to stay with friends, she paid a fisherman to take her back to the lighthouse—the pace of life was too fast, she said.

The story of the Hanging Rocks contrasts the overcrowded island of Guernsey with rural Alderney. The desperate islanders of the former rowed to the United Kingdom, attached a rope to the Hanging Rocks and pulled Alderney into the sea, intending to take the lump of much needed land home. It stuck on the sea bed and the rope parted when they were halfway, leaving the Guernsey people to return to their island empty-handed.

They certainly would not have chosen such a dangerous place to leave an island. The Channel Islands have a huge rise and fall in the tide—more than 35 feet (11 metres) on some of the big spring tides. These cause vast quantities of water to pour out of the English Channel where the maritime river is split by Alderney. One vast current, **the Race**, rushes between the island and Cap de la Hague, while another, **the Swinge**, passes through the narrow channel to Burhou. Beyond this flat island, the turbulent water surges and heaves to the distant **Casquets Lighthouse** as the tide rushes past.

Whisky and water: Shipwrecks on the many reefs have been and still are commonplace. Several yachts a year end their lives, and occasionally those of their crews, on the rocks, while the occasional commercial ship comes to grief. The most talked about of these in recent years was the "Corinna", which created mayhem when islanders discovered her general cargo contained booze. Thousands of bottles were rescued by police and customs officers who locked them in the ancient cells built for the Irish stoneworkers. But the cells have huge grilles and local people went on fishing expeditions at night catching the bottles using rods with running nooses in the strings. Many of the remaining bottles had no labels and had to be smashed—a tragedy in the eyes of many.

Alderney is described as the Cinderella of the Channel Islands—people coyly say she has no money and is extremely beautiful. What they mean is that she has two ugly sisters, and it is in caring for Guernsey and Jersey that the islanders may find salvation. It is widely thought that one day the Federation of Channel Islands must be formed. It will be totally independent of the United Kingdom, have its own bank, currency, health service, stamps, administration and legislation.

If the separation occurs, there will be bitter arguments about where to site the administrative headquarters. Alderney will say that the glass slipper fits her and that the figurehead bank, administration and federation headquarters should be on the island, supporting the others' insular functions.

SARK

To an extent Sark remains in its famous time-warp. At its best the island can still give you a feel of what it must have been like to have lived, not only in the Channel Islands, but in almost any rural community on France's Cotentin peninsula 100 years ago; to taste life as it was before the peace of the wooded countryside was shattered forever by the internal combustion engine and metalled roads. The Victorian poet Swinburne would probably continue to find Sark his "small, sweet world of wave-encompassed wonder".

All the same, a visitor should be warned that this last bastion of European feudalism can no longer claim to be almost entirely free of horseless carriages. It wasn't so long ago that the only powered vehicles permitted were the invalid car belonging to Dame Sybil Hathaway, whose rule during the German Occupation inspired a play in London's West End, and the tractor attached to an ambulance-van originally designed for a horse.

Alas, these days are long over. There are now more than 60 registered tractors in Sark—about one for every nine of its 550 permanent inhabitants. John Michael Beaumont, the Dame's grandson and the present Seigneur, would like to see the number reduced, but it seems that the omnipotence of feudal rulers isn't what it used to be either and the majority rules.

In fact Sark was never feudal during the heyday of feudalism. During the 14th and 15th centuries it was raided by pirates so often that its only inhabitants were a few hermits living in the ruins of abandoned monasteries. It was reoccupied in the 16th century when Elizabeth I gave the Jerseyman Helier de Carteret the right to colonise it and thus prevent its seizure by the French.

After an initial reconnaisance convinced him that Sark was well worth cultivating, de Carteret arrived in force with 39 families and their retainers in 1565. He divided the island into 40 pieces *(ténéments)* and 39 of these were leased in perpetuity to his followers as feudal holdings. Most of the tenants built their homes as far inland as they could to shelter from the elements and hide from unwelcome visitors. To this day the Sarkees seem to be able to live without a view of the sea.

Part of each tenant's feudal obligation to de Carteret was to mount a watch on a section of the coast as well as to provide at least one man armed with a musket for the island's defence. Elizabeth was so pleased by the way the Jerseyman had organised things that she gave him the gift of a cannon which can still be seen in the ground of the present seigneurie (well worth a visit).

Subtropical myths: The public aren't allowed into the house itself but they can wander through its grounds and inspect the large walled garden where the gardeners strive to save, from the winter gales and frost, the exotic shrubbery introduced by the Dame and her grandson.

Preceding pages: La Coupée, the link with Little Sark; tractors are the only powered vehicles permitted on Sark. Left, a Sarkee fisherman. Right, Seigneur Michael Beaumont and his wife.

The islands have many charms, but don't let anybody try to fool you that the they are almost subtropical, a silly image fostered in the days before most British holidaymakers knew what real heat was. It sadly misfired during World War II when some Britons rejected evacuees from the islands because they thought they'd be black.

The site of the seigneurie is on the old priory of St. Magloire which was founded in the sixth century and finally abandoned in the 14th, having been vandalised once too often. Some of the present houses date from the 17th century, although the bulk of it was built about 1730. It wasn't conceived to any grand plan in the way of English stately homes but grew according to the quirks of succeeding seigneurs. Dame Sybil introduced a pets' graveyard with appropriate headstones on a wall where visitors can wonder at the longevity of her animals, "Mac—a gallant ratter, 1928-43", reads one.

Unfortunately, her grandfather's main contribution was even more startling. It is a square signalling tower for semaphoring messages to Guernsey because the original round one had become overgrown by trees which he was reluctant to cut down. The tower gives the house a Wodehousian "Blandings Castle" theme, especially when the seigneurial standard (a St. George with two gold Normandy leopards in one corner) is flying. Dame Sybil is reported to have hated this glowing example of the folly school of architecture, but could never afford to have it demolished. The seigneurial doves have made the tower their own. Only the Seigneur is allowed to keep a Colombier (dove-cote) in the same way that he or she is the only person permitted to keep a bitch (although spayed bitches are now allowed).

However, under the 1951 Reform (Sark) Law the Seigneur's powers are much eroded. He can now merely delay a proposal put up by the Chief Pleas, the island's parliament, for 21 days instead of vetoing it altogether. But he does still receive Le Trezieme, a handy one-thirteenth part of any property deal done on the island. In 1980, shortly after he took office, Michael Beaumont was reported to have received £34,000 from this ancient right. He himself pays a rent of £1.79 a year to the Queen; payment is not made directly to Buckingham Palace but by cheque to the Crown Receivers in Guernsey.

The present seigneurie was originally one of the original 39 *ténéments*. Helier de Carteret himself lived at a place called **Le Manoir** which is on the opposite side of the road from the junior school and quite near the strange little building that looks like it might be a public lavatory but turns out to be the island's **prison**.

The Connetable and his assistant, the Vingtenier (so called because originally there was one for every 20 households), have greater powers that you would expect from part-time appointments: they can keep somebody in the jail for two nights, after which they have to be released or transferred to Guernsey. Its occupants are usually visiting day-trippers with bad hang-

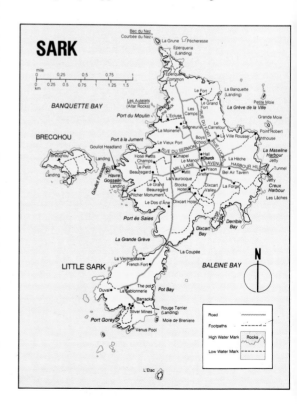

overs who might be fined by the local magistrate, known as the *Seneschal*.

Trippers, like tractors, are another grievous self-inflicted wound. In the high season, from July to September, they swarm ashore from Guernsey and Jersey on as many as 11 boats a day. During summer, at least 65,000 people, whose boat tickets include the landing tax demanded by the Chief Pleas, try to "do Sark" in about five hours. As a result, some of the better-known places become distinctly overpeopled. They take on a kind of Disneyland air and with it goes the sort of beerbottle-in-the-gorsebush littering often found in natural beauty spots in England.

Battle of the bicycles: Just how lucrative tourism has become may be judged by the saga of Sark's recent bicycle war. A great way to get around the island is by bicycle, for most of its 1,300 acres (520 hectares) is plateau fissured by narrow valleys running down to the sea. The smaller island, **Little Sark**, is a bit bumpier and bicycle with gears are preferred.

For several years now it has been possible to hire machines by the day or week from two main establishments. In the summer of 1987 the proprietor of one of these bicycle hire firms, a well-known local figure, was sent to prison in Guernsey for a month for employing children to damage or wreck the rival establishment's machines. This Fagin laid down a scale of payments ranging from a couple of pounds for a puncture or cutting the brake cables to a fiver for the complete destruction of a bicycle by hurling it down the Corvanche Chasm from **La Coupée**, the precipitous causeway improved by German prisoners-of-war labour that tops the isthmus joining Sark and Little Sark. Names are withheld to protect the guilty; bolder visitors might inquire, at their own risk, whether they are hiring from the victim or the villain.

Nowadays, if you want to avoid the trippers, it's probably best to visit during either side of the school summer holidays. Both spring and autumn are marvellous times in Sark, although the

equinox gales that sometimes sweep the Channel can make mid-September a gamble. The tortured urban soul wishing to get the best out of the island and feel the tension drain away as he bicycles through the green tunnels or walks the cliffs, should stay at least a week.

Competition of a more beneficial sort is evident in the restaurants of the island's five hotels, and it would be invidious to pick any of them out for special attention. They all tend to have good *à la carte* dinner menus with plenty of locally caught fish prepared by imported young chefs anxious to make a name for themselves. Well-selected wine cellars are also a uniform feature, although prices can be disappointingly high, given the islands' carefully cultivated duty-free image.

In l987 no fewer than three of Sark's hotels were featured in the *Good Food Guide* and four in the *Good Hotel Guide*. This isn't to say that they are without their faults and, unless you book well in advance and get one of the best rooms, accommodation can be a bit tatty and the plumbing eccentric. Some have quiet sitting rooms furnished with comfortable sofas and those wonderful hardback collections of long out-of-print novels and biographies that are always to be found in the best British country hotels. Others do not.

The **Avail de Creux Hotel**, where the food is second to none, aggravates its misfortune at being sited next to the 24-hour hum of the island's oil-powered electric generator (a night sound that is a soporific to a few and torture to most) by playing BBC Radio 2 over the piped music system in its lobby and dining room. Apart from the hotels, there are several guesthouses and altogether about 400 tourist beds available in Sark during the season.

How to get there: Sark lies eight miles (13km) east of Guernsey and, since the only aircraft permitted to land on it are helicopters engaged in mercy missions, the visitor must arrive by boat. There are three harbours, two on the east coast and one on the west which

Sark's population of about 550 is big enough to support a school.

is rarely used. Hydrofoils from Jersey and St. Malo on the Brittany coast come in to **Le Creux harbour** which was once a landlocked bay and had its narrow entrance quarried out of the granite. It dates from 1570 and is thought to be one of the smallest harbours in the world. In the 1930s a film company used it as the outdoor backcloth for Victor Hugo's *Toilers of the Sea* because they thought it was the next best thing to early 19th-century Guernsey. The company went bust and the film was never shown.

Creux is a well-sheltered place, a favourite of those yachtsmen experienced or foolish enough to sail the foggy Channel Islands' waters which wise sailors recognise as some of the most treacherous in the world. In Sark a law forbids the shooting of seagulls because of the help the birds' cries give mariners when the wind drops and their nesting rocks and headlands vanish into sudden sea mists. Until the mid-19th century, when it was finally conceded that another war with France was un-

likely, the way into Sark's harbours was a closely guarded admiralty secret.

Nowadays the main harbour for most shipping from Guernsey and Jersey is **Maseline**, just north of Creux in the neighbouring bay; it was completed shortly after World War II. This is Sark's main link with the outside world, the place where the supplies are received during the long winter months when gales bring grey seas lashing down onto its concrete quay which in the summer is a favourite spot, between boats, for line fishing with sandeel bait.

On landing, the visitor is approached by carters whose flat-bedded waggons are pulled by tractors. These carters deliver your baggage to the hotel and, if you don't mind an uncomfortable ride on the waggon, it's possible to travel with it all the way. However, your baggage will turn up quite safely and it should take you no more than 30 minutes to walk up winding **Harbour Hill** to the plateau above.

The alternative is to take the "bus" up the steep road to the **Bel Air Tavern**.

Creux Harbour, linked to the village by a tunnel.

This is a fairground-looking vehicle, though quite comfortable, also pulled by tractor; its twin benches have earned it the nickname "toast-rack". The bus company, by the way, is owned by a man who first came to Sark with the British liberation forces to supervise, with prisoners-of-war labour, the clearance of 13,000 mines the *Wehrmacht* had planted. It is quite common on Sark to meet people who fell in love with the place on first sight, whether they be residents or holidaymakers who come back year after year.

The real thing: At the top of Harbour Hill, just past the Bel Air pub, awaits a cab rank of horse-drawn vehicles to take you through the cluster of shops sometimes referred to as **The Village** to your hotel. In most cases the drivers of these Victorias and Wagonettes are horsestruck young ladies on a working holiday, but you may be lucky enough to be driven by a genuine Sarkee.

If you are and you have never heard a proper Channel Islands accent before—which is possible if you have simply passed through Guernsey or Jersey en route for the Sark boat—this may come as something of a shock. At one time all the inhabitants of the Iles Anglo-Normandes spoke a French patois which not only varied from island to island but from parish to parish.

The anglicisation of the islanders that started in earnest in the 1920s is now almost complete. Very few people under 50 speak patois and it will probably be as dead as Cornish by the end of this century. But it has left behind a distinct Channel Islands English complete with French circumlocutions and local variations. Jerseymen, for instance, can sound remarkably similar to English-speaking South Africans. Both Guernseymen and Jerseymen can instantly spot a Sarkee by the way they roll their 'Rs'. And all those islanders whose speech still owes a lot to patois sauce their English with a generous lashing of aitches.

The route to your hotel may well take you down **The Avenue** (known as the M1 to regular visitors) in which there are various shops, many of them selling such customary tourist tat as souvenir tee-shirts. A variation is the sale of "Sarkstone", an amethystine quartz made up into jewellery. Without VAT and other taxes, prices are quite reasonable. But don't imagine you are getting anything unique: the attractive purple stone is no longer mined on the island but comes from Zambia and China.

Mining has an unhappy history on Sark. Mute testimony can be found in the granite chimneys and craggy ruins growing out of the bracken and brambles down at **Port Gorey** on Little Sark, which is almost the southern tip of the island. These are the abandoned silvermines and, without the tragedy that closed them, the present Seigneur would have never inherited his fief. Perhaps it would be best to read this tale where most of it happened.

Mining for millions: To get to the mines you cross into Little Sark at La Coupée—the only dry-shod way there. There is a sign warning cyclists to dismount—though a head-on collision with another cyclist there would be a

Waiting for the postman—who arrives, of course, by bicycle.

memorable experience. Before German prisoners-of-war labour put in hand-rails, school children used to have to crawl across the causeway in high winds. One day erosion will complete its job by cutting through the isthmus. **La Grand Grève Bay** will become a strait, and the causeway itself be transformed into a bridge. On your right a steep set of steps descends to the bay, which is good for bathing and surfing when the wind is in the right direction. The climb back up makes it only worth going if you intend to stay a while.

Once across La Coupée, ride down to the **La Sablonneri**e and turn left up the lane just beyond it (the entrance to the hotel's tea gardens is on your right) and ride up to the point where there is a gate and a sign telling you that the track beyond it leads down to the **Venus pool**. This pool, 20 feet (six metres) deep and named by the Victorian artist William Toplis, who died on the island, is uncovered for two-and-a-half hours either side of a low tide. It has flat rocks around it suitable for sunbathing and in

July or August, perhaps even September, a pleasant swim might be had without needing hot tea and blankets to ward off hypothermia. Perhaps it should be noted that throughout the islands small children and fat ladies tend to stay longer in the water, apparently immune to its more bracing qualities.

To get to the old mine-workings, do not go through the gate; descend instead through the gorse to the right of it towards the inlet called **Port Gorey**. The tracks go through bracken and brambles and, in September, bushes heavy with blackberries and sloes. A slope near the top is sometimes used as a rubbish tip and, if the smell doesn't give it away, the circling crows and gulls will. (Ordinary landbirds of the thrush and blackbird variety are, by the way, unusually tame on the island.) You can already see the first of the ruins. The chimneys are the most intact. They were the air vents.

Silver was discovered on Sark in the 1830s and Cornish miners were brought over to work it. One of the

"The Window", a rock formation at Port du Moulin.

principal shareholders in the newly formed Guernsey and Sark Mining Company was the Seigneur, Pierre Le Pelley. Test bores promised an Arizona but the veins were narrow and, although the company kept a Sark silver tea set in their St. Peter Port office to impress potential investors, the big vein of ore always seemed to be just around the corner. One of the eight galleries is now extended 200 feet (60 metres) under the seabed and sometimes the Cornishmen could hear an angry sea rolling bottom boulders along its roof. Maintenance expenses were heavy. There was a constant need to install bigger and better pumps to prevent flooding.

Then the first tragedy struck. Seigneur Le Pelley was drowned with two others off the **Bac du Nez**, the island's northern point, during a boat trip to Guernsey. His younger brother Ernest became Seigneur and, in order to raise more money for the mining venture, took a £4,000 mortgage on his fief from one John Allaire, a wealthy Jerseyman with an interesting past.

During the Napoleonic wars some 25 years before, Allaire had been a British privateer, licensed by the Crown to prey on French cargo vessels in the Channel. But it is believed that Allaire found it equally profitable to run up a *tricoleur* and capture an English ship since his patois-speaking Channel Islanders were just another bunch of Frenchmen to the average British sailor. They would take booty back to Jethou, the tiny island Allaire owned between Guernsey and Sark. Like most pirates, he had a reputation for not taking prisoners and there is a story of a curse being put on him and his descendents by a women left to drown. This was the man to whom the Seigneur mortgaged his inheritance.

By 1845, 245 miners and Guernsey-man had set up a tavern there which soon acquired a reputation as a den of iniquity among the increasingly Methodist islanders. When the disaster came, some must have regarded it as divine retribution. A gallery ceiling collapsed and gallons of freezing sea-

"Mr. Pye", starring Derek Jacobi, was filmed for television on Sark.

water came crashing in. One can imagine how it was, a frantic scramble for the entrance shaft in the dark, for the lamps had gone out and the water was already chest-high and rising. Ten miners were drowned.

It was the end of the mining. It marked the beginning of the end of the Le Pelley dynasty of seigneurs, too. Ernest died two years later, a broken man by all accounts. His son, Peter Carey Le Pelley, was unable to meet the mortgage repayments on the fief. By 1852 the old pirate Allaire was dead. It was left to his daughter, a widow called Marie Collings, to foreclose on it and become the next seigneur.

So John Allaire, scourge of the Channel (when he died it needed a wheelbarrow to take his gold coin to a bank) is the present Seigneur's great-great-great-great grandfather. Thus even gentle Sark proves the theory that behind every great fortune lies a great crime. Or, in John Allaire's case, probably several great crimes were committed during the course of his life.

There is a kind of natural jetty at Port Gorey, a finger of rough granite rocks going into the sea. If, on a fine day when the rocks are not too slippery, you go to the end of it you will discover the rusted hand-rail of a landing stage which is thought to have been something to do with the mining, although the Germans may have added to or repaired it during the Occupation. At least one Cornish miner remained on the island; his name was Remphrey and his descendents are still there.

Artists' haunts: From the silver mines it is best to go back to the La Sablonnerie for further exploration of this coast. Once at the hotel, turn left and follow the road its last 400 metres or so until you come to a farmyard where most of the outbuildings appear to have been turned into living quarters—at least in the summer. Go round the corner on foot (there is a notice telling you not to take your bicycle any further) and then you turn left through the fields until you reach the clifftop gorse. The Victorians who pioneered Sark as a holiday place were mostly artists and poets of varying talent, but to a man and a woman they all seem to have been classicists. So apart from the Venus Pool there is also the **Jupiter Bath** and the **Adonis Pool** which you are now approaching.

The pool faces an islet called the **Moie de la Bretagne** and, like Venus, is visible two hours from either side of a low tide. The tide rises very rapidly. It cannot be overemphasised that, however exhilarating scrambling around the Sark coastline can be, you must be constantly aware of the state of the tide and allow yourself some leeway for taking longer than you estimated.

A deep gulley has to be crossed to reach the pool where the clear waters are well over seven feet (two metres) deep. The pool contains a slowly beckoning garden of different coloured seaweeds. The rocks around it are a strange gold tint and have been gently sculpted into saltpans.

Tides have to be watched even more carefully if you want to explore Sark's caves. One is named after Victor Hugo,

Even Sark didn't escape the sound of cannon fire.

who climbed to it on a visit during his exile years in Guernsey, but it can be reached only by boat or by swimming and is dangerous without a guide. Just north of this, however, and also on the west coast, are the **Gouliot Caves**. These tunnel into the headland between Sark and the islet of **Brecqhou** (one of the original 39 *ténéments* and most recently owned by a millionaire who flies in by helicopter). Nobody can visit Brecqhou without the owner's permission. It is ironic that the isolation that now makes it so desirable for the man who values his privacy must have made it one of the least wanted of de Carteret's original *ténéments*.

The Gouliot Caves are fantastically studded, almost like a glass mosaic with sea anemones of various colours from beetroot red to dark green. You can get to them by taking a track to the headland overlooking Brecqhou from the **Beau Regard** area or the **Hotel Petit Camp**, where the proprietor puts up a notice about the suitability of the tides.

Just before the rocky headland overlooking Brecqhou, there is a footpath dropping down through the bracken towards the right. Follow this. Your footsteps may fall on an incongruous concrete slab about six inches (15 cms) thick that has become part of the path; this is a German **mine marker**, HI. There is another one back in the bracken about another 16 feet (five metres) away.

The mines themselves have long since gone; several German prisoners-of-war lost their lives in clearing them. Further down, you may notice some iron stakes where the Germans rigged their barbed-wire entanglements.

One British commando raid on Sark had far-reaching effects. The commandos took prisoner some Germans billeted at the **Dixcart Hotel**, which is in one of the island's loveliest valleys and is where the few remaining cider apple trees can be found. Some of the Germans tried to escape; one was later found with rope around his hands and knifed to death. It was because of this incident that Hitler issued his infamous

order, not always followed by the *Wehrmacht*, that all commando prisoners must be treated as terrorists and summarily shot.

Hard on the ankles: The **Boutiques Caves**, so called because they were once used by smugglers, need a torch to explore. Boots, or at least well-fitted training shoes with a good grip, are recommended for both caves, where the abundance of boulders over which to clamber give the ankles a lot of hard work and can be dangerous.

The Boutiques are near the **Bec du Nez**, the nothernmost tip of Sark. To reach them, you have to cross **Eperquerie Common**, which is thick with bluebells in the spring, then clamber down into La Grune channel which at high tide separates **La Grune** from the rest of the island. Once you are in the channel, the cave's entrance is to your left; it is necessary to climb over a large boulder to enter it.

There's something really quite eerie about the Boutiques. You can imagine the sweating men, the kegs of brandy,

the whispered oaths. For the first 650 feet (200 metres) or so, there are quite deep pools of water trapped in craters on the floor even at low tide. A reassuring factor is that there's nearly always a glimmer of light at the end of the tunnel. About halfway along, a side entrance leads to a small beach.

On your way back across the common you might ponder that this quiet place saw, according to local legend, the *dénouement* of one of the strangest stories to come out of the German Occupation of the islands.

It seemed a straightforward case of murder followed by remorse and suicide; the batman's body was buried in an unmarked grave on the common without benefit of clergy. Then, a few months later, a badly wounded soldier in a field hospital on the Eastern Front confessed that he was the killer. While serving in Sark, he had tried to persuade the doctor to declare him unfit for frontline duty. The doctor refused. He then murdered the batman to cover his first killing. Some Sarkees will tell you that the soldier, having survived his wounds, was brought back to Sark and, before being executed, he was made to exhume the batman's body and give him a proper burial.

The locals like telling visitors stories. Some people insist that it is their favourite occupation—which is a bit unfair because, like most Channel islanders, they are an industrious lot.

It is common for a man to have two or three jobs, especially in the summer when there are tourists' bags to be carted about and bars to be waited on. And, even if there are very few pureblooded Sarkees left, there is an attitude to life that goes with living on a small island where winters aren't for the physically soft or easily bored.

There was a time when winter made a prisoner of those Sarkees who couldn't afford to decamp to Guernsey, as most seigneurs did, before the seas became too rough. Now a new tradition is catching on: the young men tend to disappear in the autumn but are back in December with money to spend. They go to England to cut Christmas trees.

Left, growing fat in a feudal system. Right, enjoying the advantages of an absence of cars.

HERM

They used to bury people in **Herm**—not just one or two people but thousands. Evidence of those burial practices can still be seen, although many of the graves have been swallowed by the sea and many more were desecrated in the 19th century.

Why our early, pre-Christian predecessors should think that Herm was an ideal place to bury their dead and to erect huge standing stones in their honour we will never know; but any visitor who believes that the old granite stones which adorn the island have arrived here by chance should think again. Someone, long ago, moved them here. Herm was a neolithic graveyard and deserves the occasional archaeological dig.

It is also a very pretty, meticulously run island where you can't pick the flowers, can't own a house, shouldn't play your transistor radio on the beach and should wash your clothes only between midnight and noon. Who said that small islands spell freedom?

Major plans: Currently leased by Major Peter Wood and his family from the States of Guernsey, Herm is very different from the other Channel Islands, possibly because the Major, who came to the island with his Yorkshire-bred wife, Jenny, in 1949, is a New Zealander. He is also very conscious that his island home stands or falls according to the whims of the tourist industry and that it has taken a lifetime to carve Herm into the quiet little paradise it is today; that is, a civilised island a mile-and-a-half long by half-a-mile wide with one large hotel (the **White House**), two pubs, a row of cottages, two shops (including a post office) and two well-run beach cafés.

There are also the puffins, of course, and the chapel and the farm and the **manor house**. But everything (apart from the puffins) had to be built or rebuilt after World War II and now have to be maintained or modernised. Major

Wood has given his life to the island and the personality of the man and, to a lesser extent his family, can't help showing through.

Herm has always lent itself to the moulding of personal visions, although one of the first people to leave his or her name behind, St. Tugual, probably never wanted to settle in the Channel Islands in the first place. He (or she) provided the name of the small chapel on the hill above **Spring Meadow**, near to the farm and the manor, and this serves as a reminder of the days when Herm was a religious outpost, well lived-in by Catholic monks who founded a monastery, improved the land so that it could fatten livestock and produce grain, and stayed there under the control of French or English dioceses for hundreds of years. Later during the 17th century, Calvinism drove them off the island.

By the middle of the 17th century the island was deserted, although the **chapel** dedicated to the memory of St. Tugual remained. It is a small, rounded,

granite room with a high stained-glass window at the far end.

Window and chapel have been tastefully restored since the Wood family came to the island but no-one can restore forgotten knowledge of St. Tugual, who remains an enigma. Indeed, it has been rumoured that Tugual was a Welsh woman who accompanied St. Magloire to Guernsey and Herm in the sixth century, who died here and whose memory was perpetuated by the building of this holy shrine which has been well looked-after by the Major, despite woodworm in the school-style wooden seats, and which is used for morning service (10:30 a.m.) every Sunday.

For the rest of the time the chapel is left open, well-lit and flooded by lilting strains of recorded choral music. This changes to the real thing on Sunday mornings, although the organist might change from week to week. A notice in the White House Hotel proclaims: "If you would like to play the organ on Sunday, speak to the manager." Cliff Richard was one of many Christians who accompanied the Major, leading the congregation in song and prayer.

Law and order: There is no rector on the island, which has a resident population of 59, (nearly twice that in summer). Similarly there is no policeman, fireman, nurse or doctor, although there are set procedures and selected men to deal with any emergency. These procedures involve mainly the island manager (Major Wood's son-in-law) and the resident accountant. Both are members of the fire-fighting team and honorary Herm constables, who between them carry the full weight of Guernsey law.

The last time the Wood family negotiated to extend its lease well into the 21st century, a report by the States of Guernsey revealed that "the finances improved dramatically from 1983 and are now achieving substantial profits". Increased prosperity means more modernisation, more holiday cottages (outhouses are being converted to allow this) and more electricity.

The main power source on the island is in the form of generators run with the aid of three diesel bus engines. This means that, at the height of the tourist season, the huge demand for electricity necessitates sacrifice. Hotel guests (and staff) are forbidden to use electric kettles and are allowed to turn on electric washing machines only in the morning. This power-saving routine has also produced a quaint tradition: all hotel guests are supplied with small gas burners in their rooms, complete with small kettle and teapot. No-one complains and the hotel brochure advises: "Please do not attempt to change the gas cylinder yourself. Bring it to reception and it will be changed for you."

The young ones: Despite having no doctor, fireman or uniformed policeman, Herm does have its own teacher and **school**. Provided by Guernsey Education, a junior/infant school teacher commutes to Herm every day, teaches a class which changes in ages and numbers each year and then, in the evening, goes home.

By the time the children are at secondary school level their parents have a

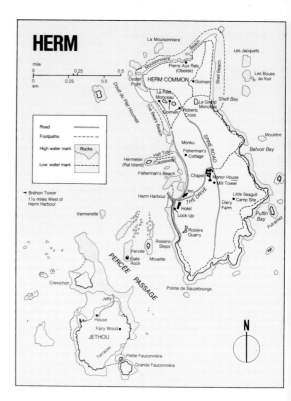

difficult choice to make: do they send them away to boarding school in Guernsey or does the whole family leave Herm, for the sake of a good education? Most parents usually leave and, for this reason, the majority of Herm employees are in their twenties—in striking contrast to most of the White House Hotel's guests.

Before the summer season it is the retired or semi-retired traveller who makes his way to Herm, knowing that no television sets are allowed in the hotel (but they are in the self-catering cottages); knowing that an evening entertainment is likely to be bridge, Trivial Pursuit or a jigsaw puzzle; and knowing that, if ever a contemporary hotel was ideally suited for an Agatha Christie murder mystery set in the earlier part of the 20th century, this is it.

With stuffed, heavy armchairs in the White House, cottages with names like Bracken, Cherry, Puffin and Primrose (where the accountant lives) close by, and pubs called **The Mermaid Tavern** and **The Ship**, all that's required to complete the scene is a corpse, Miss Marple dithering her way to the solution ("nobody leaves this island until the murder is solved") and the police inspector—who, of course, would have to be sent over from Guernsey.

Occasionally a policeman *is* required, but usually the island looks after itself extremely well. Any serious injury prompts the swift call-out of the ambulance boat *Flying Christine*, while the two special constables know that if any troublemakers arrive on Herm, they can call on volunteers to help them ship the offenders back to Guernsey, as convicts were once shipped to Australia. Alternatively, they can lock them up in one of the smallest jails in the world: a domed, beehive-shaped affair opposite the White House. This is primarily a granite ornament these days, but that wasn't always the case.

Steps to London: Herm lends itself to autocratic rule. In the 19th century John Lindsay, his son-in-law Jonathan Duncan and then Ebenezer Fernie saw

Focus of island life: the White House Hotel.

Herm not as a burial island or a tourist resort but as a working set of quarries. The harbour, opposite the hotel and the shops, was strengthened and enlarged; huge amounts of granite were exported to London (the steps that lead from Carlton House Terrace to the Mall were cut from Herm granite) and 400 labourers lived on the island with nothing else to do but work and drink.

The drinking led to fights, to gang warfare and to the prison becoming a popular place to spend the night. The search for granite and then copper, lead and silver led to many of the cromlechs and standing stones being destroyed. It was easier to take the granite from above the ground than to dig it out from below and bones were crunched underfoot or used as footballs.

Near **Rosière Steps**, where ships bring passengers to the island at low tide, an experimental mine shaft was sunk into the cliff edge and a large monolith called *Pierre aux Rats*, at the northern end of the Common, disappeared completely. Its granite was dressed and shipped to London.

As Guernsey fishermen used the stone as a navigational aid, they were none too happy, and the States of Guernsey ordered Herm Granite Company to erect a monument in its place. They did so and this odd, granite finger stands high above a grass and fern common to the north of the island. The scene is reminiscent of a badly neglected golf course.

The granite industry floundered. The granite men went bankrupt and it was left to Prussian Prince Blucher von Wahlstatt to bring his own, personal vision to Herm in the final years of the 19th century. Pine trees were planted, the manor hill was lined with dozens of eucalyptus trees and other exotic plants, and the manor at the top of the hill was extended, turreted and turned into a kind of corridored, Teutonic private asylum.

Wallabies and deer were brought to Herm and bred successfully. But neither they nor the Prince were present when the novelist Compton Mackenzie took over the lease in 1920, before moving to a tinier island nearby—Jethou (pronounced Jetoo)—in 1923. He left an island populated mainly with rabbits, cattle, a few horses and many, many species of birds. This was as much as the island was when Major Wood took over the lease in 1949.

Bird island: When the RAF Ornithological Society conducted a seven-day bird survey in the early 1980s, they indentified 92 different species, including Brent geese, guillemots, razorbills, shags and—on the "Humps", four small islands two nautical miles from Herm—puffins.

Sadly, the 90 or so pairs that were nesting there in the 1970s have now gone, however Herm is still full of visiting birdlife. It even contains a memorial to a well-loved bird, a parrot, owned by Sir Percival Perry who lived there before the World War II. The bird was strangled one night by a band of drunken fishermen and, to commemorate his passing, Sir Percival dedicated an outcrop of rock behind the hotel to honour his pet bird.

St. Tugual's, a small chapel, is a reminder that Herm was once a religious outpost.

If it is bad form to kill the island's fauna (apart from the rabbits, which overrun the place) it is terribly bad form to pick the flora. The policy of allowing it to grow, unchecked by anyone but those people who live there (a mere 59 in 1987, as mentioned), has produced an island full of blooms during summer which may be hard to control (any garden the size of Herm would be), but which is immeasurably pretty. Royal Fern, peculiar to Herm, grows here and wild iris, celandines, primroses, foxgloves plus more exotic plants such as New Zealand Flax and Japanese Cactus all thrive.

They grow especially well towards the centre of the island and either side of the path which begins above the Harbour, leads uphill towards **Le Manoir** and then runs, spine-like, towards **Primrose Valley**.

Allied to the natural prettiness of the flowers is the natural beauty of the beaches, particularly **Shell Beach** and **Belvoir Bay**. Both have cafés which are maintained with scrupulous care by

As well as tourists, the ferry brings empty milk churns for refilling.

Herm Island Ltd., which the company Major Wood established to ensure that Herm will be run as a family affair after his death.

Indeed, the cafés are so well looked-after that, just after 4 p.m. every day during the summer, one of the island's few tractors arrives pulling a refuse skip on wheels. All of the day's collected rubbish is taken to the dump near Rosière where it is either burnt or unloaded into an old quarry. There is no litter problem on Herm. Residents say litter just isn't tolerated.

Both Shell Beach and Belvoir Bay (the smaller and more popular of the two) are neither entirely sand or shell, but somewhere in between, and ideal hunting grounds for the dedicated shell collector. They are clean and slope gently down to the sea. Occasionally they attract the attention of a passing sailing ship which moors in the calm waters a little way from the land.

No swimming at all should take place within 300 feet (100 metres) of Alderney Point because of strong cur-

rents, but camping and walking along the designated paths (*not* either side of them) are actively encouraged. There are two campsites, **Seagull** and **Mermaid**, which are quite popular with Guernsey residents during the low season. They bring their own tents, put them up and live in them on weekends. This is a cheap way to enjoy repeated two-day spring and autumn holidays for not much more than the price of a 20-minute boat fare.

The food at the White House Hotel, its three cafés (there is one larger one attached to the Mermaid Hotel), the pubs and the restaurant is slightly limited, never poor and occasionally very good indeed. It is scrupulously served with the added attraction on the restaurant menu of oysters—a new, independent venture by a Guernseyman. This means that the local oyster beds provide visitors with Herm oysters at only £1.25 extra for six shellfish, which would fetch six times this amount in any major capital city.

Oysters are the island's main growth industry apart from tourism, although the Herm herd of cattle (Guernseys) makes money and the milk boat leaves for the mother island twice a day, winter or summer. During the German Occupation, however, Herm was expected to see more cattle than ever before. It was placed under the control of Guernsey's chief agricultural officer who was told to use the land as a cattle-fattening store; all fattened cattle were to be milked or eaten by or for the sake of the occupying army.

In effect it was a good idea which came to nothing. For most of the war only the Dickson and Le Barge families lived on Herm, tending a few livestock and at times oblivious to what was happening in Europe.

Letter of the law: Before tourism blossomed, one of the most lucrative ways of making money was from the sale of **Herm stamps**. The island established its own post office, designed its own stamps and for nearly 20 years issued fresh covers which were franked, with a Herm island stamp,

Fisherman's Beach: sun, sea and solitude.

before being sent on their way, via Guernsey, all over the world.

The British government allowed Herm this financial privilege until, in 1969, Guernsey intervened. The States told Major Wood that he could frank Guernsey stamps and sell stamp-size, sticky pieces of paper of a similar size to stamps (he was not allowed to call them "Herm stamps") and that, while one piece of paper could be placed on envelopes, the other could not. If ever a modern-day, Herm-issued stamp is franked at the sorting office (the hotel), Guernsey Post Office will want to know why.

Wood craft: Gravediggers, quarrymen, wallabies and now 1,800 holiday-makers a day at the height of the season—Herm has seen them all. But cars are a rarity. Three tractors, one Land-Rover and three buggy-type motor bikes with go-anywhere wheels are the only vehicles on the island.

When Major Wood took over the island (the lease is due to expire in 2027) he discovered that a ghost shared it with him. It was (is) supposedly the spirit of a 16th-century monk.

In a similar fashion, once Major Wood dies, his spirit will live on because just about everything that the island is now can be traced to his vision. Tourism is the thing, at the moment, that brings in the money and the whole island is expected to realise it. Every hotel guest has a questionnaire to fill in which includes the following: "We expect our porter to welcome you by name and be helpful and courteous. Please give comments. Our receptionists are expected to welcome you warmly, be helpful and to know your name from the moment you arrive. Please give your comments." Another 15 similar questions are asked, each one just as pointed.

Herm is a wonderful tourist paradise—if you enjoy the high standards set for staff and guests. You get the feeling that, if you complained about the noise the seagulls were making outside your window, the next day they would still be there—but silent.

Herm is a popular weekend retreat for Guernsey people.

THE LITTLE ISLANDS

Jethou: According to that great island-fancier, the author Sir Compton Mackenzie, Jethou is the *"most perfect small isle"*. He was tenant of the 45-acre (18-hectare) Crown property for seven years from 1923; wrote 14 books and innumerable articles there and saw the music magazine, *The Gramophone*, for which he was responsible, thrive. He fled to Jethou after selling the lease of Herm—just 2,600 feet (800 metres) across the sea—to Ford motor mogul Lord Perry, when financial upkeep of the larger isle threatened to overwhelm him.

Lord Perry had also made an offer for Jethou, where he wanted to grow poisonous plants for the chemical industry. Sir Compton, who always maintained that the spirits of Jethou were a benign influence on his life, later expressed thankfulness in his autobiography that he had resisted the plan. In 1958, when he heard that the island was once more up for sale, he wrote: "Jethou is the most perfect small island off the coast of Britain. If I was younger, I'd buy it again".

Over the centuries many people have coveted magical, hump-backed little Jethou, which includes the islets of **Crevichon** and **Grande Fauconnière** joined to it at low tide. It was the first Channel Island to fall into possession of the English Crown at the end of the 11th century, when the rest of the archipelago was still part of the Duchy of Normandy. The tenant (who has to be a British subject) pays no income tax—merely an annual rent of £100. All mineral and wreck rights are the reserve of the Crown, and the tenant is forbidden to keep a brothel or a gaming house, and must allow Guernsey residents to collect seaweed and sand eels.

Under the present tenant and his predecessor, both wealthy men, Jethou has become a private paradise. Visitors can no longer readily explore the "haunted" Fairy Wood, smothered in bluebells each spring, nor wonder at the 275-year-old mulberry tree—said to be the oldest of its species in the British Isles. The 24th tenant is Anthony George Duckworth, a lawyer living in the Cayman Islands. He bought the lease in 1984 for a sum "in excess of £500,000" following the death of millionaire industrialist and philanthropist Sir Charles Hayward. The sale included a granite manor house, two staff bungalows, a boathouse, jetty and slipway.

Sir Charles acquired Jethou in 1971 for £90,000 at an auction held on the island that is now part of local history. Bidding started at £50,000 between a handful of interested purchasers, standing in October sunshine above Jethou's lonely foreshore. Bids rose at the rate of £1,000 a second until all but one contender had dropped out. The previous tenants were a Jersey family, Susan and Angus Faed, with their four children, who paid £25,000 in 1964 for the lease. The Faeds ran a café to help with the cost of running Jethou, and welcomed visitors in summer. The difficulty of

Preceding pages: Lihou Island; the Minquiers, off Jersey. Left, the Ecréhous are administered by Jersey. Right, Jethou, as seen from Herm.

education for their children was the main reason for the family's deciding to give up their Robinson Crusoe life.

In the more distant past, Jethou tenants had not always been so law-abiding. The Faed's café was once the Admiral Restald Tavern, which had a hard-drinking reputation and was named after the island's first tenant of 1,000 A.D.

Brecqhou: When millionaire industrialist Leonard Matchan bought the beautiful 100-acre (40-hectare) island of Brecqhou, just off Sark, for £44,000, he acquired a tax-free private kingdom at a knockdown price, a seat in Sark's parliament, and a transport problem. The previous tenant was J. Thomson Donaldson, who bought Brecqhou in 1949 with his brother, Alastair, for £15,000. The island, with its big house and farm buildings, had been neglected for nine years, the German occupiers of Sark having no interest in its fate. The Donaldsons, founders of the Donbros clothing firm, sunk large sums into restoring and improving the property. It was ill-health that drove J. Thomson Donaldson to put Brecqhou on the market for £120,000—and to accept a much lower price for it in 1966.

Dame Sibyl Hathaway, the late and famous Dame of Sark, created the little island into a *ténément* (one of 40 freehold properties in Sark that entitles the owner automatically to a seat in Chief Pleas) when she sold it in 1929 for £3,000. Sark has no income tax, and bans cars and planes. Mr. Matchan, the busy boss of Cope Allman International, found that one of his early tasks as an island MP was to present the case for landing his helicopter on his own private domain.

Len Matchan, on reaching his seventies, also decided to sell—to the right buyer and at the right price—but he died in 1987 before the sale was completed. The "big house" is now equipped with seven bedrooms, five with bathrooms *en suite*. There is a swimming pool, two flats, four cottages, farm buildings and a private harbour. Under Sark's constitution, the

Brecqhou, just the thing to give the millionaire who has everything.

ténément can only be bought by a subject of the British Crown. An Australian and a Canadian would qualify, but not an American. This is one of the reasons why there were proposals to see Brecqhou on a long leasehold, without ruling out the option of a freehold sale. Figures between £3 million to £5 million for the property have been tossed around. Michael Beaumont, Sark's hereditary feudal ruler, is entitled to one-thirteenth of the selling price, paid to him by the buyer in return for the Seigneur's *congé*, or permission to purchase. However, after Mr. Matchan's death, the island was withdrawn from the market.

Lihou: The witches who, according to local legend, cavorted on their Sabbat around Le Catioroc headland on Guernsey's west coast would hurl defiance at the priory dedicated to the Virgin Mary on the tiny isle of Lihou. Only the ruins of the medieval Benedictine priory remain on the island, which is linked to the mainland at low tide by a causeway. But past and present tenants of the 40-acre (16-hectare) Crown property—rent is £3.50 a year—along with many of the visitors who pick their way across the rocky causeway, maintain that Lihou has a peculiar serenity.

The priory itself was not always so tranquil. In 1304 a priory servant murdered a monk, and was subsequently slain by one of the Bailiff's men sent to arrest him. When a human skeleton was unearthed on Lihou in 1962, there was speculation that these might be the remains of the monk's murderer, perhaps buried in a shallow grave.

In 1926 an iodine factory was opened on the island, but the owner had to close it when South American producers undercut his prices. During the Occupation of the Channel Islands from 1940-45, the Germans used Lihou for target practice; after the war it was bought by two ex-RAF men. An American company that wanted to build a hotel there began negotiations to buy it, but abandoned the project because no source of water could be found.

Meanwhile, a wealthy landowner

Lihou: you can walk to it at low tide.

and farmer from Sussex had become spellbound by Lihou, seeing it as an oasis of peace in an increasingly frantic world. Colonel Patrick Wootton and his wife Ann eventually bought the lease in 1961, after tracing one of the owners who had emigrated to South Africa through an advertisement in the *Cape Times*. True to his earlier vision, Pat Wootton introduced in 1965 a summer series of youth camps that annually brought young people from many different countries to spend a fortnight under canvas on the tiny isle. The Colonel believed that Lihou's remote, peaceful environment provided a spiritual breathing space for youngsters caught up with the whirling world and the need to make their way in it.

An effervescent, complex personality, Pat Wootton was one of two private individuals to sue the owners of the *Torrey Canyon* as a matter of principle after oil from the stricken giant tanker badly polluted one of Lihou's bays. After a long fight, he was awarded £750 compensation. He was almost equally incensed when Guernsey decided to ban the smaller island's "stamps" (carriage labels) after the Channel Islands took over the running of their postal services from Britain's General Post Office in 1969. He had been issuing Lihou stamps since 1966 to help fund the youth project, and protested to the Guernsey authorities that Her Majesty's postmaster-general had given him *carte blanche* to run a postal service because the General Post Office was unable to do so. The Lihou postal service went down fighting with the issue of defiant last-day covers, supported by Len Matchan's helicopter flying in from Brecqhou.

The Colonel introduced a rare breed of seaweed-eating sheep from Orkney to Lihou—part of a survival operation mounted by the Rare Breeds Survival Trust. These engaging animals flourished only too well in their new home, and took to swimming across to Guernsey and back regularly to raid local residents' gardens. The flock has since been sold by the present owners of

Gull's nest on the Ecréhous.

Lihou, the Honourable Robin and Patricia Borwick. The couple bought Lihou in 1983 for £274,500, after Pat Wootton moved to Prince Edward Island, Canada, where his wife had been partly brought up.

The Borwicks live all year round in the six-bedroom granite house built on the island by their immediate predecessors, but occupied by them only in summer. They share Lihou with their dog, their donkey and horse, and about 150 assorted ducks, peacocks, bantams and geese—the latter being particularly fond of a daily dip in the sea. The youth camps are no more, but Robin Borwick and his wife are environment-conscious people who welcome visitors—as long as they come dogless.

Les Minquiers and Les Ecréhous: The final battle to repel French invaders in the Channel Islands took place as recently as 1953. Unlike previous conflicts up and down the centuries, this was a bloodless affair between Jersey (backed by the United Kingdom) and France, fought out in the cool ambience of the International Court of Justice at The Hague. The foothold in question was two groups of rocky islets, **Les Minquiers** (pronounced Minkies) and **Les Ecréhous** reefs. Les Ecréhous lie roughly halfway between Jersey and the Normandy coast of France, while Les Minquiers are situated to the south of Jersey on the way to St. Malo.

The French government claimed that Les Minquiers were a dependency of their own Chausey group of islands, and that Les Ecréhous belonged to France by virtue of a gift in 1203. Learned legal, geographical, geological and historical arguments droned on for several weeks, culminating in a 70-minute judgement favouring British sovereignty of the region under Jersey's jurisdiction.

Jersey continued to be responsible for maintaining customs posts on both reefs. The stone fisherman's cabin at Les Minquiers, bought by the Jersey authorities for £25 in 1909, is the most southerly customs station in the British Isles. Like a similar building on the Ecréhous, acquired for £52 in 1884, it bears the Jersey coat of arms.

The periodic visits of customs officers were unresented if not exactly welcomed by the man who, as "King of the Ecréhous", became the best-known Channel Islander internationally apart from the late Dame of Sark. Alphonse Le Gastelois was born in 1914, in St. Martin, the Jersey parish to which Les Ecréhous belong, and he grew up to acquire a reputation as a loner and eccentric. He "emigrated" to Les Ecréhous in 1961 after coming under suspicion of being the perpetrator of terrifying sexual assaults on children. Fortunately for him, it was Edward Paisnel, the notorious "Beast of Jersey", who was convicted of these crimes 10 years later.

A teddybear figure in woolly hat and wellies, Alphonse lived alone on the reef for 14 years. French yachtsmen and local fishermen would bring provisions for him when they visited Les Ecréhous, and owners of summer weekend cottages on the reef trusted him with their keys, asking him to keep an eye on their properties. At Christmas, a hamper from St. Martin would arrive for the castaway aboard a Jersey government launch. As the years passed, the hermit of Les Ecréhous became something of a celebrity, the subject of articles circulating throughout Europe and of TV documentaries. Absorbed in his rocky kingdom, he accumulated a mass of papers to prove that the reef did not belong to St. Martin, but was held by him for the English Crown by right of long occupation. He finally gave up his claim in 1975 when he returned to Jersey to live more conventionally in a boarding house in St. Helier. Age and hard winters had caught up with Alphonse.

But he had a predecessor who outstayed him. Phillipe Pinel was a Jersey fisherman who lived on the reef from 1848 for 46 years, and was the first "King of the Ecréhous". He was very much a Royalist, and when Queen Victoria visited Jersey in 1857, he presented her—as one sovereign to another—with a basket he had made from dried seaweed.

DURRELL'S DEN

Early spring is bird-sexing time at Gerald Durrell's Jersey Wildlife Preservation Trust, as it is at many specialist zoos. But this zoo, built round the l6th-century Les Augrès Manor, is different. In an operating theatre, well away from the visiting coachloads of tourists, Tony Allchurch, masked and in surgical hospital green, poises his scalpel over two stately white African cranes and 10 Balinese Rothschild's mynahs. Looking on is a group of vets and birdkeepers, a biologist and even a human doctor, together with trainees from Argentina, the Philippines and Bali.

"Nowhere else in the world is bird-sexing performed on these endangered species," says Allchurch, a vet who doubles as the Trust's general administrator. "It's not as easy as it looks to figure out because there are no textbooks on the internal anatomy of rare birds. Ideally what we need is a video camera to keep a record of what we see—but we can't afford one. It's embarrassing to have to admit that we had to borrow a human doctor's endoscope because ours is broken."

Not that the zoo is poverty-stricken these days: Gerald Durrell's international fame as a naturalist, spread through his TV films and best-selling books, inspires support from benefactors the world over. One Canadian grandmother even upped sticks and moved to Jersey to become a full-time volunteer at the zoo.

But running the zoo and associated cooperative conservation ventures around the world is an expensive business. It costs the Trust, which has a Jersey staff of nearly 60, about £1 million a year just to tick over. Feeding the 1,500 animals alone costs £50,000 a year. The island's farmers try to help by donating day-old bull calves, apples and tomatoes; greengrocers supply the occasional lorry-load of bruised peaches; locals collect earwigs and snails; and the Trust has its own organic farm.

Preceding pages: coping with the boom in boating; a Guernsey lane. Left, the Jersey Wildlife Preservation Trust's founder, Gerald Durrell.

As readers of *Menagerie Manor, The Stationary Ark* and other Durrell classics know, it was never the founder's intention to set up a "simple, straightforward zoo" with the usual elephants and giraffes. "The idea behind my zoo was to aid in the preservation of animal life," he wrote, "to build up under controlled conditions breeding stocks…so that, should the worst happen and the species become extinct in the wild state, you have, at least, not lost it forever. Moreover, you have a breeding stock from which you can glean the surplus animals and reintroduce them into their original homes at some future date."

Already, Jersey-reared pink pigeons and

now has affiliates in the U.S. and Canada, 25 years ago. Smitten with "zoo-mania" from the age of two when he discovered a "zoo of sorts" in the central Indian village where he was born, he started assembling his first collection of "everything from minnows to woodlice" before he was seven. The collection became more sophisticated—"everything from eagle owls to scorpions"—when his family moved to Corfu during the 1930s. Back in London during the war years, he landed a job as a student keeper at the Zoological Society of London's country estate, Whipsnade Zoo in Bedfordshire. Then he struck out on his own, leading expeditions to collect animals on behalf of other zoos.

kestrels have been returned to their native Mauritius; thick-billed pepper-green parrots to Arizona; white-winged wood ducks to Thailand; brown rodents called *hutias* to Jamaica; and golden lion tamarins, one of the world's rarest primates, to Brazil.

Most should be sorry to leave, given the quality of care and scientifically formulated diets in Jersey's 30-acre (12-hectare) parkland complex. In the intensive recovery unit of the zoo's modern Vet Centre, you might find a Goeldi's monkey under observation after a bout of diarrhoea, or an ibis with a broken mandible recovering from surgery.

Durrell set up the scientific Trust, which

In 1957, after financing and leading 10 major expeditions to various parts of the world, Durrell decided the time was ripe to start his own zoo. He returned from a six-month West African safari to the Cameroons with a collection of "some 200 assorted denizens of the jungle" which he deposited "temporarily" in his sister's back garden in suburban Bournemouth. But he found it difficult to raise the money needed to realise his dream.

As a last resort, with three best-selling books *(The Bafut Beagles, My Family and Other Animals* and *The Drunken Forest)* under his belt and the prospect of more in the pipeline, Durrell put an unusual proposition to his publisher, Rupert Hart-Davis: why not borrow on these "as yet unconceived masterpieces"? Hart-Davis agreed to stand guarantor for £25,000 if Durrell took out a life-insurance policy for that amount ("just in case I got eaten by a lion before I could repay the loan").

Outcast in the islands: Durrell spent 18 months battling with the local planning authorities over where to site his ready-made zoo. During one cold month, a Bournemouth department store came to his rescue, offering "Durrell's Menagerie" as a Christmas sideshow in its basement. Finally, fed up with "the constipated mentality of local

ing Fort Regent, a site Durrell estimated would cost £25 million to convert into a zoo, he returned to lunch with the Major at his Trinity estate. It was "probably one of the most beautiful manor houses on the island," he recalled. "Here was a huge, walled garden dreaming in the thin sunlight; a great granite wall, thickly planted with waterfalls of rock plants; 15th-century arches, tidy lawns and flowerbeds brimming with colour. All the walls, buildings and outhouses were of beautiful Jersey granite which contains all the subtle colourings of a heap of autumn leaves."

Durrell decided Les Augrès Manor was the perfect site for his zoo. When he learned

government and frightened off by the apparently endless rules and regulations under which every free man in Great Britain has to suffer," Durrell decided to investigate the possibility of starting his own zoo in the Channel Islands.

Again, his publisher came to the rescue with an introduction in Jersey to a retired English gentleman, Major Hugh Fraser, who promised to show him around the island and help him find a suitable property. After see-

Left, meeting endangered species at close range. Above, the Trust's symbol, the Dodo; and Jambo the gorilla.

that the Major, worried about the upkeep of his vast estate, had decided to move back to England to a smaller property, Durrell agreed on the spot to rent Les Augrès with an option to buy it at a later date when the zoo became more firmly established. It took three days to get the necessary permits and, less than a year later, in the spring of 1959, the Jersey Zoo opened its gates to the public.

The early years saw quite a few casualties. Many of Durrell's favourite monkeys, for example, succumbed to a mysterious ailment known as creeping paralysis; eventually an antidote was found through massive injections of D3 phosphorous. Vitamins today feature prominently in the diets of the zoo's nearly 200 primates and many of the other species, as do locally baked nutcakes laced with aniseed.

Few of the early collection, with the exception of N'Pongo, the zoo's first female gorilla, and Bali, the first female Borneo orang-utan, survive today. N'Pongo, now over 30, is a grandmother, and still breeding. So are nearly half the zoo's 100-plus other species, including the ring-tailed, ruffed and Mayotte brown lemurs, Guenther's gecko, Telfair's skink, Cuban and Jamaican boas, and plumed basilisks. Some golden lion tamarins have become so prolific that they've had to be put on the equivalent of the

nappies, Walt Disney characters decorated the walls, and closed-circuit TV cameras recorded their movements.

N'Pongo's mate Jambo, the zoo's famous 25-stone (160-kg) silver-back gorilla, is said to be the most prolific gorilla in captivity: at last count, he had fathered 15 offspring and taken a third mate. She recently produced a daughter, Sakina (meaning "Happy Family" in Swahili), who weighed in at four lbs (nearly two kg) and was fed by her mother four hours after birth.

"The gentle giant", as Jambo was nick-named when he hit the headlines for standing vigil over a young boy who fell unconscious into his family compound, is worth, in

birth-control pill. "We'd prefer not to be giving them hormone implants," says Tony Allchurch, "but there are a limited number of places in the world which can handle these endangered species."

Few of today's new-born animals require hand-rearing, with the exception of sad souls like Gremlin, a silvery marmoset rejected by his mother after his twin died of pneumonia. But N'Pongo's first infants had their own separate nursery in the manor house, complete with incubators, wash basin, playpen, thermostatically controlled radiators, baby oil, feeding bottles and plastic pants; there was a washing machine and tumble drier for

publicity terms, all of the £4,000 the Trust paid the Basle Zoo for him in 1972—the most it has paid for any animal. He has become almost as important to the zoo as the extinct Dodo, its symbol. His image is emblazoned on its livery and the BBC's *Wildlife Magazine* has even created an annual "Jambo Award" in his honour. Jambo lives with his three mates, two sons, a daughter and two unrelated young gorillas in a large modern enclosure: inside there is underfloor heating and a spacious gymnasium area; the outside play area extends over half an acre of undulating ground with boulders, climbing frames and natural vegetation.

Like more than half the animals at the zoo, Jambo has a foster parent: an eccentric animal lover from Ohio. Under the zoo's unique single-parent adoption scheme, she contributes £500 a year toward his support—less than half of what it costs to feed him. She has also adopted a colobus monkey, a Rodrigues fruit bat and a terrapin.

Just like home: Throughout the zoological park, the Trust has tried, wherever possible, to cultivate the native habitat of the animals' wildlife— and with some success, thanks to the temperate Jersey climate. In the white-throated wallabies' paddock, for example, there are various species of eucalyptus from Australia. Elsewhere, there are

been successful. Pedro and Patronica, the first spectacled bears, successfully bred twice during the 1970s; but one of their offspring, Spencer, who spent his adolescence "holidaying" at Basle Zoo, failed to continue the line when he returned to Jersey to be mated with Inca, the resident female. Both have since been despatched to Rotterdam Zoo and been replaced by another pair on loan from other zoos.

But the Trust has had success with breeding the endangered snow leopard. Its first pair of cubs was born last summer to snow leopards on permanent loan from Seattle and Zurich.

Unlike other zoos, the Trust has set up a

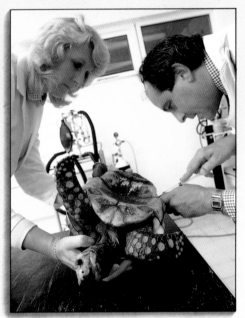

dawn redwoods and other rare species.

The gigantic red, rope-haired orangutans, inveterate nest builders, have taken to their new open-plan bedrooms. It's worth lingering at the zoo until closing time just to watch Giles and Bali and their mates prepare their beds, complete with canopies which they construct over their heads out of discarded newspapers and cardboard.

Not all the breeding programmes have

Left, the zoo's new gorilla compound. Above: left, a golden lion tamarin and family; and right, Tony Allchurch takes a blood sample from a red-footed tortoise.

mini-university next door to the zoological gardens to instruct students from all over the world in methods of caring for the wild in captivity. Over 230 trainees from 22 countries have graduated from the new International Training Centre for the Captive Breeding and Conservation of Endangered Species, started up with funds raised by the Trust's U.S. sister organisation, and opened in 1984 by the Trust's Patron, Princess Anne.

Once the zoo was out of financial danger, Durrell left its day-to-day running to the Trust, dividing his time between globe-trotting and his home in the south of France. But his work goes on.

Birdwatching guides who take parties to Alderney have a money-making ruse which they work on their clients for the cost of a pint or two of beer. A few pence per person is collected for a sweepstake to benefit the party member who sees the first magpie. If none is seen, the kitty goes to the guide. The leaders always win, even when escorting Channel Islanders: the magpie, which is numerous throughout the archipelago, can't be found in Alderney.

Moles can be, though. They also push their unwelcome mounds up in Jersey, but not Guernsey or Herm. And hedgehogs, occurring in all the islands, were introduced into car-free Sark by the Seigneur's wife, Diana Beaumont, only recently. They still get killed on Sark's roads—run over by horses and carts—possibly proving that rolling in front of a vehicle is the most popular way for a hedgehog to commit *harakiri*.

The differences in wildlife distribution between the islands are large and often cannot be explained. Jersey has 120 breeding species of bird but a mere 70 or so nest in Guernsey. Loose-flowered orchids are scarce in most of the islands, bar Guernsey, where many thousands of the plants grow in old boggy meadows. A barefooted walk across any public land can be done with impunity, except on Herm Common where the burnet rose covers the ground. Its delayed action thorns allow soft unsuspecting feet to get several metres over the inviting sward before pain strikes, making retreat an act of self-inflicted agony.

No dippers: The gap between the U.K.'s natural history and that of the islands is even wider; familiar creatures like deer, foxes, hares and badgers are missing. So too are rooks, jays and some members of the titmouse family. One ornithologist, studying dippers, arrived on a two-week research programme to find his work completed after just one telephone call. "We have no dip-

pers," he was told by a local birdwatcher.

The Channel Islands are the nail on a finger of Mediterranean species which runs along the French Atlantic coast from Portugal and Spain, pointing at the southern counties of England. The delicate plants, insects and birds which inhabit this strip of usually mild terrain struggle to maintain a toehold and their presence is sometimes threatened by slight shifts in climate.

One such shift occurred when a heat-

seeking frost of great severity sucked all life from palms, eucalyptus trees and the rocket-like giant echiums which are cultivated in the islands. The frost also wiped out most of the Dartford warbler populations, leaving large gorse slopes in Alderney, Guernsey and Jersey all but devoid of the Burgundy-coloured songster's sharp rattling notes. They have been seen by lighthouse keepers on Les Casquets, northwest of Alderney, attracted by the flashing beam on misty autumn nights, so there is a hope that this diminutive warbler, which has paid the price for not migrating south in winter, will return.

Other Mediterranean species fared better.

Preceding pages, Alderney's wild north coast. Left, Alderney bursts into bloom. Right, a shag and its young.

The green lizards living around the skirts of Jersey's Mont Orgueil Castle and beneath the defensive walls of Fort George in Guernsey escaped the frost during their subterranean hibernation, as did the Glanville fritillary butterflies which danced over the cliff paths to lay their eggs on plantain leaves the following June. Mole crickets singing their summer love songs from burrows in the sandy soils also escaped the cold.

Threat to the ormer: A marine biologist in Guernsey measures temperature changes in the ocean by calculating the ratio between a northern and southern species of acorn barnacle. They meet in the English Channel and, as the sea gets hotter or colder, their

tions of 10p per mollusc. Octopus and dolphin used also to be common but have almost vanished from local waters. Grey seals are seen rarely, fishing in sheltered shallow bays.

Nature conservation in some islands equals much which is done in the United Kingdom, while in others it is nonexistent. Guernsey and Jersey have the best records but took opposing paths to get the final results. Herm has a happy compromise between the demands of a modern farm manager and those of the vast visiting public who want to see the island's natural attractions. Alderney and Sark people tend to conserve by default, finding that leaving things wild is

respective populations change. The northern species is winning and the cause—lower sea temperatures—has hit the Channel Islands' most prized delicacy, the ormer. These huge Mediterranean relatives of the limpet are collected from beneath large rocks and, although they need 24 hours' cooking to be edible, the delicate flavour make them firm favourites. Their decline was so lamented that the States of Guernsey spent thousands of pounds on a breeding programme from which the first commercial ormers have reached the market. In 1988 they launched an "adopt an ormer" scheme, offering ormer-shaped car stickers in return for dona-

easier than war with nature—yet still attracts the tourists.

A Sarkee, asked if he should have weeded poisonous ragwort from a field in which his horses were grazing, said that he was going to do the job in a few days. This, according to a familiar story, prompted the questioner to ask if there is an equivalent word in Sark-French patois to the Spanish *mañana*, doing tomorrow what you should do today. "We have nothing for that sort of urgency," came the laconic reply.

Alderney people tend to be equally laidback. New fields are occasionally ploughed for potatoes or corn, but as summer settles on to the island the attractions of fishing, chatting to yachtsmen in the many bars, and the weekly round of drinks parties seem to distract the would-be farmer, leaving crops of inviting weeds for the finches which attract birdwatchers who follow in the autumn. The fields soon return to their former state.

Both Alderney and Sark make the most of their natural assets. They have superb cliff paths which wander through natural flower gardens of thrift, stonecrop, gorse and prostrate broom. Banks of heather grow on the more exposed sites and in sheltered valleys small woods ring to the sound of singing blackcap, garden warblers, chiffchaff and even the rare golden oriole in spring.

bours, lack of a sewage system coats the rock in white, foul-smelling guano, and hot calm days force the birds to take flight over the backs of family, friends and neighbours before reaching the peace and isolation of fishing grounds at sea.

The boat trip used to include a visit to Blue Stone Bay for a peek at naturists basking on the rocks, but the universal redundancy of bikini tops has ended the thrill of that sport. Instead, Cocq Lihou is visited by the boat and her passengers who see and hear Alderney's most recently established colony of kittiwakes calling out their onomatopaeic names as a greeting to mates on the narrow ledges.

Alderney has a boatman who takes parties of visitors on the *Beverley Rose* to see the puffins bobbing on the waters around Burhou, an island which is closed to the public from April to mid-July as a conservation measure. The trip also calls at Les Etacs where 2,000 pairs of gannets live within a beak's-length of each other, raising their chicks in a bird city which holds all the ingredients for a nervous breakdown. Overcrowding results in fights between neighbours.

Left, an ormer, threatened by temperature changes. Above, superb cliff paths lead to natural flower gardens in the dunes.

Sark's seabird ledges are observed from cliffs above Port du Moulin where guillemots huddle together on Les Autlets rock like penguins. There they incubate pear-shaped eggs which roll in tight circles if kicked by a departing parent rather than drop into the sea below. Sand crocus stick their minute heads out of the grassy banks overlooking the colony, opening in sunshine to justify the botanist's lens which must be used to see the full beauty of the tiny flowers. Little Sark, with its desolate-looking silvermine chimneys, is home to a small number of puffins in Pot Bay while fulmars have included the island's cliffs in their worldwide expansion plans.

War breaks out: Jersey's conservation movement was spilt by dissension and argument, with the result that several organizations claimed that they looked after the wildlife. La Société Jersiaise pontificated, local members of the Royal Society for the Protection of Birds could do nothing—the society's charter does not allow them to buy land in the Channel Islands—and the Jersey Conservation and Naturalists Society split the movement.

The National Trust of Jersey owns some of the best sites in the island, but like its Guernsey counterpart, is a body independent of the U.K. trust. As such, both are more responsive to local pressures than the National Trust and people's wishes are sometimes placed before the interests of wildlife. It was left to the States of Jersey to pick up the pieces, appointing a conservation officer. But, as an officer of the States, he is not free to criticise when other departments engage in unsympathetic treatment of natural habitats and conservationists in Guernsey have resisted the temptation to press for a similar post to be set up. The work of Jersey's conservation officer led to the establishment of Les Mielles and Les Quennevais conservation area with its information centre at Kempt Tower. The area is considered to be a naturalist's paradise with one of the richest sand dune habitats in Britain containing 1,000 plant species or more, including 16 listed in the Red Data Book of endangered species.

La Mare au Seigneur, known to Jersey folk as St. Ouen's Pond, has a similar reputation for migrating birds. The amazingly shy Cetti's warbler was observed through a telescope from her lounge by a keen naturalist who was able to record the first breeding record of the species in the British Isles. The nest is now in Jersey Museum. The pond is also used by vast flocks of swallows and martins, reed and sedge warblers, and many birds of prey which stop off in the island.

Two headlands in Jersey contrast the differences in climate and habitat between north and south. Les Landes in the north is the largest area of heath on the island. Due to the wind, few shrubs or trees are able to raise their heads high and dwarf scrub heath is the dominant vegetation. Glanville fritillary butterflies, a few remaining Dartford warblers and, according to local rumour, the protected agile frog occur. In contrast, Noirmont Headland on the south coast is covered with tall gorse, bramble scrub and a few evergreen Mediterranean holm oaks. Autumn squill, spotted rockrose and the declining Jersey forget-me-not are found in the area.

In Guernsey nature conservation is almost the sole responsibility of La Société Guernesiaise whose members provide the money, labour and political incentive to protect the island's natural resources. They moved into land ownership when the Silbe Nature Reserve, a wooded west coast valley in St. Peter's, was given to the society in 1975. Other sites were bought and La Société now own fields around L'Eree and Rue du Vicheries, which contain six of every 10 British loose-flowered orchids.

"They are called Jersey orchids in U.K. and Jersey," Guernsey botanists will tell you with horror in their voices. "But we call them pougencoute in Guernsey patois, meaning Pentecost or Whitsun orchid after the season in which they flower."

Splendid sites: The States of Guernsey became involved in conservation by handing management of several sites to La Société. Prize of these is a conservation area made up of a marsh, shingle bank and seashore at L'Eree. The shingle bank, owned by the States, forms a barrier to the sea at Rue de la Rocque, and is home to little robin, halberd-leaved orache, Cornish mallow and progenitor of the brassica family of cultivars, sea kale. It lies between the society's reserve at La Claire Mare—a reed bed with wader scrape and birdwatching hide—and a beach which is planned as the island's first marine nature reserve.

La Société also advises the States on the management of Port Soif Headland with its locally rare bee orchids and the area around Fort Hommet which has a low-lying seacliff habitat. One of Guernsey's oldest companies, Bucktrout Ltd, gave the management of the Vale Pond to the society. The reserve has played host to a multitude of rare migrant birds and is the site of several botanical gems including the bulbous foxtail, a grass species not found in the other islands. A hide, with access from the main road running past, overlooks the area.

Dutch elm disease has brought some of the

most severe modern changes to the Channel Islands. Elms were a large proportion of the the few trees found in Alderney and have died, along with huge stands in Sark and Jersey. But in Guernsey, where the States fear the effect of increased wind speeds on the cost of heating greenhouses, a strict felling programme and a scheme to give away trees have kept the disease in check and ensured that alternatives are planted. Many of the free trees died—through lack of care in the first two years: unprotected at ground level, they were killed by weed cutters and rabbits, or because they were the wrong species chosen for the site. Stakes and guards are now given with each tree.

Myxomatosis threatened to change the delicate habitats found on Herm when it was introduced a few years ago, killing the rabbits which ate the rank, coarse vegetation but leaving the more delicate species of plant. Here lay the quandary of Herm's management. Should they pursue modern farming techniques, which would see an end to the islands's natural assets enjoyed by so many visitors, or watch pests, weeds and people put paid to a potentially prosperous farm? The compromise was fairly reached. Large

The islands celebrate their horticultural heritage with annual flower festivals.

sections of the island, including a skirt of scrub draping the farm and the common which has a wonderful sand dune habitat, were left wild.

But intensive farming supports a top herd of cows, providing an extra bonus for tourists who can take advantage of the 8.30 a.m. "milk boat" from Guernsey to get a full day on the island. Ravens and puffins nest on the south coast, Brent geese winter in the shallow bays along the western side of Herm and white campion grows among the boulders which separate the fields.

Cliff paths, running along the highest parts of Jersey and Guernsey, mark a peculiar difference between the islands. Jersey's path is along the northern cliffs with views over the other Channel Islands; the land slopes away for eight miles (13 km) to reach the sea along the sandy south coast. Jersey's farmland faces south and enjoys a milder climate than Guernsey which faces north and needs greenhouses to protect the crops from cooler winters. Jersey farmers specialise in early outdoor potatoes and vegetables while in Guernsey the cost of higher horticultural investment is met by bigger incomes from the production of flowers and tomatoes under glass.

Real battles: Both islands celebrate the success of their horticultural industries with flower festivals in which huge wire-framed floats, mounted on trailers, are covered with blooms and drawn past great crowds of spectators. The festivals are held in August, and years ago ended with the ultimate test of design and construction of the floats—people swarmed over them, ripping out the blooms as missiles to be hurled at each other, giving the world-famous name to the Battle of Flowers. The winner was the float which best stood the test of destruction. Naturally, excitement was high, excesses taken, and a number of serious injuries occurred in the carnage.

The battles have ended but the name lives on. Other changes have seen the introduction of a few floats made from paper flowers instead of the less reliable, weather prone, field-grown marigolds, asters, carnations and hydrangeas. The floats are parked around the islands and charity collecting boxes left at the feet of the fantasy figures until, like most dreams, they fade to become charnel caricatures of their earlier glory.

There is abundant archaeological evidence to suggest that prehistoric man, mysterious builder of unfathomable architecture, found the Channel Islands as attractive a base for his operations as bankers and offshore settlers do today. The geographical accident that made these little islands into stepping stones between two hazardous mainland coasts presents modern archaeologists with something of a bonus. The archipelago was the point where, many hundreds and even thousands of years ago, different cultures crossed and met, mainly through trading. Sometimes these influences—on pottery, for example—were given distinctive local adaptations.

Bob Burns, assistant curator of the Guernsey Museum, who directed recent excavations establishing St. Peter Port for the first time as a thriving Roman trading post, points out that "island hopping" made good sense to our ancestors. "They were frightened of the sea, and naturally would stop off here on their way across the Channel."

Remarkable man: Guernsey is particularly lucky in having a number of sites that have been left very much as their prehistoric builders conceived them. They include the impressive passage graves of Le Déhus and La Varde, 42 feet (13 metres) long and 13 feet (four metres) wide. Preservation of the integrity of Neolithic chambered tombs dating back in some cases to 3,000 B.C., and the rescue of quantities of grave furniture found in them is due to one remarkable Guernseyman, Frederick Corbin Lukis. In the best traditions of the self-taught, Victorian "gentleman" scientist, Lukis had wide interests—conchology, natural history, geology, and archaeology above all.

When he was 23, he excavated La Varde in 1811 with his elderly relative, Joshua Gosselin, the first Guernseyman to make a study of prehistoric remains. Afterwards, Lukis dug up his native island with unflagging zeal for over half a century to unearth the secrets

Preceding pages, Sark's west coast. Left, Jersey's Dolmen de Faldouet. Right, Jersey's Grosnez Castle.

of a megalithic civilization. He also made archaeological expeditions to Alderney and Jersey. In those days, when archaeology was little understood, Lukis was way ahead of his time. He made detailed records of his findings, and would bribe farmers not to tamper with strange boulders found in their fields. And he astonished the locals by paying cash for earthy old pots and bits of flint.

He was one of the first archaeologists to realise that megalithic remains were not

"druids' altars" as was generally supposed, but the burial places of a much older people. His four sons inherited his enthusiasm and helped in the field work, and his three daughters made hundreds of drawings of stone monuments, urns, axes and other artefacts. Lukis died in 1871, leaving his entire collection and voluminous records to Guernsey.

The chances of turning up a completely untouched Neolithic site in a small island like Guernsey—already well worked over by the Lukis family—are pretty slim. Yet that is exactly what happened in 1978. Members of the very active archaeological section of La Société Guernesiaise (the local cultural body) spotted two large stones, near the fifth green of the golf course, whose composition suggested that they had been transported there. Following an exploratory dig, Dr. Ian Kinnes of the British Museum was called in. Over the next three years, he carried out a total excavation of the complex Les Fouaillages site for the Guernsey government's Ancient Monuments Committee.

The significance of the findings at Les Fouaillages—involving levels of human activity from 4,500 B.C. to about 2,000 B.C.—is still being assessed. But it is thought that the strange, original level could be the first stone monument ever known in Western Europe—a bridge between primi-

monuments to General Henry Conway, a former Governor of Jersey, who accepted this "feeble but sincere tribute of our gratitude".

Dubbed "Little Master Stonehenge" because of its likeness to Stonehenge, the site had been discovered two years earlier during military reinforcements of what was then Town Hill, but is now the Fort Regent leisure centre. Dauntless General Conway had the capstones and 45 megaliths—each more than 23 feet (seven metres) in diameter and weighing around 140 tons—shipped across the Channel and then transported by barge up the Thames to his Park Place estate at Henley-on-Thames. The re-erected stone

tive structures of wood and the familiar, massive dolmens. Six decorated vessels of the Bandkeramic group were discovered in association with this first stone layer. The pottery has been found so far only in conjunction with evidence of building in wood.

For lack of a Lukis, Jersey has fared less well. It was not until the opening of La Hougue Bie tomb this century that the larger island could lay claim to excavation of a significant prehistoric site that had not been pillaged, damaged or just rearranged more tastefully. In 1787, the Vingtaine de la Ville (town councillors) of St. Helier actually presented a complete group of prehistoric

circle of General Conway's "Jersey Temple" stands there still—200 miles (320 km) from the monument's homeland. In 1984 it was listed by the U.K. Department of the Environment, and a year later Jersey unveiled a plaque at Fort Regent to mark the probable site of the lost dolmen of Le Mont de La Ville.

Tomb robbers: A more fitting destiny awaited the 43-foot (13-metre) man-made mound of La Hougue Bie, because it was acquired in 1919 by La Société Jersiaise,

Le Trépied Neolithic dolmen in Guernsey, reputed to be the meeting place of witches.

which was founded in 1873. The mound, crowned by one 12th-century and one 16th-century chapel, was excavated in 1924 to reveal a chambered tomb. Dr. Arthur Mourant was a member of that excavation team as a 20-year-old undergraduate. He recalls that the structure of the passage grave was in such perfect condition that it was presumed to have been untouched since Neolithic times. But the actual contents of the tomb chambers had been scrabbled out into the middle of the floor, and all the bones and pottery broken up, indicating that at some stage looters had broken in.

The archaeological and geological museums of La Société Jersiaise today are at La Hougue Bie complex, but plans for a new extension at the society's Jersey Museum in St. Helier revolve round an ambitious presentation for the island's prestigious Old Stone Age site, La Cotte at St. Brelade. Meanwhile, the carefully preserved remains of woolly mammoths that roamed Jersey 150,000 years ago (when it was joined to the Continent), and other Paleolithic marvels languish out of public view in temperature controlled storage. The animals' skulls weigh about 300 lbs (130 kgs) apiece.

Worldwide scientific interest in La Cotte was heightened with the publication of a major report in 1987. Incorporating the work of the late Professor Charles McBurney, with contributions by scientists from five different countries, the £60 tome is edited by Dr. Paul Callow of Cambridge University and Jean Cornford. The complex site encompasses a time scale of a quarter of a million years, and records how man interacted with his changing environment.

The bones of mammoth and rhino found heaped at the foot of the site's 98-ft (30-metre) drop prove that primitive man used ravine systems such as La Cotte as "funnel" traps, stampeding herds of prehistoric beasts over the cliff edge to their deaths. Teeth that were discovered are believed to be the only true Neanderthal remains found so far in the British Isles, and more stone artefacts of the same period have been recovered from La Cotte than in the whole of Britain. While evidence of Roman occupation in Jersey continues to be slight, there have been dramatic discoveries on land and sea in Guernsey fixing St. Peter Port firmly on the Roman map for the first time. Excavations at the town site of La Plaiderie uncovered two substantial buildings with Roman roof tiles that were almost certainly warehouses. These, and a wealth of other items, establish St. Peter Port as a waterfront trading post.

Revelations of Roman activity on land were matched at sea by local diver Richard Keen's exciting discovery of a unique wreck in St. Peter Port harbour. The Gallo-Roman merchant vessel had been preserved below the silt for 18 centuries, until propwash from a new generation of cross-Channel ferries began to expose and then to erode it.

Dr. Margaret Rule, who raised the Tudor warship "Mary Rose" masterminded a successful underwater excavation in 1985. The rescue operation was a race against time to prevent the 23-metre-long vessel—never seen before out of the pages of history books—from being broken up. The recovered timbers are now being restored for reassembly and display by the Guernsey Maritime Trust.

Wine drinkers: Roman remains were also unearthed at an important Iron Age site of around 100 B.C. at King's Road, on the outskirts of St. Peter Port. Sophisticated artefacts that include a sword and sheath and a brooch have been carefully examined at Oxford University, and point to the existence of an elite community who drank wine imported from Northern Italy before the coming of the Romans.

In the past few years, Guernsey archaeologists have filled in a number of blanks from around 250 B.C. to A.D. 1250 in the island's history. Four seasons of excavations for the Ancient Monuments Committee at 13th-century Castle Cornet has built up a vivid profile of the stronghold's development, and supplied details of sieges and bloody battles with the French.

A pet ambition of Bob Burns is eventually to uncover the mystery of Corbière Castle, which used to dominate the sea below the cliffs at Guernsey's west coast. A sketch of the fortress, drawn in 1680 for an official survey on Channel Island defences for Charles II, is tantalising proof that once it was there. "A great deal has been revealed in recent years," says Mr Burns, "and there are plans to develop further sites. But the Channel Islands are full of archaeological goodies—there will be plenty left for future generations to discover."

In heathen times, in Jersey, lived a band of unscrupulous beachcombers who left nothing to chance. If stormy weather wouldn't wreck ships and sweep their cargo to shore, then stormy weather would have to be given a hand. And so, at the height of a storm, they would build huge fires above the most treacherous rocks at Corbière and L'Etacq as a signal to worried captains that here, below, was sanctuary from the wind and waves.

As the unwary captain steered his ship closer to the shore it would be caught by the tide, thrown against the rocks and torn apart. A day or two later, and the cargo would be washed ashore by tides more kindly to the St. Ouen wreckers, as they were called, than to the foreign captain and his crew. Death was inevitable: any seamen who survived the raging water would be murdered by the wreckers.

This is one of Jersey's best-known legends, which has been altered dramatically over the centuries and glamorised, particularly by Victorian writers, who were determined to give their readers value for money.

Father's curse: One account, for example, tells of an old man's vain efforts to save his daughter's life as his ship, one of five on their way from America to Spain, was lured towards Corbière in 1495. The wreckers, watching from the headland, heard the old man cry out: "Save my daughter's life and all my chests of gold will be yours. Refuse my plea and I condemn you all to die within a year." They ignored his cries and calmly watched as the ships and everyone aboard them were destroyed in the howling seas below. Exactly a year later, a black, howling storm swept in from the west and tore to pieces the islanders, their homes and the forest to the north of the bay. Only sand and tree stumps remained.

Such legends were told and retold in melodramatic style. "Even as their fiendish laughter broke out, a cresting wave swept the decks of the doomed ship and carried the

Left, old women were often suspected of sorcery. Right, stormy seas, the stuff of legends.

young girl into the depths of the sea," was one 1856 version. But the legends contained nuggets of truth. At one time the Seigneur (lord) of St. Ouen, who could claim any wreckage thrown on to the beaches bordering his property, had an arrangement with his parishoners whereby they would be paid for anything brought to the manor. And contemporary records show that in 1494, or thereabouts, one Spanish ship (not five) carrying wine was wrecked off Corbière and

that many hundreds of barrels were washed ashore, to be purloined by the lord.

From this story the legend grew and to it were added other elements of truth—as well as the tale of the old man's curse. For at one time there was a forest to the north of St. Ouen, and old maps show a château near L'Etacq where, today, there is only sea. The forest disappeared long before the 15th century, the château in more recent times.

The legend contains a name which appears in many Channel Island stories —de Carteret, hereditary lords of St. Ouen. The regularity with which their name appears should surprise no-one who knows Channel

Island history: over the centuries the family has bred easily and regularly (Margaret de Carteret, for example, gave birth to 20 sons and a daughter in the 15th century) and it was Helier de Carteret who, in 1565, took 40 parishoners with him to populate Sark.

Presumably Pierre de Carteret, who (legend has it) lived in Sark in the 18th century, was some distant cousin, although the islanders hated him and called him a witch. Known locally as "*le vieux diable*", he was said to have employed small devils and spoken to them in their own language. He built a boat in a barn one morning and the Serquiaise watched in amazement as he launched it at Creux harbour. How he man-

their bodies, and would shout relentlessly across the sea to the small priory of Lihou "*Tcheit d' la haout, Marie d' Lihaou*" ("Fall from up there, Mary of Lihou").

There seems to be shreds of truth behind such tales: certain weird men and women did meet, in both Guernsey and Jersey, for devil worship. In rigidly puritanical islands, any hint of scandal was seen as a sign that the devil was in someone, and the best way of removing him, it was thought, was to burn the afflicted person and to scatter the ashes to the four winds. In Guernsey, the condemned man was burnt alive in the aptly-named "Vale of Misery". In Jersey, he was tied to a post in the market square, strangled from

aged to get it into the water they never knew because the barn was far from the sea and the boat was too large to get through the door. They decided that he had used black magic.

However, there is no record of his having been to trial for "*l' horrible et énorme crime de sorcellerie*" although between June 1, 1550, and the end of October, 1661, over 170 Channel Island "witches" were tried. Tales about their antics abound. They danced naked at La Rocqueberg in Jersey, for example, and bewitched passing fishermen into joining in their fun. They met at Le Catioroc, in Guernsey, where they rubbed *le verjus au diable*, a hallucinatory cream, on

behind, then burnt.

All such executions attracted huge crowds, not least because public execution was one of the few forms of recreation the courts allowed. There was also the remote possibility that the devil might come down and whisk away his favourite son or daughter before the executioner had earned his pay.

A Guernsey legend, set in 1640, illustrates this belief. An old woman "of four score years and more" was sentenced to death for sorcery although she was convinced that no human hand could kill her. As she was escorted down the steps from La Tour Beauregard toward *La Vallée de Misère*, a great black raven appeared. The old woman threw a length of black cotton towards the bird which flew away, holding tightly to one end, while the woman, clinging to the other, was lifted into the air. It seemed to the waiting crowd that the witch would make good her escape until a young man, standing on higher ground, threw his staff at the bird which, stunned, immediately released the thread. The old woman fell back to earth where she was recaptured and burnt. The lad, lauded as a hero, enjoyed his triumph over evil but within a year he, too, had died—choked to death in his sleep.

Sadly, from a storyteller's point of view,

a passing witch in the belief that to do so protected them from evil.

If such superstitious practices didn't work, there was always the ultimate deterrent, death, as the *greffier* (chief clerk of the court) was well aware. While writing down the court's verdict in the ledgers, as the magistrate sentenced yet another islander to death, the *greffier* would doodle in the margin pictures of the condemned man hanging above the flames. The more people condemned (for example, three of the Massi family in 1624), the larger the picture. These sketches can be seen in the States' archives.

In Guernsey the most prominent witch-hunter was Amice de Carteret, bailiff and

there were no witch trials in 1640. But why quibble with fact when there is a good moral tale to tell?

The sting at the end of that tale served as a reminder to islanders that the devil was a vindictive loser who would exact a terrible revenge when crossed. For this reason, they heated nails in a pan over the fire on Friday evenings to deny him access to their houses, or they carried quicksilver (mercury) when they went fishing, or spat on the shadow of

Left, devil worship on Guernsey. Above, frogs dancing on the witches' Sabbath; and the end of a supposed witch.

magistrate, a member of the St. Ouen de Carteret family with a tally of 35 witches burnt and 19 banished between 1601 and 1635. In Jersey, the chief scourge was George Paulet, bailiff at the end of the 16th century, who ordered the execution of 18 witches from 35 trials. Paulet's daughter, coincidentally, was married to a de Carteret.

The devil gets everywhere, of course, which is why, when making dough, Channel Island housewives traditionally make five dents in the pastry before placing it to rise, make a sign of the cross and say "*au nom de feu, soit*". Presumably, if it doesn't rise, no-one has been listening.

SAILING CLOSE TO THE WIND

Show a landsman a chart of the Channel Islands and you might persuade him that its printer had been incompetent. So many rocks, heads and treacherous wave-washed reefs are marked that they could be taken for the smudges of poor workmanship. The truth, of course, is that the reefs really are there, so it's lucky that today's yachtsmen have the benefit of modern cartography and a buoyage system to help them through the chaos of rugged granite and unpredictable water. Certainly, if a complete picture of its hazards were not available, the entire Channel Island sea area would be as lethal to strangers as an unmapped minefield.

That sounds like a daunting introduction to the delights of island waters, but anyone who has cruised them will quickly say that the dangers ordinarily do no more than add spice to the routines of sailing. The interest of coping with the navigational challenges outweighs the inconvenience of extra vigilance.

Flood tide perils: Besides what may be described as fixed hazards, island waters also try to intimidate with their famous tides. These can have a range of well over 32 feet (10 metres) between low- and high-water and they move so many cubic miles of sea that tremendous forces are exerted by their flux and reflux. The influence spreads throughout the area but nowhere is it felt more powerfully than around Alderney, particularly in the passages north and south of the island, the Swinge and the Race. On the flood tide the whole Atlantic Ocean does its best to force its way into the English Channel and in doing so it creates fearsome tidal streams which have been logged at almost 10 knots.

Such conditions occur only in restricted zones on the very biggest of big spring tides, but the Swinge or the Race on only average form can be monsters if the weather is less than perfect. A wind howling against a contrary tidal flow can whip up the sea so that it looks more like a white-water river in full spate than a cruising ground for pleasure craft. Overfalls (a word which is sprinkled liberally over charts of the islands) make matters even worse where tidal runs scour rough ground on the seabed.

Again this sounds like bad public relations for the islands; but, in practice, conditions suitable only for Cape Horn veterans are rare. In summer the chances are that even the

narrows with the most fearsome reputations will be docile. Under the influence of light airs the short, tumultuous, confused seas that make such good background for bar-room chats are transformed into glassy glides as clear as chalkland brooks. Care is still needed if swift currents are not to push a boat off its intended heading and into trouble, yet on many days the sun will beat down, the breeze will be gentle and bikinis may even be more in order than oilskins.

Serious sailing: Once the physical threats, real and imaginary, of the islands have been braved, what is left for the yachtsman visiting Jersey, Guernsey or the smaller isles?

Preceding pages, sailboarding off Guernsey. Left, anchored off Alderney. Right, preparing to cast off from St. Peter Port.

The answer rather depends on where the yachtsman is coming from, because the Channel Islands are the objective for two distinct boating invasions. One originates in France, the other in the United Kingdom.

Le yachting is a passion among many Frenchmen—including those going to sea for the first time. It's not surprising, therefore, that the passage seems to be the crucial matter for the southern visitors who pour out of St. Malo and other Breton ports throughout summer.

Many take their sailing so seriously that they make it a point of honour not to use their auxilliary motors until it is absolutely necessary, so any yacht flying the *tricoleur* should be allowed plenty of searoom as she leaves or enters port. Once on dry land, of course, the Continental visitors can soak up what for them is the English atmosphere and enjoy shopping for duty-free whisky or chain-store woollens.

Merely getting afloat can also be the main concern of the British yellow wellie wearer but it is more likely to be tempered by thoughts of enjoying islands which blend with France and make an excellent staging post on the way to it. Alderney, the hospitable if slightly bleak northern isle, is the logical first landfall for the English armada, and during the summer it's not unusual for the down-to-earth pubs near Braye Harbour to be full of the patrician accents of off-duty professionals temporarily disguised as matelots.

There's nothing wrong with this, although after a particularly heavy cross-Channel influx it's easy for the average holidaymaker to close his eyes and imagine that he has gatecrashed the headquarters of a more than averagely pukka yacht club.

Meeting of equals: Boating can, however, be a great leveller, and when the ketch of the retired doctor from Devon and the sloop full of students from Paris are tied up alongside each other it may be in one of the marinas in Jersey or Guernsey. The latter island has a new 800-berth marina which occupies pride of place in a £16 million land reclamation project next to St. Peter Port Harbour; this is the home of two older berthing areas, including the Victoria Marina, which is where the visitor is most likely to find himself.

In addition to these States of Guernsey facilities, there is a 250-berth marina in private ownership at Beaucette. This was created in the 1960s when visiting Royal Engineers were good enough to blast a channel linking a disused quarry with the open sea. The entrance they cut in the granite is less than 66 feet (20 metres) wide, so a cool head is required during the final approach to this most sheltered of havens.

Topless sunbathers: Jersey's main marina, which first opened its watergate in 1981 and is at the inner extremity of St. Helier Harbour, has only 400 berths. It has nevertheless established quite a reputation, having won the five gold anchors, the top award of the National Yacht Harbours Association. That might come as a surprise to those more used to five-star hotels than five-anchor marinas; the view of the crowded pontoons from the adjacent Victoria Pier is enticing only when the decks of the yachts below are decorated with topless sunbathers. All marinas, with their craft packed together like sampans in some exotic anchorage and washing fluttering from a cat's cradle of rigging, tend to look like floating slums.

However, from the yachtsman's point of view, the sardine-can environment offers plenty of companionship of the right sort and every facility from hot showers to a café serving bacon and egg breakfasts. It's easy to see why marinas are a better bet than a drying mooring half-a-mile from the high-water mark on a featureless expanse of glutinous grey mud.

The choice of places to tie up may begin with modern facilities but it does not end with them. Throughout what geographers (but never locals) might call the archipelago are many sheltered mooring places, a large number of which are protected by stone piers dating from the last century or earlier. Braye Harbour and its massive Admiralty Breakwater in Alderney is an example on the grand scale; altogether more modest, though no less interesting, are havens such as Gorey on Jersey's east coast, Creux in Sark and Herm's fittingly tiny harbour. Just what is on shore at these and other mooring places varies enormously, but the pilot books which explain in precise detail how to approach them in safety are often full of useful information.

Perhaps the best way to enjoy the sheer cliffs of Sark, Jersey's sunbaked southern coast or the low-lying, reef-strewn west of

Guernsey is to find a temporary anchorage where the hook can be dropped for lunch, a swim or sunbathing. Again, pilot books explain where you can venture safely, so don't be too surprised if someone has beaten you to what the chart suggested was going to be a secluded spot. Often the first to the best anchorages are islanders, many of whom are just as keen on sailing as their U.K. and French counterparts.

Warm welcome: Happily, there's not too much "them and us" feeling, and visitors are made welcome. The welcome is extended on land as well, the islands' yacht clubs taking their tradition of reciprocal hospitality very seriously.

Perhaps this is one of the reasons why so many yachtsmen in transit decide to make the Channel Islands their cruising ground for an entire holiday instead of heading on to France or, in the case of the French, England's Channel coast. It is possible to use the islands as mere stopping-off points but much is missed in doing so. Lost, for example, would be the magical experience of slipping quietly past the rocks of Maître Ile and Marmotière at Les Ecréhous to find the

St. Brelade's sailboarders: the islands' protected bays suit first-timers.

peace of the offshore reef's enclosed anchorage set in the midst of a wasteland of kelp and sandbanks. Lost, too, would be the pleasure of cautiously exploring Les Minquiers, the 12-mile (19-km) long rock and shoal plateau south of Jersey which Hammond Innes used as the setting for his novel *The Wreck of the Mary Deare*. Certainly, storms in the area have claimed enough ships over the centuries to make the islands an exciting place for experienced divers.

Although the Channel Islands have been a classic destination for sailors from both sides of the Channel for decades, they are now the starting point for many yachting holidays. Skippered and "bareboat" charters can be arranged to begin at St. Helier or St. Peter Port and the charter firms are only too eager to point out that hiring an expensive hole in the water is more cost-effective than owning one and pouring money into it 12 months a year.

Evidence of how important the sea is to Channel Islanders is provided by everything from the high level of boat ownership to Guernsey's publicity-conscious hosting of international powerboat racing and the prestigious Swan European Regatta for £750,000 superyachts.

Skimming the surface: There is, though, one growth sport *par excellence* which puts sailing within almost anyone's reach. Sailboards are everywhere, both on the sheltered waters of enclosed bays and off surf beaches such as Jersey's St. Ouen, where the swells roll in from mid-Atlantic. There are conditions suitable for windsurfers of all levels of competence because, in anything short of a full gale, there always seems to be a protected shore where conditions are safe. And tuition is no problem in the main islands: there are schools where lessons are given and equipment—including buoyancy aids and wetsuits—is hired.

It's even possible to learn the rudiments of the sport without getting your feet wet. Windsurfing simulators on the beach let you get the feel of board and rig before going out on the water. And, if even that sounds like hard work, wait for the big winds and big seas and watch the funboard sailors. At home even among pounding breakers, they have adapted and extended the repertoire of ordinary surfing to suit their custombuilt wave-jumping sailboards.

FACTS FOR FISHERMEN

Limpet shells by the hundred unearthed at La Hougue Bie, the site in Jersey of a miraculously preserved New Stone Age burial chamber, suggest that Channel Islanders have always had an appetite for seafood. At first, of course, the sea merely supplemented a meagre diet, but eventually regular links with mainland Britain led some medieval wide-boy to the realisation that fish could also supplement income. Conger eels abounded then as they do now and, salted or dried, they found eager buyers across the English Channel. The *saleries* and *éperqueries* (the centres of the salting and drying trades on shore) became such big business that Jersey in the Middle Ages was often referred to as the "Isle of the Congers".

Paradoxically, success with exports of Friday fare led indirectly to the decline of the islands' fisheries. In the 16th century the immense riches of the cod banks of Newfoundland were first discovered and canny Jersey and Guernseymen recognised that, if there were profits in moderate quantities of dried conger, there were fortunes in unlimited quantities of dried cod.

Vessels were equipped, fishermen waved farewell to families and a new era of prosperity began. Channel Island fishing became an activity carried on far from home, although the profits of the operation found their way safely back to Jersey and Guernsey.

While island ships and companies were busily supplying Catholic Europe with cod from the other side of the Atlantic, the home fisheries declined. Declined, that is, until another rich source of revenue was found lurking on the muddy seabed between Jersey and the Norman coast: 1797 was the year of the oyster and soon after the shellfish were discovered, their lucrative exploitation was in full swing. Again, the catches were for the English market and again it looked like a triumph for Channel Island know-how and business acumen.

Preceding pages, the seas around the Channel Islands can be very treacherous. Left and right, the enormous tidal range offers a wide variety of fishing.

The French, traditional and often official enemies, saw things rather differently, and the fleets of dredgers working just off the beaches of France were often harrassed by craft flying the *tricoleur*. In 1822, when 300 boats, 1,500 fishermen and 1,000 shore workers were supported by the Jersey fishery, separate fishing zones eased the rivalry.

"The Battle of the Oyster Shells" of 1838 was, therefore, an insular rather than an international affair, being based on an early

attempt at conservation. The "battle" was joined by 120 oyster smacks which set off to fish protected beds off Grouville, pursued— rather improbably—by the Constable of St. Martin in a rowing boat. The Lieutenant-Governor of Jersey was also involved, calling out the garrison and the militia to march on Gorey, the oystermen's home port. Cannon were fired and 96 skippers found themselves in jail, but, ironically, the only casualty of the otherwise comic-opera episode was the Lieutenant-Governor. He caught a chill which worsened and he died of complications a few days later.

Efforts at control finally gave way to a

free-for-all and, by the close of the 19th century, Channel Island oysters had gone the way of the North American buffalo. You can still find empty oyster shells on the beaches, but the only live ones you will find are those being nurtured carefully in recently established "farms" on the foreshore. The price of greed over the oyster fishery resulted in having a fleet with nothing to catch and for more than half a century fishing was small-scale and for the home market.

Shellfish boom: Gradually, however, lobsters—those blue, heavy-clawed crustaceans which boiling transforms to red-shelled gourmets' delights—became the focus of the harvest of the sea, laying the foundation of today's Channel Islands fishery. A stroll nowadays around Jersey's St. Helier Harbour, St. Peter Port in Guernsey or Braye in Alderney will reveal sturdy wooden boats, often with flared bows that betray French origin, in the 10- to 20-metre category. These crabbers were acquired to cash in on the shellfish boom which began in the 1960s when local enterprise fixed its gaze on the prices fetched by lobsters and crabs in high-class restaurants. The kelp-covered reefs of coastal waters were the first zones to be bombarded with string upon string of baited lobster pots, but the bigger boats soon ventured further afield, seeking their valuable quarry in the English Channel and even off the Scottish coast.

Typically, today's crabbers are based in Jersey or Guernsey but use Alderney as an operating port while fishing the Channel during neap (small) tides. During these restricted fishing periods it's all systems go.

Setting and lifting as many as 700 50-pound (23-kg) pots each day, crewmen clad in the traditional blue denim fishing smocks of the islands or in vivid yellow oilskins carry on working in almost any condition short of a severe gale. The catch, which now consists primarily of the brown edible crab, with its flat, pie-crust shell, is stored on board in water-filled *viviers* before being unloaded in bulk. Some of the tangled, writhing mass of carapaces, claws and legs may eventually grace island tables, but most of the shellfish are destined for the longer voyages to France, Spain and Portugal where the top prices are paid.

The deckhands of the modern fishing industry are something of a race apart because of the trips which keep them from home for days at the time. It's tempting to think of them as direct descendants of the oystermen and cod catchers of former ages; but, in spite of the seafarers' oiled wool jersey and guernsey sweaters, which they sport on shore as well as at sea, their attitudes are conventionally 20th century. A visit to a fishermen's pub—such as La Folie Inn on the very edge of St. Helier Harbour—will confirm this.

The shellfish fleets of the Channel Islands are the big money earners and other forms of commercial fishing—such as trawling—are relatively unimportant. This, of course, is excellent news for that other category of fisherman, the angler. Sea angling is important in all the islands. Once a way of putting a little extra on the table, it is now a major leisure activity, for both islanders and visitors. The main islands already have accomplished charter boat skippers who can put their clients' bait right on the fish's nose and Alderney has an international reputation as a shore fishing centre where record-breaking ballan wrasse and monster grey mullet are landed. The latter are now caught with the lightest of light tackle which would not be out of place in the hands of a freshwater coarse angler.

This is a far cry from the methods of old, when the mullet man would set off not only with his tin of *chervie* (ground bait) but also with a rod and line strong enough to yank the top lip off this delicate, shy fish. The technique in those days was to swing hooked mullet under your jacket as soon as they left the water. Loose scales from captured fish were thought to scare the rest of the shoal.

Throwing them back: The use of modern tackle is not the only way in which local sport fishing has leapt into the latter part of the 20th century. There are many serious anglers, including some of the charter skippers and dedicated specimen hunters, who return a high proportion of captured fish to the sea. This is especially good news in the case of slow-growing species such as bass, but many hooked tope, congers and rays also live to fight another day. Conservation, however, is taken far enough and no further: so far, there have been no reports of the big turbot (which are often tempted by live sand eel baits fished over offshore banks) being returned to the depths.

Alderney, with its half-mile breakwater as a superb vantage point, may have the premier reputation as a shore angling centre. However the other islands should not be ignored by the fishermen who like to keep their feet on dry land. Jersey, for example, offers excellent pier fishing from St. Catherine's Breakwater, and everywhere you will find rocky points from which pollack, mackerel, garfish and a host of other varieties can be caught from the shore.

Bear two things in mind, though: there's nothing but sea between the islands and America and the entire area has an enormous tidal range. The first factor means that huge swells sometimes sweep up exposed rocks;

the second means that it is all too easy to get cut off as the tide rises. Care and, above all, local advice are the things to take.

Most parts of the world are content with two forms of fishing: commercial and sporting. As in so many other things, the Channel Islands are different. If you hear someone talking mysteriously about "going down the tide" he will be talking about low-water fishing, an activity made possible by the enormous tidal range which can pose such a threat to the unwary.

Above, the lure is the high prices fetched by lobsters in high-class restaurants.

Low-water fishing is a complex business because it is no single pursuit but a whole range of them. These vary from putting baited lines (trots) on winter beaches to catching razorfish with salt—yes, salt. This is something visitors often try, setting out sceptically for the low-tide mark armed with a salt pot and the knowledge that they are looking for keyhole-shaped burrows in the sand. If they have been instructed properly they discover that adding the salt to the keyholes is as effective as it is meant to be and up pops the razorfish (a plump mollusc in an elongated shell) shooting out like a missile from a silo. He is, of course, a victim of chemical warfare, preferring to take his chances in the open instead of being pickled in his lair.

Hunting the ormer: In the same breath as mentioning "going down the tide", islanders are likely to speak of ormers, ear-shaped shells which stick themselves to rocks with their own brand of superglue. Tourists may be fascinated by the ormer because of its beautiful mother-of-pearl interior, but for Jersey and Guernseymen the little beasts are sought for their meat.

Anywhere but at the Minquiers, that massive reef 10 miles (16 km) south of Jersey, finding sufficient for a meal is a real challenge, involving hours of wading and rock turning. However, ormers are held in such esteem that attempts are being made to breed them in captivity and an "adopt an ormer" scheme was launched in 1988. All sponsors got in return for their 10p contributions were a car sticker and a sense of virtue, but they were assured that their money would be put to good use in a marine conservation area near Port Saumarez in Guernsey. What's more, ormers are protected by rigidly enforced closed seasons. Guernsey, where the season is restricted to a few winter days, is a particularly bad place to break the rules. Illegal ormering is regarded almost as seriously as an act of high treason.

As if the sea weren't a big enough place for every conceivable type of fishing, both Jersey and Guernsey offer facilities for freshwater angling, game and coarse. The venues include reservoirs and, in the genuinely idiosyncratic style of the islands, Jersey's South Canal, which is a flooded German antitank defence in the meadowland bordering St. Ouen's Bay.

ISLAND FARE

In total the Channel Islands cover just 100 square miles (259 sq. km), an area larger than a city and its suburbs. Yet, included in that area are 314 restaurants and cafes, 498 hotels and guest houses and 60 inns. All serve food for holidaymakers or locals and make a good living by doing so.

More statistics: according to the most recent Channel Islands' census, 80,212 people live in Jersey, 55,482 in Guernsey, 2,130 in Alderney, 550 in Sark, 59 in Herm and two on Jethou. This means that, on paper at least, there are 872 eating places for a population of 138,435 people—or 158 people for every pub, hotel or restaurant.

Such odds in the diner's favour would spell death to restaurants anywhere else in the world. But in the Channel Islands, the population nudges two million during the summer, giving the restaurateurs a chance to make their money. Many, however, have been trying to extend their restaurant's life by earning a good local reputation that will stand them in good stead for the rest of the year. This means a visitor will often enjoy a better meal out of the tourist season than in it and, what's more, stand less chance of coinciding with a party of fussy, old-age pensioners on a strictly guided tour and a strictly limited menu. Autumn or spring (particularly during the food festivals) are seasons for the gourmand.

Guernsey and Jersey import a great deal of food from the continent. Their markets and shops (including supermarkets) offer tremendous selections of cheese, fish, shellfish and fruit. The islands' unique position of *not* being owned by the British and *not* being part of the EEC gives them access to a range of foodstuffs hard to find elsewhere.

The same can be said of Alderney, an island which, though it seeks tourists, doesn't always get them. But Alderney is more than a tourist centre: it is a retirement island. People sell up and move there to enjoy their last few tax-free years in peace,

and, since one joy of retirement is good food, Alderney possesses at least one superb restaurant and several others that wouldn't look out of place in London or Paris.

Herm, meanwhile, *has* to offer good food to its visitors, even if choice is limited. Without tourism the island would die and the leaseholder, Major Peter Wood, knows that poor service and poor food kill the trade. He demands dedication from his staff and so, even when the food is disappointing, the

waiter is sure to be servility personified.

The last of the major islands, Sark, remains an enigma. Repopulated by Jersey in the 16th century, it has watched the other islands move firmly into the 20th century. Good food may be found there; where to find it is another matter.

Fruit and Vegetables: Of all Channel Island recipes, *des pais au fou* is most renowned, although its Jersey-French name hides a dish which could never be described as glamorous. If ever a cheap meal of various beans, pig's trotters and belly has been refined by countless generations of cooks into something finer, this is it. The dish sounds

Preceding pages, eating out in Jersey. Left, Channel Islands potatoes are a big export. Right, visitors at work.

better in French than in the islanders' name for it—*bincrock*.

So, too, do other dishes, including *d'la soupe de congre* (conger eel soup), *d'la Bouanne soupe* (Sark pottage, traditionally made with mackerel, gooseberries, shredded cabbage, milk and ham) and *d'la soupe de caboche* (cabbage soup). If the soup doesn't appeal, try the bread. Cabbage loaves (*des pains à caboche*) are superb. The bread is baked wrapped in cabbage leaves which are then pulled away to leave a sweetish, doughy, heavy bread—brown and ripe.

Other local vegetable dishes include Guernsey baked potato pudding (*houichepoté à patate*), Jersey baked carrot

maintain the tradition by fermenting their own cider. One or two enterprising growers are also trying to resurrect the art of cider-making on a commercial basis.

More popular in island pubs are local beers, which are both cheaper and sweeter than their U.K. equivalents. The trendy set, meanwhile, drink vast quantities of *grolsch*, a Scandinavian lager imported in vast quantities in flip-top bottles.

Sweetmeats: Another apple-based dish the islanders are known for is *bourdelots* or apples baked in shortcrust pastry. They are delicious and, like cabbage loaves, should be cooked wrapped in cabbage leaves—the island's version of modern-day tinfoil.

pudding (*du podin d'carotte*), tomato soup (*d'la soupe des tomates*) and parsnip pottage (*panais à la Graisse*). Such dishes were extremely popular during the German Occupation, when meat was scarce and vegetables were at a premium.

Today, perhaps, because vegetables and fruit grow so easily on the islands, they are rather taken for granted. At one time nearly every farmer had his own orchard and cider press. Apples were as plentiful as today's tomatoes, and Jersey cider had a great reputation. Not so now. But the huge, granite cider presses remain and can be seen in some of the larger gardens, while a few farmers

Jersey black butter, another delicacy, sounds best in the native tongue (*du nier beurre*), although in either language the name is confusing: black butter isn't made from milk but from apples. Before 1914, most islanders made it regularly and looked forward to autumn when a huge brass pan of new cider would be placed on the outhouse stove. To this would be added peeled, cut apples, sugar and liquorice, plus a variety of

Above, a St. Peter Port fishmonger. Following pages: a Sark carriage; waves pound Cobo; taking in the sun at St. Brelade's Beach; a Sark dovecote.

spices. The pan would be stirred constantly, day and night and the spices added right at the end of the marathon. Two or three brawny young, farmers would be called to stir the stiff, tacky mixture.

The phrase "brawny, young farmers" is used deliberately because the Jersey Young Farmers Club is the mainstay of the traditional *sethe d' nière beurre* (black butter night). Every November they spend 24 hours or more making enough black butter to last them and their families from one end of a year to another. It tastes sweet and syrupy and can be spread quite happily on bread or bread cake (*gâche à fouée*) to be enjoyed with a glass of cider or a cup of tea.

Jars of black butter, carrot butter and tomato sauce can all be bought at the Witches' Cauldron, St. Ouen. But, if you are looking for different types of bread to spread them on baked by different local bakers, look long and hard. Le Brun's bakery has a virtual monopoly of all breadstuffs made in Jersey and the island government even agreed to help set up the vast new bakery at the Rue des Près Trading Estate in St. Saviour. Guernsey, meanwhile, has a tradition of independent bakeries including the Maison Carré in St. Peter Port's shopping arcade, which has become something of a cult eating place for the middle-aged.

One of the tastiest sweetmeats is *gâche* (pronounced "gosh" and consisting of flour, butter, eggs, candied peel, sultanas, milk and sugar). Guernsey *gâche* in Jersey tastes different to Guernsey *gâche* in Guernsey, however; this is because each island jealously protects the purity of its own distinctive breed of cattle, which means that the milk of each island tastes slightly different to that of the other.

Because of the high cream content, Channel Islands milk tends to leave grease marks on top of tea or coffee. Just close your eyes and enjoy the taste. This high cream content also means the milk sours quickly and dissuades Jerseymen (but *not* Guernsey cheddarmen) from turning it into cheese.

Jersey wonders (*des mervelles*), Guernsey hearts (*des p'tits tcheurs*) and local biscuits (*des galettes*) are also worth sampling.

Meat and fish: Channel Islanders, being inventive, have learnt to make the most of their seafood resources. *Moules* (mussels) are popular and appear on every menu, although they have to be imported. Ormers (similar to oysters) are a traditional delicacy which, at one time, were farmed extensively, with the best ones being sent to U.K. markets and the rougher ones being sold locally. Nowadays fishing for them is rigidly controlled for their preservation.

Even lobsters and crabs (mainly spider crabs) are not as plentiful as they used to be and are no longer cheap: locally caught lobster (*l'homard*) are more expensive than quality meat imported from the continent. Inevitably, demand has outstripped supply. As many as 4,000 lobsters a week were pulled from Guernsey pots in the 1860s and even a decade ago; they were so prized that Belgian businessmen would fly to the islands, buy half-a-dozen, and fly back home that same day to sell them at extortionate rates in their restaurants.

Crab is getting scarcer, too, and Canadian crabmeat is occasionally flown in to satisfy demand. Limpets, although lilliputian compared to lobster, are an alternative treat when cooked for half an hour in a saucepan and served with vinegar. The problem is, of course, that you have to cook an awful lot of limpets to satisfy a hungry man. What recommends them is that, along with whelks and shrimps, they are freely available.

Islanders have an extraordinary ability to turn anything that can be swallowed into food. An Alderney dish, for example, became popular when the locals, realising that all around them flew a rich source of food no-one had thought to capture, created sparrow pie. You can still find recipes for it, or, a much more tempting prospect, *des pigaöns* (boiled pigeons).

When you can't turn your environment into meat, you may be able to turn it into drink instead. The Blayneys have done so successfully at St. Mary, in Jersey, where they have reintroduced vines to the island and produce their own wines (passable light whites). One enterprising Guernsey grower has tried his hand at fermenting wine, although his concoction, *vin de Castel* (pronounced Cattell) doesn't compare too favourably with a glass of hock or Muscadet.

Anyone braving the Guernsey Tomato Centre can try a glass of tomato wine. It is worth tasting, though perhaps not so much for its piquant flavour as for its providing an enduring talking-point.

TRAVEL TIPS

DESTINATION CHANNEL ISLANDS

GETTING THERE

Air: Migrating birds stop off in the Channel Islands to rest their wings before flying home. So do more than a million tourists each year, and over half of them keep coming back. Most visitors are from the British Isles and travel by air because it is quick and easy. In summer, direct flights operate to Jersey from around 30 regional airports in the U.K. Fewer operate to Guernsey and Alderney, but traffic to and from mainland Europe is increasing steadily.

The islands' policy of attracting out-of-season conference business means that flights can be fully booked at the most surprising times. So forward planning is advisable. Those who can plan far enough in advance should be able to save by buying an APEX ticket. Out-of-season, remember that fog can sometimes cause flight delays or cancellations.

Sea: Journeys by ferry from the south coast of England can take up to nine hours and the crossing is sometimes rough. Reserve cabin accommodation on night sailings. On-board facilities include duty-free shops, bars, restaurants and cafeterias and amusement machines.

Fast hydrofoil services run between the islands and to St. Malo. Connections with Herm and Sark are by boat only. Cherbourg and some of the small Normandy ports can also be easily reached by ferry. The crossing from Jersey to Carteret takes as little as 40 minutes. In Alderney, boat trips are run to the bird colony on Burhou island.

A full list of the various air and sea links appears on page 281.

INSIDE CHANNEL ISLANDS

GETTING ACQUAINTED

Passports: British subjects and citizens of the Irish Republic do not require passports or entry visas. Common Market nationals may travel on either passports or identity cards, as may nationals of Austria, Switzerland, Monaco and Liechstentein. Nationals of other Western European countries and North America need a valid passport but no entry visa. Citizens of other countires should contact the nearest British Embassy or Consulate about visa requirements.

Weather: The islands owe a great deal to their maritime situation. The surrounding waters, warmed by the North Atlantic Drift, reach 17° or 18°C in August. This helps reduce the risk of frost or snow, but it also keeps the summer temperatures a little lower than parts of England, with June to September maximums averaging 20°C.

The warm, wet air can cause fog, especially in winter—though the strong southwest winds soon cause it to disperse. Jersey and Guernsey usually vie for the highest sunshine totals in the British Isles. The islands average eight hours a day during summer. Mean rainfall per year is about 100mm during each winter month and 50mm during each summer month. The islands, particularly Jersey, have one of the greatest tidal ranges anywhere in the world (40ft/13 metres).

Clothing: Despite the islands' self-promotion as sun, sea and sand resorts, it's best not to have great expectations about the weather: the climate, being temperate, is unpredictable. Think about bringing some rainproofs and a couple of woollens just in case the weather changes. Unwary tourists caught in a downpour can usually dive into the nearest shop and buy a plastic mac which, though unattractive looking, is cheap and gives good protection.

Leisurewear is accepted almost anywhere, except in the better restaurants and hotels where men will be expected to don a jacket and tie for dinner. One of the best ways of seeing the islands' beauty is on foot, so a pair of stout shoes is useful.

Topless sunbathing, although not widespread, is accepted on the beaches; but baring all is not. In the towns, service might be refused to anyone clad solely in a swimsuit or not wearing a shirt. Smart, casual dress must be worn to gain admission to the many nightclubs and discotheques: those in jeans or training shoes are likely to be turned away.

Time: Like everyone else in the United Kingdom, Channel Islanders set their watches and clocks to Greenwich Mean Time (G.M.T.), adding an extra hour in March for British Summer Time, and then reverting back to G.M.T. in October. The accepted reason for changing the clocks is to provide daylight saving for farmers and school children in winter.

When it is midday (G.M.T.) in the islands, it is 7a.m. in New York, midnight in Wellington, 1 p.m. in Paris, Madrid and Rome, 8 p.m. in Hong Kong, Manila, Beijing and Singapore, and 9 p.m. in Tokyo.

The pace of island life is faster than it used to be.

Sometimes in conversation the older farmers and residents use the expression "time past" (or *temps passé*). This refers to a bygone era, now almost part of folklore, when many of the customs and traditions, particularly on the farm, were kept alive and everyone worked a day that lasted from sunrise to sunset. Nostalgia, though it is sometimes overdone, does keep islanders aware of the present and their future.

Shopping Hours: Shopkeepers don't take long siestas, despite the continental influence. Most open their premises from 9a.m. to 5.30p.m., Mondays to Saturdays—although in Guernsey, on Thursdays, and Alderney, on Wednesdays, it is usual practice to close early (12.30 p.m). In Jersey, most establishments remain open all day on Thursdays, except for a few small family-run businesses and the markets.

Lunchtime closing is rare in the two larger islands, but standard in Alderney. During summer, many shops catering for tourists—perfumeries, tobacconists, souvenir shops and larger U.K. chain stores such as Boots and Woolworths—reopen in the evenings, especially in St. Helier. It's worth noting that there are no 24-hour stores. Newsagents, rota chemists and some grocers open Sundays, but opening hours vary.

What To Buy: Pick up any brochure and the image created is that the islands are a paradise for bargain hunt-

ers. True enough, duty is low and the absence of Value Added Tax (15 percent on the mainland) makes luxury goods, perfume, tobacco, wines, spirits and jewellery in most cases quite a bit cheaper. But when it comes to buying cameras, clothing and electrical goods, the buyer should beware. Visitors sometimes find that the bulk purchasing power of the national chain stores enable them to buy goods cheaper in the U.K. than in the Channel Islands because discounts are greater than the sales tax savings. A freight surcharge is also added to many goods sold in the Channel Islands.

For traditional gifts or souvenirs, try some of the unusual items manufactured from giant cabbage stalks at L'Etacq Woodcrafts in Jersey; Guernsey or Jersey milk cans; and pottery and glassware, woodcarvings or soft toys produced by local craftsmen.

Traditional Alderney, Guernsey or Jersey sweaters are favourites among souvenir hunters and should last for years. They can be bought direct from the manufacturers: Channel Island Knitwear Co. (20226) or Hall and Son Ltd., (44504) in Jersey; Le Tricoteur and Co. Ltd., Guernsey (26214); and Channel Jumpers Ltd., Alderney (2202).

Many visitors also buy jewellery, especially in St. Helier where the number of shops has proliferated. One chain of stores offers a cashback refund as an inducement to customers if they can find a similar item they have purchased cheaper in other stores in the island.

Customs Rules: It is difficult to take maximum advantage of the duty-free shopping in the Channel Islands. On returning home, British and Irish residents can take only a limited quantity of goods through the green customs channel: spirits, 1 litre; wine, 2 litres; tobacco, 250 grams, 50 cigars or 200 cigarettes (double if you live outside Europe); perfume 2 fl.oz.; toilet water, a quarter litre. Problems can arise when watches, jewellery or cameras are purchased: the maximum customs' allowance is £32 worth, so any surplus should be declared. Citizens of other English-speaking countries in transit through the U.K. can often carry back more generous allowances.

Animals: Rabies is a very real danger to these small communities, especially because so many yachts sail to and fro between the islands and France. There is a total ban on the import of all animals from everywhere except the U.K. and Republic of Ireland.

Banks: While there are around 100 banks in the Channel Islands, most are set up to take deposits or investments. Foreign exchange dealings, therefore, have to be carried out in one of the British high street clearing banks such as Barclays, National Westminster, Lloyds, Midland, The Royal Bank of Scotland or the TSB. There

are no building societies in the islands.

Normal hours of business for banks in Jersey and Guernsey are from 9.30 a.m. to 3.30 p.m., Mondays to Fridays; some close later on Fridays and a few open on Saturday mornings. In Alderney, banking hours are from 10 a.m. to 1 p.m. and 2 p.m. to 3.30 p.m. weekdays; the two banks here are Midland and National Westminster. They also have offices in Sark, open between 10 a.m. to midday and from 2 p.m to 3.00 p.m. Mondays to Fridays. Most hotels and shops will accept travellers' cheques or Eurocheques.

The most commonly accepted credit cards are Access (MasterCard) and Visa. American Express and Diners Club aren't so ubiquitous. Most proprietors of the smaller hotels and guesthouses will expect accommodation bills to be paid in cash or by cheque.

Money: There's plenty of it floating around in the Channel Islands. The big power boats and luxury yachts in the marinas are visible evidence of high *per capita* incomes. Consumerism lurks conspicuously round many corners, in the shape of a Ferrari, Porsche, Lamborghini or Range-Rover. The expansion of the finance sector, in particular, has brought big salaries and more spending power.

The island governments will do all they can to protect standards of living and financial security—even to the extent of operating outside the sterling area if nec-

essary. However, at present the pound is still the official unit of currency and, as if to assert their independence still further, the bailiwicks of Jersey and Guernsey issue their own money. The notes are in £1, £5, £10 and £20 denominations while coins are 1p, 2p, 5p, 10p, 20p, 50p and £1.

British money is also in circulation and both bailiwicks accept each other's currency. But make sure that you exchange all local coins and notes before leaving the islands; they aren't accepted as legal tender elsewhere.

French francs are readily accepted in many shops. Other currencies must be exchanged at a Bureau de Change office or bank.

Public Holidays: The Channel Islands enjoy the same public holidays as the U.K. with one extra—Liberation Day on May 9—to commemorate the end of the German Occupation in 1945. Alderney does not enjoy the extra holiday.

The other holidays are: New Year's Day (January 1); Christmas Day (December 25); Boxing Day (December 26). Good Friday and Easter Monday fall in March or April. Two spring bank holidays in May and a summer bank holiday at the end of August also change annually. Alderney's summer bank holiday is at the beginning of August.

Language: English is the language spoken and used by most people today, although the islands' tradition is very French. Each has its own dialect, forms of ancient Norman French called Jersiais, Guernsiais, Auregniais and Sercquiais. Basically they are conversational languages, and pronunciation and words differ greatly between the islands.

Until World War II these dialects were widely spoken and true French was used to conduct much written business. With the great influx of English-speaking people after the war, the dialects declined rapidly.

They are kept alive today by local societies, occasional letters in the newspapers, weekly talks on local radio and by two dictionaries produced by Dr. Frank Le Maistre in Jersey and by Mrs. de Garis in Guernsey.

One way in which the local language is preserved is in place names. When the most recent Ordnance Survey Map of Jersey was produced in 1981, traditional place names were used wherever possible and the (often more commonly used) English equivalents were put in brackets. This policy achieved its aim, but visitors get a hard time: if they look on the map for First Tower (a region of St. Helier in Jersey) they will find 'Premier Tour'.

Names: Most surnames have French origins; *Poingdestre*, for instance, means "right-fisted". Many begin with 'Le' or 'L' meaning "the" (e.g. *le Liévre*, the Hare; *L'arbalestier*, the Cross Bow; *L'anglois*, the Englishman—pronounced 'Longwah' in Jersey and 'Longlay' in Guernsey).

Others begin with 'De' 'De La' or 'D' meaning "from". These people were nobility who fled to the islands during the French Revolution, (e.g. *de la Mare*, from the marsh; *de la Haye*, from La Haye in France, meaning hedge; *de Gruchy*, from Gruchy in France).

Older names have Frankish origins (e.g. *Renouf*, from Regenwulf; *Mauger*, from Maethelgaer).

Electricity: Standard 240 volts A.C. sockets in most hotels take square-pin 13-amp. plugs. In older properties, in the smaller islands, round-pin plugs may still be in use. Good adaptors should fit either type.

Car Hire: Self-drive rates are just about the lowest found anywhere. One reason for this is that some car manufacturers have been using the islands as a back door into the British market; by registering the cars in the islands and hiring them out for a few months, dealers have been able to sell "nearly new" cars to mainland customers at quite a big discount because of the saving in car duty normally added to new cars in the U.K.

Off-season, a week on the road in an economy car can cost as little as £35, unlimited mileage and liability insurance included. The daily rates in summer for a small car—Fiat Pandas, VW Golfs and Ford Fiestas are the ideal vehicles for the narrow roads—would be from £6 a day in Guernsey and Alderney and around £8 a day in Jersey. That is a lot

of incentive to get mobile and explore at limited expense. Many companies compete in the hire business and it pays to shop around.

Hire cars are instantly recognizable as a large letter 'H' is affixed next to each number plate. Local motorists says this stands for "Horror"—a description of the way hire cars are sometimes driven by visitors who have difficulty adjusting to the different road conditions, one-way systems and reduced speeds.

Poor signposting also creates problems. The directions to destinations only a few miles part appear at best intermittently or not at all. There is a good chance of getting lost, although sooner than later a major junction will pop up and reference can be made to one of the sketchy maps provided free with the rental car. For those who want to know where they are at all times, buy an Ordnance Survey Map or Perry's Guide.

The rural beauties of the islands can only be appreciated by venturing into the small country lanes. In Jersey alone there are 500 miles of road to unravel. Most firms hire cars to people over 20 or with at least one year's driving experience. Some also impose a maximum age limit. A valid licence with no endorsements for dangerous or drunken driving in the past five years is also required.

Cycling: Visitors seem to enjoy pottering around the parishes on rented pushbikes, particularly on day excursions to the smaller islands. A little more puff is needed to circumnavigate Jersey than Guernsey by bicycle since distances from A to B are obviously greater and the hills longer and steeper in Jersey. Cycles can be hired from as little as £2 per day. Couples could have double the fun for twice the price on a tandem. (See page 283).

Scooters: Scooters or mopeds (small motorized two-wheelers) can also be hired on the two larger islands. Helmets must be worn. (See page 283).

Buses: While a car is the most economical way of getting around, buses are usually the only viable alternative for non-drivers. The Jersey Motor Transport and Guernseybus operate islandwide services from central terminals at the Weighbridge, St. Helier, and the town of St. Peter Port. Anyone planning to use the buses regularly during their stay will find it cheaper to buy a Rover ticket which allows up to seven days' unlimited travel. Off-season and Sunday services on both islands are reduced. Airport routes run frequently during the year. Alderney no longer has a bus service.

Taxis: Waiting areas for rank cabs can be found at the ports and in the towns. Private taxis can be ordered by phone from one of the companies listed at the back of the telephone directory, especially when planning an evening out. Extra charges

apply for late-night collection, waiting time etc. The taxi is the main transport link between the airport and St. Anne's in Alderney. Sark has no motorized vehicles; taxis there are literally horse-powered.

Train: Except for a couple of model railways and a short track run by a steam enthusiast in Jersey, the only passenger train in the islands is for tourists and runs from Braye to Mannez Quarry and back in Alderney. Tickets are return only which means the fare is double if visitors decide to alight for a look around the quarry (not particularly interesting). Old London Underground carriages are now used in addition to roofed-in goods wagons powered either by a steam locomotive called "J.T. Daly" or a diesel engine known as "Elizabeth".

Inter-Island Travel: A full listing of services by air and sea between the islands and France appears on page 281. Herm is only two miles and Sark nine miles from Guernsey, making them both easily accessible by ferry. An air taxi company, Aurigny, has its operations base in Alderney and it's much faster to get one of their little, yellow Trislander planes for a visit from Jersey or Guernsey instead of going by sea.

The French ports of Carteret, Port Bail, Granville and St. Malo are just a short ferryride from Jersey.

Traffic Laws: Yellow lines painted across roads at

intersections mean "stop and give way". It is sensible not to ignore them: particularly in Guernsey where many roads are of a similar size and the difference between a major and a minor road isn't always obvious. Yellow arrows before a junction in Guernsey and Alderney indicate that a junction is ahead and brakes should be applied.

The only stretch of road with more than one lane is Victoria Avenue, the dual-carriageway coming from the west into St. Helier.

The "filter-in-turn" is one of the most efficient systems in use and certainly helps keep traffic flowing where a number of roads meet. These occur at larger junctions where vehicles from each direction take it in turn to cross or join the traffic flow from other directions.

Long yellow lines painted the length of a kerb are areas where parking or stopping is prohibited day and night. A number of zones in St. Helier, including the high streets, are pedestrianised and closed to traffic. Only permit holders can get access to the main street in St. Peter Port .

Speed Limits: In Jersey, less so in Guernsey, many well-to-do people like to own fast cars; but, unless they take them to Europe or the U.K. regularly, there's not much chance to put the foot down since speed limits are so low. Jersey's is 40 m.p.h. but drops to 20 m.p.h. in certain sign-posted areas. In Guernsey it is not permitted to go faster than 35 m.p.h. on open roads, 25 m.p.h. on built-up areas and five m.p.h. in some places. Alderney has a similar maximum speed limit of 35 m.p.h. except in St. Anne's where 20 m.p.h. is the norm and only 12 m.p.h. up the main street.

Parking: Parking in towns can be frustrating as visitors vie with local commuters to get spaces. It is free in Guernsey and controlled by a disc clock obtainable from the police station or tourist information office; hire car firms should also provide them. Time of arrival has to be set on the clock which must then be left on the dashboard for traffic wardens to see. Parking zones are indicated by special blue signs and vary from 15 minutes to 10 hours. Jersey operates a similar system and, depending on the area, parking is allowed for periods between 20 minutes and three hours.

A number of concrete edifices in the shape of multistorey car parks have sprung up in Jersey to help alleviate the parking problem and congestion in St. Helier. Metered parking here costs 15p an hour, except from 5.30 p.m. to 8.00 a.m. and on Sundays when it is free. (Maximum stay restrictions operated in some of them). The same rate applies in other "pay and display" areas. Special spaces are reserved for disabled drivers.

Petrol: It is doubtful whether the surprisingly low cost of petrol in the Channel Islands can be correlated with the high ownership of cars. Premium grade costs around 23p a litre, the cheapest in Europe.

Diesel oil is sold at most garages but not unleaded fuel. For some reason petrol cannot be purchased on Sunday in Guernsey.

Telephones: Cordless or otherwise, telephones provide a lifeline to the outside world. The States of Jersey and Guernsey are spending millions on the installation of new, highly sophisticated digital telephone systems, basically to provide their respective finance industries with quick and efficient connections to international money markets in all corners of the globe. Of course, other subscribers also benefit from the improved service.

Very occasionally a ship will drag its anchors in the Channel and accidentally sever the undersea telephone cables joining the islands with the U.K. When this happens, panic and pandemonium result. Calls have to be made via a microwave link but only a limited number of lines are available.

Generally, visitors should experience few problems making calls home or abroad, even from the smaller islands (whose services are handled by Guernsey Telecoms). Area codes for the U.K. and main cities in most countries are found at the back of the telephone directory. There are plenty of public call boxes in street kiosks, pubs, restaurants, hotel lobbies, shops and at the ports.

International calls can be dialled direct from any public phone—the newer ones take 50p pieces, which makes things a little easier for long-distance conversations, as well as 10p and 5p coins. Local calls are cheap: 6p in Guernsey and 5p in Jersey. International telegrams (or telemessages, as they are now called) can be sent by dialling 190.

Postal Services: Each bailiwick has its own postal system and issues its own stamps. Look out for red mailboxes in Jersey and blue ones in Guernsey. Those with a deep sense of heritage might like to see what is claimed to be the oldest postbox in the British Isles, found in Union Street in St. Peter Port.

Only local stamps are valid for sending mail out of the islands. Guernsey postage is used in Herm and Sark, although mail will be franked locally. Alderney also has its own postage but Guernsey's are used for the higher values.

Unlike the U.K., mail is not divided into first and second class service— there is only one class. At the time of writing the standard rate for a letter or card sent to the mainland or to an address in one of the other islands in 15p. Letters weighing up to 20 grammes, or postcards, cost 22p to European countries and go by air automatically. Airmail rates to other parts of the world vary according to weight and size.

The main post offices are open from 9 a.m. to 5.30 p.m. during the week and close at lunchtime on Saturdays.

Most sub-post offices shut early one day a week.

Jersey and Guernsey stamps are sought after by philatelists and collectors throughout the world. There are five or six new issues every year, many coinciding with special anniversaries and events. These can be bought at philatelic bureaux in the main post offices in St. Helier and St. Peter Port.

Media: All English national newspapers and numerous foreign papers, together with a vast selection of magazines and periodicals, arrive daily on a special early-morning delivery plane, except during fog or bad weather. A small supplement is added to the price of a paper to cover freight.

For the latest news, B.B.C. local radio stations in Jersey and Guernsey have regular broadcasts and programmes with plenty of local flavour. Other BBC services and output from continental stations can be picked up easily, including a new FM music station, Radio Force 7, based in St. Malo and targeted at Channel Island audiences.

High-powered transmitters relay clear pictures from the four British T.V. channels into the majority of homes and hotels. More regional news can be obtained by watching Channel Television bulletins on ITV (Channel 3). Some sets can receive teletext information (Prestel, Ceefax etc.) and with special aerials French TV broadcasts can be picked up.

For what's on, when and where, consult the *Jersey Evening Post*, the *Guernsey Evening Press* or the fortnightly *Alderney Journal*. In the summer various holiday papers and publications are also produced.

Health and Emergencies: It is advisable to take up a medical insurance as private consultations and prescriptions are not covered by the reciprocal health agreements between the Channel Islands and many other countries, including the U.K. In Jersey, however, visitors can get free treatment at special morning medical clinics held at the General Hospital, from 9 to 11 a.m., Mondays to Fridays and 10 to 11.30 a.m., Saturdays, May to September; and on Mondays, Wednesdays and Fridays, October to April. Prescriptions issued at one of these clinics cost 50p, and are dispensed at the hospital pharmacy.

In-patient care is provided free-of-charge in Jersey, Guernsey and Alderney. The majority of visitors who seek treatment are those suffering from sunburn. Plants, animals and marine life in the islands are quite harmless so the likelihood of being stung or bitten by a "wee beastie" is remote.

Crime: Despite the image portrayed by the B.B.C detective series "Bergerac", neither Jersey nor the other islands have high crime rates. Most wrong-doers are apprehended by the police fairly quickly. Not everybody can be trusted, so keep valuables out of sight and lock car doors.

Useful Numbers: Dial 999 in an emergency for police, fire, ambulance or sea rescue. In Herm dial '0' for the operator.

Jersey
Police HQ 75511
Beach guards (summer only) 82032
Ambulance HQ 72222
Fire Service 37444
General Hospital 59000
JMT (buses) 21201
Samaritans 25555
Daily Diary 1882
Automobile Association 23344
Flight Enquiries 43925
Directory Enquiries:
- local & U.K. 192
- international 100
Telegrams 190
Ship arrivals/departures 1883
Weather 1885

Guernsey
Ambulance HQ 25211
Fire HQ 24491
Hospitals 25241
Police Hotline (to report crime) 28822
Automobile Association 22984
Samaritans 23731
Weather Report 64033
Alarm Call 191
Telegrams 100
Directory Enquiries 191
Guernseybus 24677
Guernsey Hotel and Tourism Association—
Bed Bank 39062
Flight Enquiries 37682

Alderney
Police Station 2731
Fire Station 2672
Hospital 2822
Flight Enquiries 2888

Sark
Medical Officer 2045

ON THE MOVE

TRANSPORT

Portsmouth and Weymouth or Torquay:

British Channel Island ferries from Portsmouth; day and night sailings, using two ships both of which carry cars; cabins available. From Weymouth, car ferry service (in summer only) takes about six hours. Reservations: 0705-819416 or 0202-681155. Direct sailing times from Portsmouth to Jersey—about nine hours, and Guernsey—about eight hours.

Torbay Seaways car ferry from Torquay, May to September. Reservations: 0803-214397. Direct sailing times from Torquay to Jersey—nine hours, and Guernsey—about eight hours.

Condor Hydrofoils from Weymouth to Jersey via Guernsey, summer only. Reservations: 0305-761551. Crossing time, Jersey—three-and-a-half hours and Guernsey—two hours. Passengers only. Can be rough.

Services to France, Guernsey, Alderney and Sark from Jersey
By Sea:
Passengers only:
To St. Malo.
Condor Hydrofoils (0534-71263). Crossing time 1 hr. 5 mins.
Emeraude Ferries (74458). Crossing time 2 hrs. 30 mins.
Vedettes Armoricaines (30773 and 20361). Crossing time 1 hr. 30 mins.
Vedettes Blanches (74458). Crossing time 1 hr. 15 mins.
To Carteret.
C.N.T.N. (Jersey) Ltd. (53737). Crossing time 40 mins.
To Granville.
Vedettes Blanches, (74458). Crossing time 1 hr. 5 mins.
Vedettes Armoricaines (30773 and 20361). Crossing time 1 hr. 5 mins.
Vedettes Vertes Granvillaises (74458). Crossing time 1 hr. 5 mins.
To Port-Bail.
C.N.T.N. (Jersey) Ltd. (53737).
To Guernsey, Alderney, Sark and Herm.
Condor Hydrofoils (71263).
To Guernsey and Sark.
Vedettes Blanches (74458).
Car/Passenger Ferries:
To Guernsey.
British Channel Island Ferries (38300). Crossing time 1 hr. 30 mins.
To St. Malo.
Commodore Travel (71263).
Emeraude Ferries (74458). Crossing time 2 hrs. 30 mins.

By Air:
To Paris. (Charles de Gaulle)
Jersey European Airways (77400 or 45661). 1 hr 20 mins.
Air France (42592). Weekends, summer only.
To Dinard.

Jersey European Airways (77400 or 45661).
To Cherbourg.
Aurigny Air Services Ltd. (35733 or 43568). 30 mins.
To Guernsey.
Aurigny Air Services Ltd. (43568 or 35733).15 mins.
Jersey European Airways (77400 or 45661).
To Alderney.
Aurigny Air Services Ltd. (43568 or 35733). 20 mins.

Direct Air Services to Jersey and Guernsey from the U.K.: Airports from which it is possible to fly direct to Jersey are shown below with the airlines and their reservations telephone numbers. A letter (G) indicates that the airline also flies to Guernsey.

Aberdeen—British Airways (0224-574281).
Belfast—British Midland Airways (G) (0232-225151).
Birmingham—British Midland Airways (G) (021-236 0121).
Bournemouth—Jersey European Airways (0202-292755).
Brighton—South East Air (0273-462222).
Bristol—Dan-Air Services (0345-100200).
Cardiff—Dan-Air Services (0345-100200).
Coventry—Bristish Midland Airways (021-236 0121).
East Midlands—British Midland Airways (G) (0332-810552).

Edinburgh—British Airways (031-225 2525).

Exeter—Air U.K. (G) (0345-666777); Jersey European Airways (0392-64440).

Glasgow—British Midland Airways (G) (041-204 2436).

Leeds/Bradford—Dan-Air Services (0532-432645/6).

Liverpool—British Midland Airways (051-494 0200).

London Heathrow—British Airways (01-897 4000); Air U.K. (G only) (0345-666777).

London Gatwick—Dan-Air Services (0293-785622); Guernsey Airlines (G only) (0293-546571).

London Stansted—Air U.K. (G) (0345-666777); Jersey European Airways (0279-815151).

Luton—British Midland Airways (G) (01-581 0864).

Manchester—British Airways (061-228 6311); Guernsey Airlines (G) (061-228 2890).

Newcastle—Dan Air Services (091-261 1395).

Norwich—Air U.K. (G) (0345-666777).

Plymouth—Brymon Airways (G) (0752-707023).

Southampton—Air UK (G) (0345-666777).

Teesside—British Midland Airways (0642-219444).

(Note: some of the above services are seasonal only).

Air Services from Eire and Europe:

Cork—Aer Lingus (021-274331); Dan-Air Services (021-961277).

Dublin—Aer Lingus (G) (Dublin 377777).

France: Paris Roissy 1—Jersey European Airways (42 96 02 44); (General Agent Air France).

Dinard—Jersey European Airways (99 46 22 81); Aurigny Air Services (99 56 42 29).

Cherbourg—Aurigny Air Services (G) Chambre de Commerce et d'Industrie ((33 22 91 32).

Morlaix*—Britair ((98 62 10 22).

Deauville*—Alta ((31 88 31 28).

Nantes*—Stellair ((40 04 04 62).

Germany: Dusseldorf—British Airways (0130-3636). May to October 1988.

Frankfurt—D.L.T. (Saturdays and Sundays; May 7—September 4, 1988) c/o Lufthansa.

Netherlands: Amsterdam—NLM City Hopper (020-495070 or 493252).

(* indicates this service is seasonal).

Inter-Island and French Excursions between Guernsey (STD 0481) **and**:

Alderney: Aurigny Airlines (23474), Condor Hydrofoil (26121).

Carteret: Service Maritime* (28680).

Cherbourg: Aurigny Airlines (23474), Sealink British Ferries* (26121), Service Maritime (28680).

Dinard: Aurigny Airlines (23474).

Granville: Europe Aero-Fret* (35547).

Herm: Herm Express Ferries (21342), Herm Ferry

Launches (24678), Travel Trident (21379).

Sark: Isle of Sark Shipping (24059).

St. Malo: Condor Hydrofoil (26121)

(* indicates this service is seasonal).

Travel to Alderney

Air: There is a choice of daily flights from Southampton and Bournemouth. There are also flights from Exeter via Bournemouth and frequent services between Guernsey and Jersey and flights to Cherbourg and Dinard. For further information contact:

Aurigny Air Services (0481-822886);

Air Camelot (Bournemouth) (0202-570008).

Rail-Air Link: Waterloo to Southampton Airport (Southampton Parkway) express services every two minutes past the hour—journey time one hour. For further information ring: Aurigny Air Services (0481-822886).

Sea: Alderney can be reached by a direct service from Torquay via Torbay Seaways or from Weymouth (seasonal) or Portsmouth to Guernsey by British Channel Island Ferries and then by Condor Hydrofoil on Sundays, Tuesdays and Thursdays (May to September). For further information on sailing dates and times telephone: Torbay Seaways (0803-214397) or 0481-822433); any British Channel Island Ferries Office; Condor Hydrofoils (0481-26121).

Rentals:

Jersey (STD 0534)

Car Hire:
Aardvark Hire Cars, Esplanade, St. Helier (36558).
Abba Car Hire, Airport Road, St. Brelade (44131).
Austin/Rover Car Hire, St. Martin's Garage, St. Martin (54302).
Avis Rent-a-Car Ltd., St. Peter's Garage, St. Peter (83288).
Caledonia Car Hire, Caledonia Place, St. Helier (71072).
Castle Cars Ltd., St. Saviour's Road, St. Helier (23928).
Charles Street Car Hire, Charles Street, St. Helier (21242).
Dolphin Travel (Handling Europe) Ltd., Gloucester Street, St. Helier (27727).
Doubleday Garage Ltd., Stopford Road, St. Helier (31505).
Drive Hire Ltd., Esplanade, St. Helier (39222).
Europcar, Arrivals Hall, Jersey Airport, St. Peter (43156).
Falles Hire Cars Ltd., Longueville Road, St. Saviour (77011).
Fauvic Hire Cars Ltd., Fauvic, Grouville (52540).
Forum Garage, Esplanade, St. Helier (33623).
Freelance Hire Cars, Esplanade, St. Helier (24777).
Grosvenor Hire Cars, Grosvenor Street, St. Helier (25732).
Hallmark Cars Ltd., Airport Road, St. Brelade (44131).
Harringtons Garage Ltd., Route des Genets, St. Brelade (41363).
Hertz Rent-a-Car, Rue Cappelain, St. Peter (45621).*
Hireride, St. John's Road, St. Helier (31995).
Holiday Hire Cars, Parade, St. Helier (20464/5).
Ideal Hire Cars, Springfield Annexe, Janvrin Road, St. Helier (25129).
Leisure Drive Ltd., Perth House, St. Aubin (43236/7).
Jersey Motor Co. Ltd., (Stanley's Cars), Gloucester Street, St. Helier (23924).
Joyride Self Drive Hire, Gorey Hill, Gorey (53863).
J. Urquhart & Sons (C.I.) Ltd., Kensington Place, St. Helier.
Kingslea Hire Cars, Esplanade, St. Helier (24777).
Melbourne Car Hire, Route des Issues, St. John (62709).
Polar Self Drive, Beaumont, St. Peter (24577).
Premier Hire Cars, D'Aubert's Garage, St. Brelade's Bay (42283).
St. Bernards Hire Cars, Gorey Filling Station, Gorey (55513/5).
St. Mary's Garage Ltd., St. Mary (82533).
Southern Autos Ltd., David Place, St. Helier (24651).*
Sovereign Cars, Esplanade, St. Helier (71238).
Warren Cars, Esplanade, St. Helier (36557).
Weighbridge Car Hire, Caledonia Place, St. Helier (76122).
West Park Cars Ltd., Lord Coutanche House, Esplanade, St. Helier (26557 or 25756).
Zebra Hire Cars, Howard House, Esplanade, St. Helier (36556).

Motor Cycle Hire:
Cross Motor Cycles, New Street, St. Helier (33911).
Dolphin Travel (Handling Europe) Ltd., Gloucester Street, St. Helier (27727).
Kingslea Motor Cycle Hire, Esplanade, St. Helier (24777)

Scooter/Moped Hire:
Dolphin Travel (Handling Europe) Ltd., Gloucester Street, St. Helier (27727).
Doubleday Garage Ltd., Stopford Road, St. Helier (31505).
Hireride, St. John's Road, St. Helier (31995).
Kingslea Moped Hire, Esplanade, St. Helier (24777).
Polar Cars Ltd., Caledonia Place, St. Helier (38028).

Bicycle Hire:
Dolphin Travel (Handling Europe) Ltd., Gloucester Street, St. Helier (27727).
Doubleday Garage Ltd., Stopford Road, St. Helier (31505).
Hireride, St. John's Road, St. Helier (31995).
Kingslea Cycle Hire, Esplanade, St. Helier (24777).

Lawrence de Gruchy Ltd., Don Street, St. Helier (72002).
The Hire Shop, St. Aubin's Road, Millbrook (73699).

Push Car Hire:
Dolphin Travel (Handling Europe) Ltd., Gloucester Street, St. Helier (27727).
Doubleday Garage Ltd., Stopford Road, St. Helier (31505).
Hireride, St. John's Road, St. Helier (31995).
Kingslea Pushchair Hire, Esplanade, St. Helier (24777).
The Hire Shop, St. Aubin's Road, Millbrook (73699).

Wheelchair Hire:
The Hire Shop, St. Aubin's Road, Millbrook (73699).

Nursery Accessories Hire:
The Hire Shop, St. Aubin's Road, Millbrook (73699).

Guernsey (STD 0481)
Car Hire:
Avis Rent-a-Car, Ville au Roi, St. Peter Port (35266).
Luxicar, Glategny Esplanade, St. Peter Port (711952).
Attenborough Garage Ltd., Braye Road, Vale (44030).
Hertz (TI Cars Ltd.), Ville au Roi, St. Peter Port (38008).
Harlequin Hire Cars, Belval, Vale (44350).
Godfrey Davis Eurocar, Airport Forecourt (37638).
Silverline, North Esplanade, St. Peter Port (21629).
Sure Drive, Les Caches, St. Martin's (37321).
Ruette Braye Motors, P.O. Box 28, St. Martin's (37661).
Sarnia Hire Cars, Stanley Road, St. Peter Port (23933).
Motor House Ltd., The Grange, St. Peter Port (26846).
Falles Hire Cars, Braye Road, Vale (45766).
L'Islet Motors Ltd., L'Islet, St. Sampson's (45873).
Fort Road Motors, P.O. Box 180, Fort Road, St. Peter Port (37670/38706).
Easy Rent, Landes du Marche Garage, Vale (56555).
Economy Cars, Rue de Pre, St. Peter Port (26926).
St. Peter Port Garage, Rue de Pre, St. Peter Port (24261).
Kingslea Car Hire, 30 Charroterie Mills, St. Peter Port (27018).
Airport Garage, La Planque Lane, Forest (64104).

Motor Cycle And Motor Scooter/Moped Hire:
Millard & Co. Ltd., Victoria Road, St. Peter Port (20777).
Island Motor Company, Grande Rue, St. Martin's (35533).

Bicycle Hire:
Rent-a-bike, The Bridge, St. Sampson's (Adult Tricycles and Tandems) (49311).
T.G. Moullin & Sons Ltd., St. George's Esplanade, St. Peter Port (Summer only) (21581).
Millard & Co. Ltd., Victoria Road, St. Peter Port (20777).
Perrio's Chescot, Route Carre, L'Islet, St. Sampson's (Plus Tandems) (45217).
Wheel House Cycle Hire, Lindale, Rue Maze, St. Martin's (Plus Tandems) (36815).
Island Motor Company, Grande Rue, St. Martin's (35533).
Galaad Cycle Hire, Hougue du Pommier, Castel (53322).
St. Peter Port Garage, Rue de Pre St. Peter Port (24261).
Wembley Cycle Works, Rohais, St. Peter Port (21489).
Belle Greve Cycle Hire, 4 Connaught Terrace, Victoria Avenue, St. Sampson's (23253).
West Coast Cycles, Les Querites, Rue de la Hougue, Castel (Free delivery and collection) (53654).

Alderney (STD 0481-82)
Car Hire:
Grand Self Drive, c/o. Grand Island Hotel (2848).
Alderney Hire Cars, Braye Street (2611).
Riduna Garage, Braye Street (2919).
Alderney Motors, Marais Square (2727).

Bicycle Hire:
Pedal Power, Les Rocquettes (through archway at rear of B.

Machon's Fruit and Veg. Shop). (2286).
Salvatores Cycles, c/o. Le Courier Restaurant, Victoria Street (2689).
Le Blanquage, Melford

House, Le Blanquage (2000, ask for Dennis)
J.B. Cycle Hire, Ollivier Street (2294).

___

Tent Hire: Mr. Bohan,

Longy Road (2762).

___

Sark
Cycle Hire:
Jacksons, The Avenue (2161).

FOOD DIGEST

WHERE TO EAT

Places to eat in the Channel Islands cater for most palates and pockets. Variety is the thing: you can dine by candlelight, sip aperitifs on a seafront terrace, meet friends in a bustling bistro, go Greek, pick up a pizza, take away good old British fish 'n' chips or enjoy a simple pie and a pint in a country pub. The best menus feature high quality local produce, vegetables and especially seafood. Most meat is imported.

Find the right restaurant specialising in marine cuisine and something close to a perfect meal is likely to be served. Bass, plaice, sole and shellfish are landed in the morning and are on the plate by lunchtime. A summertime feast might include mussels poached in white wine, a lobster or dressed crab salad with Jersey new potatoes, washed down with a chilled Muscadet, and a bowl of strawberries topped with a dollop of thick cream.

Because of so much healthy competition for the brisk, year-round trade from businessmen, locals and tourists, owners and chefs do not like to be outdone by the restaurant next door. The islands have a reputation for gastronomy that goes far beyond their shores. The number of excursionists from France who come over just to eat a good lunch is testimony enough to the quality and variety of food on offer.

Portion control is unheard of and long menus in many establishments should be scrutinised. Extra dishes of the day—*Plats du jour*—are often chalked up on a blackboard in a corner somewhere and shouldn't be missed.

Chefs also tend to like writing their menus in French and a certain amount of inventiveness goes into describing a dish in that language. *Sole Bonne Femme* is understandable, *Sole Deauville* is not. Don't be afraid to ask what the ingredients are. Wine lists are normally comprehensive.

The traditional Sunday lunch is a great favourite with locals. Set menus in many hotels and restaurants are good value.

Time a trip to coincide with Jersey's annual Good Food Festival in May when many of the establishments put on special gastronomic menus and food fairs are held in St. Helier.

The following restaurants and hotels have been chosen as good places to dine. Alphabetical symbols at the end of each entry denote average prices per head for a full evening meal, excluding wine, or a one- or two-course lunch where indicated. Many restaurants offer extensive *à la carte* menus and feature set menus, normally of four or five courses for dinner, three at lunchtime. Special Sunday lunch menus are cheap and popular with residents and visitors throughout the year.

House wines are usually available at around £4 a bottle, although delving deeper into a wine list will reveal better quality German, French, Italian, Portuguese or Spanish wines at extremely reasonable prices. Table bookings at all establishments during the tourist season are advisable.

Visitors could plan a gastronomic tour of the islands without running out of choice. The Jersey Restaurateurs Association alone has more than 250 members.

A—Under £5
B—Under £7

C—Under £10
D—Under £15
E—£20 and over.

Jersey (STD 0534)
Around St. Helier:
Candlelight Grill: Hotel Revere, Kensington Place (38773). Modern cuisine, not cuisine moderne, with generous portions and interesting tastes. Finish with an Irish coffee prepared by the patron. The set dinner menu is good value. D

Victoria's Restaurant: Grand Hotel (72255 or 22301). Acknowledged to be one of Jersey's top restaurants. Try Smoked Salmon Romanoff, breast of chicken with spinach and brandy snaps filled with fruit. Dancing too. Jacket required. E

O'Fado: 20 The Esplanade (71920). A real Portuguese restaurant. Fresh fish like baby hake deep-fried, grilled squid with coriander and vinho verde to drink. D

Top of the Town: Hotel de France, St. Saviour's Road (38924). Speciality international menus feature at weekends. Many inventive dishes on the *à la carte*. Informal but smart. D

La Buca: The Parade (34283). The Italian influence goes way beyond pasta. Customers are lavished with lots of attention. D

Bombay Brasserie: Anley Street (76565). Among a number of ethnic restaurants this is one of the best. The manager, Shan Gill, originates from the Northwest Frontier so besides *tikkas* and *tandooris* there's also more regional Indian cuisine. C

Lido's Wine Bar: 4—6 Market Street (22358). Animated and very busy with outside tables to capture the Continentals. A variety of quiches and salads, as well as hot food on the clever lunch menu. Open until 9 pm. No evening meals. A

Pizza Express: 59/61 Halkett Place (33291). Go on a Wednesday night, eat pizza and listen to jazz. A

Albert Ramsbottom: 90 Halkett Place (78772). Fat-free English fish and chips served in a nautical setting. Substantial portions. A

Le Pommier: Pomme D'Or Hotel, Weighbridge (78644). Clean and central. Ideal stop for a lunchtime snack, quick evening meal or just tea and coffee. A

La Bastille: 4 Wharf Street (74059). A focal point of the annual French foodfair in May. Soups, salads and seafood appear on a well-balanced menu of hot and cold dishes. Lunch only. A

Out of Town:
Old Masters Restaurant: Little Grove Hotel, Rue de Haut, St. Lawrence (25321). Luxurious country hotel with a fine restaurant. Imaginative dishes—try the blueberry pie to finish. Not too expensive for quality.

Longueville Manor: St. Saviour (25501). Widely regarded as Jersey's top and most exclusive place to eat. However, the set dinner menu won't cost an arm and a leg. Chef Barry Foster's menu is quite unique. E

Château La Chaire: Rozel Valley, St. Martin (63354). Quiet and peaceful, set in a wooded valley, its important to look out for the signpost. Pannelled dining room and quality cuisine. D

Red Rose Restaurant: Oaklands Lodge Hotel, Augrès, Trinity (61735). Features a number of promotional menus throughout the year. Comfortable and with good service. D

The Old Court House Inn: St. Aubin (46433). Known as one of the settings in the TV detective series, *Bergerac*, it is lively and popular. Special menu for weight-watchers plus plenty of fresh fish. D

Seacrest Restaurant: Petit Port, Corbière (42687). In early summer, the sun sets in front of the terrace. Fairly formal though worth a visit for the roast duck, seafood and local produce. Flambé dishes are very good. D.

Apple Cottage: Rozel Bay, St. Martin (52111). Cosy and seafood is excellent value. *Pièce de resistance* is the sea bass with fennel and garlic. D

Borsalino Rocque: Fauvic, Grouville (52111). Always busy, especially for Sunday lunches, and notable for the relaxed, bistro-style atmosphere. Many *à la carte* dishes to choose from. Disco after 10.30 p.m. to work the meal off. D

Jersey Pottery Restaurant: Gorey Village, Grouville (51119). Seafood salads and home-made pastries, this is a place well worth stopping at for lunch. Open-air surroundings under the vines. Closed evenings and weekends. C

Guernsey (STD 0481)
In and Around St. Peter Port:

Da Nello Restaurant: 46 Pollet Street (21552). Reputation for its locally caught fish, charcoal grilled steaks and friendly service. 15th-century inn modernised. C

Dario's Restaurant: 56 Lower Pollet (25055). Bistro-type Italian restaurant with exclusive menu including French specialities and Italian wines. Good value. C

La Frégate: Les Côtils (24624). Fairly pricey but only food of the highest quality is prepared and served by professionals in luxurious surroundings. D

Le Nautique Restaurant: Quay Steps (21714). International à la carte. The accent is on local seafood and marine delicacies. D

Partners Restaurant: Warwick House, The Pollet (26624). Relaxed atmosphere, extensive à la carte. Burgers, pizzas and a summer lunchtime salad bar. Very popular. C

La Piazza Restaurant: Trinity Square (25085). The Piazza specialises in fresh Italian dishes and local fish. Veal T-Bone is rosemary and coquilles St. Jacques Bretonne are specialities. D

Le Recolte Restaurant: 7 Contrée Mansell (22640). Guernsey's original bistro. The cuisine includes French and Italian dishes besides traditional ones like Egg Florentine, Moules à la creme, Veal Normandie, Chicken Estragon or Surf & Turf. C

Bistro Valentino Top Bar/Pizzerie: 9 North Esplanade (27529). Selection of pizzas including takeaways. Popular late night venue. Large selection of fresh salads or daily specials at economic rates. A

Villa Dante Restaurant: 44 Lower Pollet (23246). Excellent menu with fish specialities and superb seafood platters. Ideal setting for special celebrations. C

Out of Town:
Le Gouffre Restaurant: Le Gouffre, Forest (64164). Situated in one of the island's most picturesque locations, Le Gouffre offers an interesting and varied à la carte menu with reasonably priced wines. C

Marina Restaurant: Beaucette Marina, Vale (47066). A French-style restaurant in a unique position on the north side of the island. Plenty of seafood. D

Rocquaine Bistro: Rocquaine, Torteval. (63149). Watch the sunset and enjoy a seafood supper. Morning coffee and bar meals served daily or à la carte menu. Bar open to non-diners. C

La Trelade Hotel: Forest Road, St. Martin's (35454). Local seafood a speciality. C

Alderney (STD 0481-82)
Nellie Gray's: Victoria Street, St. Annes (3333). Popular with the locals and business people. BBQ lunches in the garden during summer. À la carte seafood dinners. D

Le Courier Restaurant: Victoria Street, St. Annes (2689). Nationality of the chef has a lot to do with Italian influenced cooking. Coffees, teas, lunches and evening meals served. C

First and Last Restaurant: Braye Street (3162). Visiting yachtsmen flock here to enjoy the harvest of the sea including crabs and scallops. D

The Marais Hall Hotel: Marais Square, St. Annes (2683). A local landmark known for its traditional Sunday lunches and meals for the family. B

Herm (via operator)
The Ship Inn: White House Hotel (22159). Carvery-style buffet is an added feature in the evenings. Lobster, crab, fish and steaks are specialities. C

Sark (STD 0481-83)
La Moinerie Restaurant: (2089). Bar lunches available. Local lobster and crab usually available. A

Stock's Hotel: (2001). Two restaurants to suit most palates and pockets. Local fish, shellfish and Sark-grown produce. Reservations are essential. C

Hotel Petit Champ: (2046: All meals are cooked to order using fresh ingredients. Lobster and local fish specialities. Recommended in many restaurant guides. C

RECIPES

These suggestions come courtesy of Jersey's Federation of Women's Institutes and Mrs. Eva Le Page.

Mother Eve's Pudding
If you would have a good pudding, observe what you are taught.

Take two pennyworth of eggs, when 12 for the groat.

And of the same fruit that Eve had once chosen,

Well-pared and well-chopped, at least half a dozen.

Six ounces of bread (let your maid eat the crust!)

The crumbs must be grated as small as the dust.

Six ounces of currants from the stones you must sort,

Lest they break out your teeth, and spoil all your sport.

Five ounces of sugar won't make it too sweet,

Some salt and some nutmeg will make it complete.

Three hours let it boil without flurry or flutter,

And then serve it up without sugar or butter.

Des Fliottes

A very filling Jersey speciality still served in many island homes on Good Friday, is known as *Fliottes* (unlike the so-called "Wonders", there is no anglicization for this dish).

Ingredients:
Half lb. flour
One quart of milk
Quarter lb. sugar
Pinch of salt
Two eggs
Knob of butter

Method:
Mix the flour, sugar, eggs and salt, adding sufficient extra milk to make a thick batter. Put the quart of milk to boil in a large saucepan, adding the knob of butter. When the milk is boiling, drop in batter by the tablespoonful, allowing the *Fliottes* to float separately. Simmer for some minutes until

cooked. Serve hot with some of the milk or sprinkle some sugar over it.

Des Mervelles (Jersey Wonders):

Ingredients:
One lb. plain flour
Quarter lb. butter
Quarter lb. sugar
Three large eggs

Method:
Rub fat into flour, add sugar, then eggs, allow to stand for one hour. Cook in deep fat, the same heat as for chips. Makes 25 to 30 wonders.

Guernsey Gache

Ingredients:
One and a half lbs. plain flour
A pinch ground ginger
10 ozs. butter or margarine
Quarter nutmeg
One and a half teaspoons cooking salt
12 ozs. fruit and 2 ozs. peel
One oz. fresh yeast and one teaspoon honey
Quarter pint milk and quarter pint warm water

Method:
Put flour, ginger and salt into mixing bowl. Mix yeast and honey in a cup until mixture is creamy—add tepid water and milk. Put into centre of flour, sprinkle flour on top, leave until it cracks. Cut butter into small pieces, start to mix until it looks like satin. Add fruit and nutmeg. Re-knead, add more water if needed. Cover, put to rise for one hour until well risen. Knock back again, put into well-buttered tin—three one-lb. loaf tins. Leave to rise again for half

an hour or until well risen. Put into hot oven Reg. 6 or 425°F.

Guernsey Bean Jar (Serve four)

Ingredients
One pig trotter or piece of beef shin
One large onion
Parsley and thyme
Salt and pepper
Large potato; cut into small pieces
One carrot; cut into small pieces
Half lb. butter beans or haricots or (halves of each item).

Method:
Soak beans overnight, wash and drain. Put in large casserole, a layer of beans, onions, parsley and thyme. Repeat until filled. Put in meat, fill with water, cover, put into oven at 300°C, 150°C or Reg. 2 for seven to eight hours. Add salt when beans are nearly cooked.

Conger Soup

Ingredients:
Head and tail of conger
Salt
A small shredded cabbage
Two shallots
One bunch of mixed herbs
Borage leaves
Marigold leaves
Parsley and thyme
Plain flour
One quart of milk
Petals of marigold
One pint of green peas

Method:
Wash head and tail of conger well; put in a large saucepan, cover with water, add salt, bring to the boil and simmer for one hour. Remove fish, strain liquid and

return to saucepan, add a small shredded cabbage, the shallots finely sliced, bunch of mixed herbs chopped up, borage leaves, marigold leaves, parsley and thyme and boil until tender.

Thicken with two dessert-spoons of plain flour and cook for five minutes. Add one quart of milk and one oz. of butter and bring nearly to boil (but do not boil). Petals of marigold glowers are then thrown into the soup which is now ready to serve. When green peas are available one pint of these added to soup improves the flavour.

Du Nier Beurre (Black Butter)

This traditional apple pre-serve is still made in one or two Jersey parishes. Hun-dreds of pounds of peeled apples, gallons of cider, a huge pan and plenty of wood for an outhouse fire, are needed along with many willing volunteers to turn a real *Séthée D' Nier Beurre* or Black Butter Night into a special occasion with sing-a-longs and lots of merri-ment. In fact it takes a whole day for the apple, cider and spices to cook and reduce down to a thick, tasty jam, which is then put into jars and shared among the help-ers and the surplus sold. The event happens in the apple season—late November—but not necessarily every year. It is sometimes diffi-cult to get a sufficient quan-tity of fruit as commercial orchards are no longer a part of the agricultural scene. The preserve can be made in the comfort of a modern kitchen. The recipe is as follows:

Ingredients:
Two lbs. sour apples
Five lbs. sweet apples
Four quarts cider
10 lbs. white sugar
Four lemons
One dessertspoon mixed spice
Half stick liquorice

Method:
Boil cider until reduced to half. Add peeled, cored, sliced sweet apples, a basin-ful at a time. Add liquorice and lemons, minced. When all are well-cooked, add sour apples. Cook until thick, then add sugar and cook again, stirring frequently-When very thick and dark-add spice; bottle and cover as for jam.

IN TRANSIT

Many visitors return to the same hotel time and time again, mainly because they get value for money and a friendly welcome from staff who remember them from their previous holiday. This, of course, applies to the Brit-ish more than other nation-alities. About 80 percent of all the visitors come from the U.K. where the islands have built up appeal as sunshine resorts. "Favoured by the British, flavoured by the French", one advertising slogan puts it quite aptly.

Mass tourism has never hit the archipelago and proba-bly never will because of Government controls limit-ing the total number of holi-day beds available at any one time. There are around 25,000 in Jersey, 12,000 in Guernsey and fewer on the smaller islands. The choice of accommodation ranges across the spectrum—from the luxury international ho-tel with a string of awards displayed at its entrance to the humble British seaside guesthouse, quality self-ca-tering apartments, holiday villages and camp-sites.

Controls are such that each of the bailiwicks has its own registration and grading system that applies to all premises taking paying guests. Some 500 establish-ments in both Jersey and Guernsey are graded and assessed annually by a team of tourism department in-spectors. The schemes are designed to ensure that basic standards are met and proper facilities provided; unfortu-nately, they aren't compa-rable with grading systems in other countries. Visitors can choose where they want to stay by consulting official lists of the registered accom-modation in tourism bro-chures produced every year and sent free when their enquiry is made.

Jersey is soon to introduce

a new grading system. At present, there are two hotel registers with four grades each and one guesthouse register with three grades. The hotel registers indicate the style of the establishment rather than its standard. First-register hotels indicated by asterisks in the official list generally have more amenities and better service than those in the second register, which are denoted by diamond-shaped marks.

Guesthouses fall into categories A, B or C. Similarly, grade A, guesthouses have more facilities and generally higher standards of sevice than grade B or C guesthouses.

Guernsey's system is slightly simpler: it has only one hotel register and each entry is awarded between one and five crowns. Guesthouses, on the other hand, have four instead of three grades, from A to D. Over 20 percent of the accommodation available in Guernsey are in self-catering units, also graded A to D. Jersey's tourism industry relies more on conventional hotel accommodation and there is far less self-catering; but in recent years a number of high quality conversions of existing buildings have been carried out for this purpose.

There are not many accommodation choices in Alderney. Nevertheless, each establishment is inspected and approved ones are published. Details of the registered hotels, guesthouses, holiday cottages and flats on Sark and Herm can be found in Guernsey's accommodation guide.

The hotel and guesthouse tariffs quoted below and approximate rates for a person sharing a room on a half-board basis (bed, breakfast and evening meal). In most places, bed and breakfast terms only would also be available by arrangement with the proprietor. The number of persons accommodated are shown.

Prices generally fluctuate according to the season and are usually subject to annual cost of living increases. Substantial savings are possible by booking accommodation and travel together as part of a tour package.

Because there is only a limited amount of space, reservations for a holiday between May and September need to be made well in advance, otherwise choice could be limited. During the season, only certain hotels accept mid-week bookings. Visitors who decide to take a break "on spec" during the season can usually find somewhere to stay, although it is likely to be in the higher or lower price brackets—check before travel is arranged. The shoulder months, March, April, May or September and October, are, weather permitting, good times of year to travel to the Channel Islands—rates are lower and accommodation easier to find.

The islands prohibit the import of trailers or motorhomes and there are no caravan sites. Camping is allowed only on recognised sites where facilities are provided; no camping is permitted elsewhere.

Jersey (STD 0534)
Hotels:
Le Chalet: Corbière, St. Brelade (41216). Charming view of lighthouse or St. Ouen's Bay from every room. 63 beds. £20—£35.

Le Couperon de Rozel: Rozel, St. Martin (62190). Situated in picturesque harbour setting with good restaurant. 65 beds. £22—£36.

Littel Grove, Rue de Haut, St. Lawrence (25321). Elegance and luxury in a traditional granite country house. 28 beds. £55—£70.

Château La Chaire: Rozel Valley, St. Martin (63354). Peace and quiet, fine food and wine in an English ambiance. Some rooms have jacuzzis. 29 beds. £35—£45.

Mountview: New St. John's Road, St. Helier (78887). Overlooks the town. Convivial atmosphere. 82 beds. £16—£30.

Beau Rivage: St. Brelade's Bay (45983). Right on the beach. Recently renovated and modernized. 63 beds. £17—£32.

Fort d'Auvergne: Havre des Pas, St. Helier (73006). Part of a group of family-run hotels on the southern side of town. 136 beds. £17—£25.

Monte de la Rocque: St. Aubin (42942). Enjoy one of the best views of Jersey high above St. Aubin's bay. Modern decor and good food. 48 beds. £15—£35.

Maison Gorey: Gorey Village, St. Martin (53351). Situated in the heart of this pretty village; plenty of good restaurants and pubs in the vicinity. 56 beds. £16—£27.

Samares Coast: St. Clement (23411).Combines

ideal seaside location with prize-winning gardens. Also has purpose-built self-catering apartments. 99 beds. £13—£25.

Uplands: Mont a L'Abbe, St. Helier (20460). Not far out of town, in a quiet setting. Solar-heated pool. Noted for good service and food. 55 beds. £17—£24.

Idlerocks: Bonne Nuit Bay, St. John (61633). One of the prettiest parts of the island, ideal for walkers and anglers. 20 beds. £23—£30.

Maison Herault: Bulwarks, St. Aubin (42760). Right on the beachfront with unspoilt views. 23 beds. £15—£21.

Guesthouses with private facilities:
Alton: Rouge Bouillon, St. Helier (26100). Central and comfortable. 70 beds. £14—£22.

Grange Court: Roseville Street, St. Helier (22357). Close to the beach and town centre. Good value. 57 beds. £17—£22.

Elmdale Farm: Ville Emphre, St. Lawrence (34779). In the heart of the country with fine restaurant, bars and pool. 46 beds. £19—£24.

La Croix: Rouite de Millais, St. Ouen (82110). Away from it all in the northwest corner. Good home cooking. 25 beds. £14—£19.

Lavender Villa: Coast Road, Grouville (54937). Golf course, beach and spectacular Gorey Castle all within easy walking distance. Friendly and welcoming. 34 beds. £15—£23.

Undercliff: Bouley Bay, Trinity (63058). Quaint, old-

world guesthouse standing in large wooded grounds 600 feet (200 metres) from small fishing harbour. 21 beds. £16—£22.

Panorama: High Street, St. Aubin (42429). Ideally situated close to old harbour, beach, main bus routes and lots of restaurants. Bed and breakfast only. 33 beds. £16—£32.

Guesthouses without private facilites:
La Bonne Vie: Roseville Street, St. Helier (35955). Small, friendly and inexpensive. 30 beds. £9—£13.

Sabots d'Or: High Street, St. Aubin (43732). Originally built in 1776 in one of Jersey's oldest streets. Good spot. 22 beds. £14—£17.

Argilston: Mont Nicolle, St. Brelade (44027). One of Jersey's only proper vegetarian restaurants is run from the premises. Popular place to dine and stay. 17 beds. £21—£24.

La Plate: Midvale Road, St. Helier (33530). Budget accommodation in a family-run establishment. £9—£13. Bed and breakfast only.

Self-Catering:
Begerac's Hawaiian: Portelet, St. Brelade (45991). A new complex with south-facing beaches in the vicinity. 34 units. £250—£400 week for four-person apartment.

Southlands: Beaumont (23783). Across the road from the beach in the middle of St. Aubin's Bay. Eight three- to five-person apartments. £200—£375.

Woodlands Farm: Mont à L'Abbé, St. Helier (61345). Three well-equipped and decorated apartments on a dairy farm. From £145—£205 for a three-person unit or £215—£350 for a five-person unit.

Camp Sites:
Beauvelande Camp Site: St. Martin (53575). 200 persons. £2.50—£4 per person per day.

Rozel Camping Park: Summerville Farm, St. Martin (51989). £2—£3.50 per person per day.

St. Brelade's Camping Park: Route des Genets, St. Brelade (41398). £2—£4 per person per day.

Guernsey (STD 0481)
Hotels:
St. Pierre Park: Rohais, St. Peter Port (28282). Built by a Jersey brewery, this is Guernsey's most elegant hotel. Set in its own parkland with a nine-hole golf course, tennis courts, three restaurants and indoor pool; a treat to stay there. 276 beds. £50—£60.

Belle Luce: La Fosse, St. Martin (38764). Old fashioned comfort and excellent food. Situated near all the south coast bays. 70 beds. £20—£35.

Hougue du Pommier: Hougue du Pommier Road, Castel (56531). Guernsey farmhouse, built in 1712, modernised to include pitch and putt golf course, restaurant, solar-heated pool, on a 10-acre (-hectare) estate. 94 beds. £17—£30.

Dunchoille: Guelles Road, St. Peter Port (22912). Spacious gardens, patio, pool and other facilities. 47 beds. £16—£25.

Guesthouses with private facilities:
Les Piques Farm: Les Piques, St. Saviour (64515). An old Guernsey farmhouse down south. Friendly welcome and home-cooking. 21 beds. £15—£17.

Spes Bona: Les Vardes, St. Peter Port (25149). An attractive house with good views. Only five minutes' walk to town centre. 16 beds. £13—£15.

Guesthouses:
La Fosse Farm: Rue des Près, St. Peter in the Wood (63315). Good value and homely. 19 beds. £11—£13.

Le Jardin des Fleurs: Courtil du Milieu, Le Variouf, Forest (38213). Near lovely cliff scenery. Pleasant place to stay. 19 beds. £12—£14.

Les Montagues: Candie Road, St. Peter Port (24251). Georgian house, five minutes from town and adjacent to Candie Gardens and Beau Séjour. 19 beds. £12—£15.

Ikati: Le Varchin, St. Martin (38754). Guesthouse serving vegetarian and wholesome food. 14 beds. From £10.

Bed and Breakfast Guesthouses:
Ivy Cottage: Rue Marquand, St. Andrew (38113). Small and homely. Evening meals on request. 13 beds. £9—£11.

La Buena Vista: 58 Hauteville, St. Peter Port (23681). Ideal holiday base at budget price. 21 beds. £9—£10.

Furnished self-catering:
Close der Mer: Grandes Rocques Road, Castel (57726). A few yards from popular sandy beach. Seven four-person cottages. £100—£280 per week.

La Grande Mare: Vazon Bay, Castle (56576). Sports facilities on site and hotel with good restaurant alongside. Ten three-to four-person cottages. £180—£400 per week.

La Madeleine: Saumarez Street, St. Peter Port (26933). Twelve self-contained, modernized town flats, with views over port, taking two to six people. £95—£285 per week.

Mille Fleurs: Rue du Bordage, St. Peter in the Wood (63911). Three bungalows in the grounds of an old farmhouse. Four to six persons each. £125—£340 per week.

Perelle Bay Cottages: Perelle, St. Saviour (64981). Each of the three cottages has a double and a twin-bedded room. Right on the west coast. £100—£300 week.

Alderney
Hotels:
Sea View: Braye Street (2738). Overlooking Douglas Quay and Alderney's most popular beach. Good food and comfort. 47 beds. £20—£25 Bed and breakfast.

Belle Vue: Butes Road (2844). One of the island's best known, family-run hotels situated in the town. 43 beds. £23—£25.

Georgian House: Victorian Street (2471). Limited

but comfortable accommodation; elegant restaurants. Eight beds. From £25 during low season.

Victoria: Victoria Street (2754). Good amenities at a reasonable price. 17 beds. £15—£17.

Guesthouses:
The Town House: High Street (2330). Value for money in a central location. 19 beds. £18.

Braye: Braye Street (3256). Open year-round. Near the sea. 12 beds. £17.

Self-catering:
Mount Hale: Arsenal (2842). Victorian buildings modernised as two-to six-person holiday flats. Terms on application.

Pine Springs: La Vallée (2848). Norwegian log villas with pool. Four to seven persons. Price on application.

Sark
Hotels:
Aval du Creux: Harbour Hill (2036). Good food, wine and company in a unique location. 28 beds. £25—£30.

La Moinerie: (2089). Proprietor meets boat at the harbour—a nice touch. Good farmhouse fare. 23 beds. £16—£20.

Petit Champ: (2046). Food writers recommend it. Not too ostentatious. 36 beds. £25—£30.

Guesthouses:
Beauregard: (2073). Good views as the French name implies. Excellent cuisine. From £18.

Les Quatres Vents: (2247). Inexpensive. £10—£15.

Self-catering:
La Vaurocque: (2020). Seven cottages sleeping two to six persons. £150—£350 per week.

Herm
Hotels:
The White House: (22159). Overlooks the harbour and close by the island's two shops, a pub and restaurants. Peaceful. 85 beds. £28—£38.

Furnished Self-catering:
Dairy Cottages: Belvoir House, Fisherman's Cottage and Pennywort Cottage (22377). Fully equipped cottages or flats for two to six persons. Apply to G.B. Wood. £85—£400 a week.

ACTIVITIES

THINGS TO DO

Castles, Museums And Art Galleries

JERSEY
Elizabeth Castle: St. Aubin's Bay (23971). Open daily between 9.30 a.m. and 5.30 p.m. from March until October. Jersey Militia Museum, tableaux depicting events during the 17th century. A recent exhibition "Granite and Gunpowder" illustrates the defences of Jersey over the last 400 years and there is an audiovisual presentation of the "History of Elizabeth Castle". Pedestrians can walk across a causeway at low water or use the privately owned ferry service in a World War II landing craft. (Fares do not include entry to the Castle).

German Underground Hospital: Meadowbank, St. Lawrence. Exhibition and Museum of the Occupation. Open March to early November. Open twice weekly from February 1 to March 5, and from early November to late December, on Thurs-

days from noon to 5 p.m. and Sundays from 2 to 5 p.m.

Grève de Lecq Barracks: Grève de Lecq. Military barracks built at the time of Waterloo. Owned and restored by The National Trust for Jersey. Exhibition of militaria and Jersey horse-drawn vehicles. Open April to September (inclusive) on Tuesdays, Wednesdays, Thursdays and Fridays from 2 to 5 p.m.

Island Fortress Occupation Museum: 9 Esplanade, St. Helier. Open from 10a.m. seven days a week, Easter to November (inclusive). Sir Francis Cook Gallery (Jersey Heritage Trust), Route de Trinité, Augrès, Trinity. Temporary exhibitions and a permanent collection of the work of Sir Francis Cook (63333). Open only as advertised.

Jersey Battle of Flowers Museum: La Robeline, Mont des Corvées, St. Ouen. See animals and birds made of wildflowers. Open daily 10 a.m. to 5 p.m. including Sundays from March 1 to November 30.

Jersey Motor Museum: St. Peter's Village. Open

daily from 10a.m. to 5p.m. from March to end October. Veteran and vintage cars; Jersey steam railway exhibition, motorcycles, aero engines; and also World War II Allied and German military vehicles.

Jersey Museum, (Société Jersiaise): 9 Pier Road, St. Helier (75940). Open all year, Mondays to Saturdays from 10 a.m. to 5 p.m. Victorian period rooms; maritime, local history and coin displays including Lillie Langtry room; Natural History Gallery; paintings by local artists and of Jersey interest.

La Hougue Bie Museum (Société Jersiaise): La Hougue Bie, Grouville (53823). Open Tuesdays to Sundays from 10 a.m. to 5 p.m. from mid-March to end October. Agricultural, Archaeology and Geology, and German Occupation Museums, massive Neolithic tomb, medieval chapels and railway exhibition.

Mont Orgueil Castle, Gorey: Four tableaux with commentary depicting the Castle's history as well as a small museum room. Open daily from 9.30 a.m. to 5.30 p.m. from mid-March to approximately the end of October. Floodlit nightly Easter to end of October.

St. Peter's Bunker: Occupation Museum, St. Peter. Open daily 10 a.m. to 5 p.m. from March to end of October. Largest collection of German Occupation military and civilian exhibits in Jersey. Housed in a seven-roomed German bunker.

GUERNSEY:

Castle Cornet: Castle Emplacement, St. Peter Port (21657 or enquiries 26518). The castle was founded by King John in 1206; buildings date from the 13th to the 20th century and it was the scene of many battles. Royal Guernsey Militia Museum, Maritime Museum, Armoury, Picture galleries, 201 Squadron Museum and museum shop. Noonday gun fired daily. Open 10.30 a.m. to 5.30 p.m. Closed November 1 to March 31.

Château des Marais: Castle Lane, St. Peter Port (26518). Castle is surrounded by a moat and large outer bailey. Being restored by the States Ancient Monuments Committee.

Coach House Galleries: Les Islets, St. Peter's (65339). Farm buildings which provide an attractive setting for an art gallery on two floors with an etching studio and pottery workshop alongside. Open 11 a.m. to 5.30 p.m. in season (March—December). Admission is free.

Colognoli Galleries: 9 The Grange, St. Peter Port (26193). This gallery holds a regular exhibition of prints, photographs and paintings by 10 local artists. Open from 9.30 a.m. to 5.30 p.m. Tuesdays to Saturdays.

Folk Museum (National Trust of Guernsey): Saumarez Park, Castel (55384). The National Trust of Guernsey's Folk Museum contains a rich collection of Victoriana, furniture, china and early household equipment set out in a series of rooms arranged around an attractive 18th-century farm courtyard. Open 10 a.m. to 5.30 p.m. (last tickets 5 p.m.) daily. Closed mid-October to mid-March.

German Military Underground Hospital: La Vassalerie Road, St. Andrew's (39100). Complex of concreted tunnels hewn out of solid rock by slave workers of many nationalities under the control of German Occupying Forces, 1940-1945. Occupation relics and newspapers on view. Open May until September, from 10 a.m. to noon; from 2 to 5 p.m. in April; and 2 to 4 p.m. in October. In November, it opens from 2 to 3 p.m. on Sundays and Thursdays.

German Occupation Museum: Forest (38205). Tells the story of the German Occupation of Guernsey, 1940-1945, with visual tableaux, a lifesize street, bunker rooms, cinema, tea-rooms and garden. Open 10.30 a.m. to 5.30 p.m. April to October. Sundays and Thursdays, 2 p.m. to 5 p.m. October to April.

Guernsey Museum and Art Gallery: Candie Gardens, St. Peter Port (26518).

Opened in 1978, the island's first purpose-built museum made a big enough impact to win the national Museum of the Year Award in 1979. The exhibition depicts the story of the island and its people. Open 10.30 a.m. to 5.30 pm., and until 4.30 p.m. in winter. (Closed Christmas week).

The Gun Museum: No. 8 Westerbrook, South Side, St. Sampson's (49102). The Gun Museum has a collection of handguns and rifles, both antique and modern. Open 10 a.m. to 4 p.m.

Maritime Museum: Rocquaine Bay, St. Peter's (65036 or enquiries 26518). Built as part of the island's defences against Napoleon in 1804 on the site of an ancient castle. Restored in 1975 as a maritime museum featuring the shipwrecks on the treacherous Hanois Reef nearby. The fort is situated on a small islet connected to the shore by a stone causeway. Open 10.30 a.m. to 12.30 p.m. and 1.30 to 5.30 p.m. Closed from mid-October to mid-April.

St. Saviour's Tunnel: St. Saviour's (64679). The St. Saviour's Underground Tunnel complex was carved out of solid granite by European and Russian slave labour. Open 10 a.m. to 6 p.m. daily.

Studio Gallois: Paintings of Guernsey by Brenda Munson, Lower Forest Lane, St. Peter Port (21496). This exhibition of about 30 oil paintings of Guernsey features St. Peter Port lanes, steps, old buildings, rooftops and chimneys. Country farms and beaches are also shown by this local artist, who has exhibited abroad and has works in many international collections. Open 10 a.m. to 5 p.m. Closed on Sundays.

Guernsey Telephone Museum: "Hermes", La Planque, Cobo Road, Castel (57904 when open). The State of Guernsey have run the local telephone service since it started in 1898. Run voluntarily by Guernsey Telecommunications staff, the Telephone Museum opened in 1976 at the former Castel Manual Exchange. The displays, some working, include undersea cables, switchboards, teleprinters, telephones and other plant. Open 7 to 9 p.m. on Tuesday and Wednesday evenings. Admission is free.

Tomato Museum: King's Mills, Castel (54389). The tomato centre features a living museum showing how the growing of tomatoes has developed over the past 100 years. Try some Guernsey tomato wine in the restaurant. Open 9 a.m. to 5.30 p.m.

Victor Hugo's House: Hauteville, St. Peter Port (21911). Home of the famous French political exile, Victor Hugo, Hauteville House is as unique as its former owner. Open daily, except Sundays and bank holidays, from 10 to 11.30 a.m. and 2 to 4.30 p.m. Closed from October 1 to March 31.

ALDERNEY

Museum: Covers the history of the island from the neolithic age to the present day. Natural history section.
Bird Museum: The only

one of its kind in the Channel Island—it is situated in a Victorian fort on Raz Island.

Fortifications: A historical feature of the island, dating back to Victorian days. Tours can be arranged.

Places of Interest

JERSEY
Samaréz Manor: Rock and Water Gardens, and a half-acre (0.2-hectare) Herb Garden. Herb courses and guided tours of the house.

Jersey Zoological Park: Trinity. Founded by Gerald Durrell, author, broadcaster and naturalist. A sanctuary for the breeding and conservation of rare and endangered species of wildlife.

Jersey Lavender: Near Red Houses, St. Brelade. Six acres (two hectares) of scented lavender.

Jersey Pottery, Gorey Village: Set in beautifully laid out gardens. You will enjoy watching the skilled potters and handpainters.

La Mare Vineyards: In the vicinity of Devil's Hole, St. Mary. It is the first vineyard in Jersey, set in the grounds of an 18th-century farmhouse.

Le Moulin de Quetivel: St. Peter's Valley. Watermill restored to working order by The National Trust for Jersey.

L'Etacq Woodcrafts: L'Etacq, St. Ouen. See Jersey giant cabbage products being made.

Eric Young Orchid Foundation: Victoria Village. A unique private collection of orchids.

Howard Davis Park: St.

Saviour. One of the best of Jersey's public gardens.

Kempt Tower: Five Mile Road, St. Ouen. Features information and natural history displays connected with the conservation area around Les Mielles.

The Fantastic Tropical Gardens: St. Peter's Valley. Tropical plants are laid out in various settings illustrating their countries of origin.

Heatherbrae Farm: St. John. Watch Jersey cows being milked.

Jersey Butterfly Centre: Haute Tombette Carnation Nursery, St. Mary.

Shire Horse Farm Centre: Champ Donné, St. Ouen.

St. Matthew's Church: Millbrook. Renowned for its Lalique glass.

Fort Regent Entertainment and Sports Centre, St. Helier: This 22-acre (nine-hectare) converted fortress can be reached by cable car, escalator or car. Funfair, museums, cafés, an indoor-heated pool, shows and sports facilities attract families on a rainy day. Good views from the rampart walks.

GUERNSEY
The Guernsey Aquarium: La Valette, St. Peter Port (Tel: 23301). Collection of seawater, freshwater and tropical fish.

Chapel of St. Apolline: St. Saviour's medieval chapel built in 1392.

Guernsey Clockmakers Ltd: Les Vauxbelets, St. Andrew's (36360). Local craftsmen create clocks and barometers.

Guernsey Copper Craft:

Rocquaine Bay, St. Peter's (65112). A display of copper and brassware. Also see craftsmen at work.

Déhus Dolmen: Paradis, Vale (enquiries to 26518). Fine example of a prehistoric chambered tomb with side chambers.

Friquet Flower and Butterfly Centre: Le Friquet, Castel (54378). The main attraction is the butterfly house where visitors can walk among free-flying butterflies from all over the world in their natural habitat.

Gold, Silversmiths and Jewellers: "Bruce Russell", Le Gron, St. Saviour's (64321). This is the only gold and silversmiths workshop in Guernsey.

The Guernsey Herb Garden: Ashcroft Hotel, Sous l Eglise, St. Saviour's (63114 or 65684). Over 400 herbs grow in the garden.

Little Chapel: Les Vauxbelets, St. Andrew's. The Little Chapel is famous as the smallest church in the world. Made from shells and pottery, the Chapel is a replica of the Shrine at Lourdes.

St. James: College Street, St. Peter Port (711360 administration; 711361 box office). St. James is Guernsey's principal concert and assembly hall.

Old Guernsey Market: Market Street, St. Peter Port. From May to September on Thursday afternoons. Evening entertainment from July to early September.

Oatlands Craft Centre: Braye Road, St. Sampson's (49978). Watch glass- blowers and glass-engravers, silversmiths, patchworkers and potters at work.

Tropical Vinery and Garden: St. Saviour's (63566). Four greenhouses containing exotic flowers and trees, including hibiscus, bougainvillaea, bananas, coffee etc.

Guernsey Zoo: La Villiaze, St. Andrew's (39176). Mainly smaller and less well-known mammals and birds are housed.

Beau Séjour Leisure Centre: St. Peter Port. A focal point for visitors when the weather's bad. Sports facilities, theatres and pool all under one roof.

ALDERNEY
The Alderney Railway: The only working railway in the Channel Islands, is operated by Railway Society members at weekends and bank holidays. Follows a coastal route from Braye Bay to Mannez Quarry.

SPORTS

Angling: With their varied coastlines and clear waters rich in marine life, the Channel Islands are ideal locations for sea anglers, particularly from mid-summer to the end of autumn. More than 70 different species of fish have been caught in local waters, including sharks (not inshore!), conger, rays, turbot, bass and bream.

No permission is needed to fish from the coastline or harbours and fellow anglers and tackle dealers are always pleased to offer help on where to go. Boat trips with experienced skippers who know many of the marks are

good value. Cost is about £15 per day per person and includes bait, tackle and refreshments .

The offshore reefs near Jersey like the Ecréhous, the Minquiers and Paternosters are rich grounds. Guernsey has become a mecca for deepwater wreck anglers.

Alderney is acknowledged to be one of the top places for shore fishing in the whole of the British Isles.

Freshwater fishing is limited but possible in the reservoirs. Temporary permits are issued by the water authorities in Jersey and Guernsey.

For boat fishing trips contact:
Jersey (STD 0534)
John Thompson (63679);
Wayne Latham (39664);
Wally Rondel (61620);
Bill Crowley (74037 and 74875).

Guernsey (STD 0481)
Roy Taylor (37959);
Dave Longlois (26307);
Arnie Brehaut (63730);
Dougal Lane (27161).

Alderney (STD 0481 82)
Roddy Hayes (contact through tourist information 2994).

Sark (STD 0481 83)
George Guille (2107)

Bird-watching: Wide ranges of habitat and a mild climate are reasons why birds use the islands during spring and autumn migrations. Look for Dartford warblers, short-toed treecreepers, firecrests, and Brent geese. For those who are not experienced enough to spot the difference, field guides containing location maps are available. Contact ornithologists Tim Earl (Guernsey 64504) or Mike Stentiford (Jersey 61114).

Botany: With their mild winters and warm summers, the islands boast nearly 2,000 species of flora, of which 400 or more are winter-flowering. Botanical societies on the bigger islands have published various leaflets and information packs which list contact names for guided rambles. Further details from Jersey Historical Tours (76066) and Hêches Herbs in Guernsey (63545).

Flying: A company based at Guernsey Airport offers fulltime training courses for private pilots (contact G. Dunster 37217). The Jersey Aero Club (43990) does not offer residential courses but flying lessons are available. Qualified private pilots are welcome to fly into Jersey, Guernsey or Alderney.

Gardening: Gardens in the islands are rarely without colour. In spring, the fields and hedgerows are transformed by daffodils bursting into bloom. From then on tulips, camellias, magnolias, hydrangeas and many other bedding or evergreen plants can be seen in the parks and gardens. Once a week during summer, private gardens in Jersey and Guernsey are open to the public in aid of charity. Ask for Jersey's *Floral Island* leaflet.

Golf: Demand for the game exceeds supply. Local residents wanting to join a club in Jersey can expect to be on the waiting list for up to 15 years. Perhaps the only way to play a full round of 18 holes on the two links courses in Jersey and one in Guernsey is to strike up a friendship with an existing member and get invited along as a guest player. The only other way is to show proof of membership of an affiliated club.

Otherwise, frustrated golfers can relieve a little tension on Jersey's driving range, two "pitch and putt" courses, and on a number of private short courses in Guernsey. Alderney's only golf course (nine-hole) normally quiet and uncrowded. Rates are very reasonable and clubs can be hired.

Further information:

Jersey
Eighteen holes:
La Moye Golf Club, St. Brelade (42701).
Royal Jersey Golf Club, Grouville (51042).
Nine holes:
Jersey Recreation Ground, Grève d'Azette No clubs hired. (21938).
Western Golf Range, Five Mile Road, St. Peter (82787).

Guernsey
Eighteen holes:
Royal Guernsey Gof Club, L'Aneresse, Vale (47022).

Alderney
Nine holes:
Alderney Golf Club, Route des Carrières (2835).

Horse Riding: One way of reaching the heart of the countryside is on horseback. Treks and escorted hacks along a well-maintained circuit of bridle paths, through valleys and up small lanes, and along cliff tops or dunes, normally last two or three hours and can be arranged through several of the stables. Riding on the beach is also permitted in Jersey but not between September 11 to 30. For more information contact:

Jersey
Bon-Air Stables, St. Lawrence (63154).
Broadlands Riding Centre, St. Peter (44337).
Sorrel Stables & Saddlery Centre, St. Peter (42009).

Guernsey
Guernsey Equestrian and Saddlery Centre, St. Sampson's (25257).
West Riding and Trekking Centre, St. Saviour's (63719).

Scuba Diving: Qualified divers can explore the mysteries of the deep in the clean, cold waters around the islands. Introductory dives and certificate courses are also available for those who want to learn the sport. The currents are often strong so don't dive unaccompanied. More fish will be seen with a mask and snorkel than with scuba gear—temperate species always seem to be scared off by the bubbles. For boat dives, equipment hire and courses, contact:

Jersey
The Watersports Centre, First Tower (32813).

The Underwater Centre, Bouley Bay (61817).
Jersey Sub Aqua Club, South Pier (81078).
Dive and Ski Sports, Francis Street (36209).

Guernsey
Fletcher Sports (24114).

Alderney
Brian Markell (2633).

Surfing: Surfers from many places flock to St. Ouen's Bay in Jersey to ride the big Atlantic swells. On several occasions the island has played host to major competitions and invitational events.

Jersey surfers travel around the world in search of the perfect wave and are among the best at their sport in the British Isles. Surf can also be found on Guernsey's west coast and in Alderney. A number of beach concessions hire boards and wetsuits. Jersey also has surfing schools at the Watersplash (82844) and Sands (83707).

Windsurfing: Islands are normally ideal locations for windsurfing and this archipelago is no exception. Wind strength and direction varies from day to day and it is quite feasible to move from bay to bay to find the best conditions. Beginners, intermediate and advanced wave sailors are catered for. Qualified instruction is available at schools in the three largest islands. A basic certificate course lasts five hours.

Jersey
Wind and Water Windsurfer Schools, St. Aubin

and St. Brelade (43777)
Longbeach Windsurfing Centre (25362).
Guernsey
Windsurfing International, Cobo (53313).
Windsurfing Surfari, Pembroke Bay (48069).

Alderney
Alderney Windsurfing (Tourist info. 2994).

Yacht Charter: Some sailing experience is necessary to charter a boat, or alternatively, skippers who know the local waters are available. The freedom to sail between the islands or to France makes a holiday afloat a worthwhile proposition. All marinas offer pontoon moorings and support facilities. Boats can be hired by the hour, day or week.

Contact:
Jersey Cruising School (51983) or
Guernsey and Herm Leisure Travel (21897).

NIGHTLIFE

Jersey and Guernsey, of course, offer more in the way of entertainment than the smaller islands—dining out, cabarets, going to a discotheque, film-shows, concert recitals and drama productions are the main choices.

In the summer many hotels lay on after-dinner entertainment for their guests, usually variety acts or singers. One hotel group has a travelling show that performs at different premises every night of the week.

Cabaret and dance shows at various nightspots are

popular with British tourists. The Art Centre in St. Helier has photographic and art exhibitions, touring theatre company productions and much more. St. James Hall in Guernsey has an extensive programme of entertainment, mostly of a formal nature.

Beau Séjour Leisure Centre, Guernsey, and *Fort Regent Sports and Entertainment Complex*, on the neighbouring island, bring in international variety acts, comedians, bands, on a regular basis during the season. The theatre at Beau Séjour has touring acts and individual artistes.

Many of the clubs and societies in the islands, add to the nightlife in pubs, particularly those associated with pure entertainment such as folk, jazz or country and western music.

The latest films either change weekly or run a season in the two cinemas in Jersey, one in Guernsey and Alderney's island hall.

For younger people, there are plenty of clubs and discotheques, and live bands play regularly. For the under 18s, who are not permitted to drink alcohol, some special discos serve soft drinks only.

Discotheques: Entrance fees for most clubs and discos are around £2. Drink prices are not excessive as in some continental resorts—everything except cocktails is under £1.
Guernsey
The Golden Monkey, Weighbridge, St. Peter Port (26755).
Bonapartes, Les Croutes,

St. Peter Port (22393).
Barbarellas, Anns Place, St. Peter Port (25349).
Pierrots Nightclub, St. Pierre Park, St. Peter Port (28282).
The Gap, Albany Hotel, St. Peter Port (28762).

Alderney
Belle Vue Hotel, The Bute (2844).

Public Houses: There are lots of quaint pubs with friendly landlords where a game of darts and a pint of the local brew can be enjoyed. Jersey is reputed to have a bar for every day of the year.

In the two larger islands, many pubs have been modernised to attract a younger and more upmarket clientele. Most pub lunches range from a simple toasted sandwich to a full-scale feast of fish or meat.

There is no uniformity in the two bailiwicks as regards pubs operating hours; indeed, the licensing laws are rather complicated. Jersey's pubs operate the longest hours—all day during the week, closing at 11 p.m., and on Sunday from 11 a.m. to 1 p.m. and 4.30 p.m. to 11 p.m. In Guernsey, drinking is permitted during the week throughout the day until 11

p.m., but not a drop can be touched on Sundays except in restaurants.

Alderney's laws are perhaps the most sensible: pubs open from 11 a.m. to 2 p.m. and 5 p.m. to midnight in the week (at their discretion, landlords can keep the premises open until 1 a.m.); midday to 2 p.m. and 8 p.m. to midnight on Sundays.

Pubs hours for Herm and Sark are similar to Guernsey's. There's no drinking-up time in the islands, as there is in the U.K. Clubs and discotheques also close surprisingly early: 11.45 p.m. in Guernsey and 12.45 a.m. in Jersey.

FESTIVALS

EVENTS

Jersey
Festival of Pool: Professional and amateur players take part in this popular tournament. February.
Jazz Festival: Long weekend of jazz featuring well-known artists. March.
International Air Rally: Attracts competitors from the U.K. and Europe. May.
Spring Festival: A month-long festival, throughout the island, of special markets, shows and exhibitions, dancing, concerts and bands. May.
Good Food Festival Week: Food and wine tastings, cookery demonstrations, food displays and gala events held all over the

island. May.
Festival France-Jersey: French-style food fair and cultural events with street theatre and concerts. June.
Floral Island Week: Flower shows, walks and talks. The island floral competition also judged. July.
Battle of Flowers: A high spot for the holiday season, this internationally renowned floral carnival takes place on the second Thursday every August. Funfair and other events during the week culminate in a spectacular parade of large and small floats decorated with fresh and paper flowers, bands and firework displays. Call 30178 for details and entry prices. August.
International Folklore Festival: This is a three-day

programme of concerts and ceilidhs in People's Park and throughout the island. September.
Battle of Britain Week: Highlight is a spectacular air display. September.
Darts Festival: Up to 1,000 players participate. October.

Guernsey
Liberation Day Celebrations: Street fairs and processions. May.
International Dance Festival: Held at Beau Séjour and attracts entrants from all over the world. Competitions and displays of many dance styles. June.
Festival of Music: This annual festival features a varied programme of musical events by leading French musicians held for many

years at Notre Dame church. July—August.

Viaer Marchi: Guernsey evening at Saumarez Park. July.

Round Table Harbour Carnival and Regatta: Man-powered flight, tug-of-war, dinghy races and boat parade in Victoria Marina. July.

Agricultural and Horticultural Shows: South Show features the Miss Guernsey Competition, the West Show—a gymkhana, and the North Show—the Battle of Flowers. Second to fourth weeks of August.

Battle of Flowers: Not as big as the Jersey version, features a float parade and agricultural fair in Saumarez Park. Brings the crowds. Third or fourth Thursday in August.

Powerboat Week: Guernsey is now established on the world powerboat circuit and will host the Formula One Championships in 1988 as well as sponsor the London Boat Show. Spectating is best from another boat. September.

Battle of Britain Week: Similar display to Jersey. September.

Guernsey Festival of Chess: International competition. October.

Air Rally: Private aircraft fly in from all over Europe. October.

Alderney

Alderney Week: Attractions include attempts at man-powered flight off Braye Quay, a daft raft race, town crier and strong-man competitions. Begins with a cavalcade and ends with a torchlight procession to a firework display and bonfire on The Bute. First week of August.

Milk-a-Punch Sunday: Each customer gets a glass of milk punch—a heady combination of eggs, milk, rum, sugar and nutmeg— from noon to 2 p.m. Pubs rival each other to see who can make the best and strongest grog. First Sunday every May.

Sark

Mid-summer Flower Show: When the island is in full bloom, the best kept gardens are judged by a visiting team of experts; also special exhibits and a flower arranging competition. June.

Sark Cattle Show: Judges from the other islands are invited to inspect the local herd. July.

Water Carnival: Fancy dress and superteam competitions, sideshows and races on land the first day. Decorated boats, swimming events, raft races and a flying machine contest at Creux Harbour the next day. Miss Water Carnival chosen by visitors. Mid-August.

Autumn Show: Agricultural and horticultural event. September.

DIPLOMATIC MISSIONS

The Channel Islands are too small to warrant their own diplomatic representation overseas. The interests of foreign nationals living and working in the islands, as well as visitors, are handled by Consuls in each bailiwick.

Consular Offices in-Jersey:
Denmark: Honorary Consul—John W. Huelin, Val La Give, Le Mont du Val la Give, Grouville (54165).

France: Consul—M. L. Vannini, Philip Le Feuvre House, La Motte Street, St. Helier (26256).

Germany: Honorary Consul—Mr. R.A. Norman, c/o. Commodore Shipping 28 Conway Street, St. Helier (71263).

Ireland: Consul—Mrs. P. O'Neill (75122).

Norway: Honorary Consul—Mr. John W. Huelin (54165).

Portugal: Consul—Mr. Antonio Alvares, 8 York Street, St. Helier (77188).

Sweden: Honorary Consul—Mr. John W. Huelin (54165).

Netherlands: Consul—Mr. R.R. Jeune, 18 Grenville Street, St. Helier (74343).

Vice-Consuls in Jersey:
Belgium: Hon. Vice-

Consul—Mr. D.A. de Ste. Croix, 18 Grenville Street, St. Helier. (74343).
Finland: Hon. Vice-Consul—Mr. D.O. Moon, 18 Grenville Street, St. Helier (74343).
Latvia: Hon. Vice-Consul—Advocate R.A. Falle, Piermont House, 38 Pier Road, St. Helier (79494).
Italy: Foreign Consular Agent—Mr. Renzo Martin c/o. Les Arches Hotel, St. Martin (54083).

Vice-Consuls in Guernsey:
Belgium: Vice-Consul—Mr. A. de Garis, White Rock, St. Peter Port (24480).
Denmark: Vice-Consul—Mr. S. Marcussen, La Chaumiere, Rue de la Douzaine, Fort George, St. Peter Port (24355).
France: Vice-Consular Agent—Mr. M.G. Flouquet, c/o. P. Drake (44460), or Mr. R. Le Prevos, c/o. Piette Ltd., St. Peter Port (23756).
Italy: Vice-Consular-Agent—Mrs. L. Edwards, La Moule, La Hurette Road, Kings Mills, Castel (75000).
Netherlands: Vice-Consul—Mr. G. Norman, c/o. Norman Piette Ltd. (23756).

TOURIST OFFICES

The bailiwicks of Jersey and Guernsey compete with each other as holiday destinations so enquiries have to be directed to the appropriate tourist office and not to a central bureau covering the whole Channel Islands. Information on how to get to the islands and where to stay is normally sent free-of-charge (surface mail only) to any part of the world on request.

The tourism departments provide help in finding accommodation but do not make bookings or reservations. Public information and accommodation desks in Jersey and Guernsey are manned during normal office hours out-of-season, during weekday evenings, all day Saturday and on Sunday mornings and evenings, in summer.

Enquiries in writing or by phone should be directed to:
The States of Jersey Tourism Committee, The Weighbridge, St. Helier, Jersey, Channel Islands (0534-78000).
Guernsey Tourist Board, P.O. Box 23, White Rock, Guernsey, Channel Islands (0481-26611)
States of Alderney Tourist Office, Alderney, Channel Islands (0481-82-2994).
Sark Tourist Office, Sark, Channel Islands (0481-83-2345).

In addition to these main offices, Jersey is the only one of the Islands to have offices in London and Paris. Contact:
Jersey Tourism, 35 Albemarle Street, London W1X 3FB (01-493-5278).
Maison de Tourisme de L'Ile de Jersey, 19 Boulevarde Malesherbes, 75008 Paris (4-742 9368).

In other parts of the world, the main offices of the British Tourist Authority can deal with enquiries concerning the Channel Islands. However, write directly to the tourism departments in the islands if up-to-date information is unavailable. The B.T.A offices in English-speaking countries are:
Australia (Sydney) 4th Floor, Midland House, 171 Clarence Street, Sydney, NSW 2000 Tel: (010 61 2) 29 8627.
Canada (Toronto) 94 Cumberland Street, Suite 600, Toronto, Ontario M5R 3N3 Tel: (010 1 416) 961 8124.
Hong Kong Suite 903, 1 Hysan Avenue, Causeway Bay, Hong Kong Tel: (010 852) 5-764 366/764 371.
New Zealand (Auckland) 8th Floor, Norwich Insurance House, CNR Queen & Durham Streets, Auckland 1 Tel: (010 649) 31446.
Singapore 05-03 Singapore Rubber House, 14 Collyer Quay, Singapore 0104 Tel: (010 65) 535 2966.
South Africa (Johannesburg) 7th Floor, JBS Building, 107 Commission Street, Johannesbury 2001, RSA. British Tourist Authority, PO Box 6256, Johannesburg 2000, RSA Tel: (010 27 11) 29-6770.
USA
New York 3rd Floor, 40 West 57th Street, New York NY 10019 Tel: (010 1 212) 581 4700.

Chicago
John Hancock Centre, Suite 3320, 857 North Michigan Avenue, Chicago, Illinois 60611 Tel: (010 1 312) 787 0492.

Dallas
Cedar Maple Plaza, 2305 Cedar Springs Road, Dallas, Texas, 7520—1814 Tel: (010 1 214) 720 4040.

Los Angeles
World Trade Center, 350 South Figueroa Street, Suite 450, Los Angeles, California CA 90071. Tel: (010 1 213) 628 3525.

LITERATURE

FURTHER READING

The following list of books include some which are out of print but may be found in public libraries.

Balleine, G.R: *The Bailiwick of Jersey*. Hodder and Stoughton.

Balleine, G.R: *A History of Jersey*. Staples Press.

Barber, A: *Walks with a Car in Guernsey*. Bailiwick Publications.

Barber, A: *Walks with a Meal in Guernsey*. Bailiwick Publications.

Barber, A: *Walks with a Bus in Guernsey*. Bailiwick Publications.

Barber, A: *Explore Herm*. Guernsey Press.

Barber, A: *Explore Sark*. Guernsey Press.

Binney, M: *Victorian Jersey*. Save Britain's Heritage.

Bisson, S: *Jersey our Island*. Batchworth.

Bois, F. de la: *Walks for Motorists: Jersey*. Frederick Warne.

Bois, F. de la: *Constitutional History of Jersey*. States Greffe, Jersey.

Borwick, Robin: *A Brief Guide to Lihou Island*. Guernsey Press.

Closs, A: *Tastes of the Channel Islands*. Ampersand.

Coysh, V: *Alderney*. David and Charles.

Coysh, V: *The Channel Islands: A New Study*. David and Charles.

Cruickshank, C: *The German Occupation of the Channel Islands*. Oxford University Press.

Dobson, R: *Birds of the Channel Islands*. Staples Press.

Earl, T: *Explore Guernsey*. Local Heritage.

Garis, M: *Le Dictionnaire Angllais—Guernesiais*. Phillimore.

Hathaway, S: *Dame of Sark*. La Haule Books.

Hawkes, K: *Sark*. David and Charles.

Jean, J: *Jersey Sailing Ships*. Phillimore.

Jee, N: *Guernsey's Natural History*. Guernsey Press.

Jee, N: *Guernsey Cow*. Elek.

Jee, N: *Landscape of the Channel Islands*. Phillimore.

Johnston, D.E: *The Channel Islands : An Archaeological Guide*. Phillimore.

Kendrick, T.D. and Hawkes, J: *The Archaeology of the Channel Islands*, two volumes. London and

Société Jersiaise.

Lake, C: *Images of the Past*. La Haule Books.

Lake, C: *These Haunted Islands*. Guernsey Press.

L'Amy, J.H: *Jersey Folklore*. La Haule Books.

Le Maistre, F: *Le Dictionnaire Jersiaise—Français*. Don Balleine Trust.

Lemprière, R: *Portrait of the Channel Islands*. Robert Hale.

Lemprière, R: *History of the Channel Islands*. Robert Hale.

Lemprière, R: *Customs, Ceremonies and Traditions of the Channel Islands*. Robert Hale.

Lemprière, R: *Buildings and Memorials of the Channel Islands*. Robert Hale.

Le Sueur, F: *A Natural History of Jersey*. Phillimore.

Le Sueur, F: *Flora of Jersey*. Société Jersiaise.

Lloyd, B: *Explore Jersey*. Local Heritage.

McCammon, A: *The Coinage of the Channel Islands*. Spink & Son.

McCormack, J: *The Guernsey House*. Phillimore.

Marr, L. J: *A History of the Bailiwick of Guernsey*. Phillimore.

Marr, L. J: *Guernsey*

People. Phillimore.

Marr, L. J: *Bailiwick Bastions: The Fortifications of the Bailiwick of Guernsey*. Guernsey Press.

Maugham, R. C. F: *Jersey Under the Jackboot*. New English Library.

Mayne, R. and J. Stevens: *Jersey Through the Lens*. Phillimore.

Millard, Robin: *The Magic of Sark*. Guernsey Press.

Mollet, R: *A Chronology of Jersey*. Société Jersiaise.

Ramsey, W.G: *The War in the Channel Islands Then and Now*. After the Battle.

Robinson, G. W. S: *Guernsey*. David and Charles.

Sinel, L. P: *The German Occupation of Jersey*. La Haule Books.

Stevens, J: *Old Jersey Houses*: Vol. 1. Phillimore. Vol. VI. Phillimore.

Stevens, J: *A Short History of Jersey*. Société Jersiaise.

Stevens, P: *Victor Hugo in Jersey*. Phillimore.

Stoney, B: *Sibyl, Dame of Sark*. Burbridge.

Syvret, M. and . Stevens J.: *Balleine's History of Jersey*, revised and enlarged edition. Phillimore.

Thorne, Nicholas: *Money Chain*. NorSou.

Toms, Carel: *Walking about St. Peter Port*. Guernsey Press.

Toms, Carel: *Country Walks by the Sea*. Guernsey Press.

Walker, Desmond: *Bedlam in the Bailiwicks*. (novel) Guernsey Press.

Wood, A. and M: *Islands in Danger, 1940-45*. Evans, London.

ART/PHOTO
CREDITS

Continued from page v

ham, whose career has encompassed reporting for the *Jersey Evening Post*, co-editing an adventure travel magazine, working as a freelance journalist in Australia and acting as public relations manager for Jersey Tourism. Like Le Garsmeur, he is acutely conscious that the once rural islands are now facing the familiar urban problems of traffic control, sufficient housing and better services for a burgeoning population. The pervasive presence of the offshore finance industry, Abraham believes, has made people in general much more money-conscious. Everyone is aware that successful economic growth has brought them unprecedentedly comfortable life-styles and no-one wants to derail the gravy train before it has accelerated to maximum speed. How does he feel about the claustrophobia induced by living on a small island? "It's there," he says, "but the islands' natural beauty always helps alleviate the problem and so does looking out in all directions at the Atlantic horizon."

In putting together this book, Apa Publications experienced at first hand the helpfulness and hospitality for which the islands are renowned. However fierce their rivalry towards one another, they show only kindness towards visitors. We would like to thank in particular **Diane Needham** of Jersey Tourism and **Evan Ozanne**, deputy director of the States of Guernsey's Department of Tourism and Recreation; their assistance proved invaluable.

Thanks, too, go to the many people who helped us track down the fascinating photographs and illustrations that portray the islands' chequered history: to the Société Jersiaise, to the *Jersey Evening Post* and the *Guernsey Evening Press*, to the Jersey Heritage Trust, to the islands' fine museums, and to **Richard Mayne** for allowing us access to his comprehensive collection of Occupation photographs.

Apa Productions' editorial manager **Vivien Kim** efficiently coordinated the book's production in Singapore—also an island, though a very different one from Jersey, Guernsey, Alderney, Sark and Herm. She couldn't have done it all alone of course; Apa house-editors **Evelyn Chan**, **Gloria Maschmeyer** and **Audrey Simon**, all shared vicariously in the process of guiding this book from raw manusripts to its ultimate glossy format.

—Apa Publications

INDEX